MARITIME SECURITY OF INDIA: THE COASTAL SECURITY CHALLENGES AND POLICY OPTIONS

MARITIME SECURITY OF INDIA: THE COASTAL SECURITY CHALLENGES AND POLICY OPTIONS

Editor

Dr SURESH R.

Associate Professor & Hon. Director
V K Krishna Menon Study Centre for International Relations,
Department of Political Science,
University of Kerala,
Thiruvananthapuram,
Kerala

Vij Books India Pvt Ltd

New Delhi (India)

Published by

Vij Books India Pvt Ltd
(Publishers, Distributors & Importers)
2/19, Ansari Road
Delhi – 110 002
Phones: 91-11-43596460, 91-11-47340674
Fax: 91-11-47340674
e-mail: vijbooks@rediffmail.com
we b: www.vijbooks.com

Copyright © 2014, Suresh R.

First Published : 2014

ISBN: 978-93-82652-36-6

Contents

Preface

The oceans have become crucial to any nations security and engagement with the outside world. The growing significance of maritime resources and of sea-lane protection, as well as the concentration of economic boom zones along the coasts, has made maritime security more critical than ever before. The maritime challenges include non-traditional threats such as climate change, transnational terrorism, illicit fishing, human trafficking, and environmental degradation. The over exploitation of marine resources has underlined the need for conservation and cautious management of the biological diversity of the seabed. The creation of a global ocean governance mechanism is sine quo non for the peaceful exploitation of ocean resources. The assertive pursuit of national interest for relative gain in an increasingly interdependent world is neither a formula for harmonious maritime relations or for peaceful utilisation of ocean resources to the benefit of mankind.

In the emerging global order maritime security assumes great significance. Soon after India's independence, the decision makers were under the impression that security threats could come only from across land borders. Therefore coastal security was not taken seriously for a long time. Though much of the weaponry for the 1993-terrorist attack on Mumbai entered the country through the sea, the seriousness of coastal security continued to be largely ignored till the terrorist attack on Mumbai in 26 November 2008.

Coastal security is one of the subset of maritime security. The coastal security has become an urgent necessity especially in the context of Mumbai terrorist attack and the threat it poses to the national security. In the post cold war period the threat to the security of nation states emanates mainly from non state actors. Unlike the attack from state actors the non state actors mode of attack is different. It demands a constant vigil throughout the land and maritime borders. The recent Italian marine issue adds a new dimension to the security of the coastal people engaged in fishing.

When we look into the coastal security a convergence of the national security concerns and human security concerns is visible. The overall development of the coastal area would lead to better human security and better human security would result in enlisting the support of the coastal community to ensure national security programme, especially the coastal security. However the task of guarding the vast coastline, unlike our land borders, is a complex issue involving multiple stake holders such as shipping, fisheries, offshore exploration and production, tourism, and scientific community. In short, it is not only about protecting the coastal terrain and territorial waters from direct attacks by state actors or non state actors, but also safeguarding the interests of all stake holders.

This edited book is a collection of selected papers presented at the two days ICSSR National Seminar on Maritime Security of India: The Coastal Security Challenges and Policy Options organised by the Postgraduate and Research Department of Political Science, Sree Narayana College, Kollam, Kerala on 13 & 14 August 2013. Almost all aspects of the coastal security dimension of maritime security of India are well explored in this collection. The contributors include academics, defence experts and policy makers.

SURESH R.

Contributors

1.   Professor Nalini Kant Jha, Professor & Dean School of Social Sciences & International Studies, Pondicherry University, Pondicherry.

2.   Dr. Navniit Gandhi, Freelance Writer/Author/Political Analyst, Mumbai.

3.   Professor Mohanan Bhaskaran Pillai, Professor & Coordinator, UGC Special Assistance Programme Dept. of Politics & International Studies, Pondicherry University, Pondicherry.

4.   Miss. Anu Unny Assistant Professor, Department of Political Science, University of Kerala, Thiruvananthapuram, Kerala.

5.   Professor B Vivekanandan, Former Chairman, Centre for American and West European Studies, Jawaharlal Nehru University, New Delhi.

6.   Professor K.R. Singh (Retd) Jawaharlal Nehru University, New Delhi.

7.   Commodore R.S. Vasan, Indian Navy (Retd) Head Strategy and Security Studies, Center for Asia Studies, Chennai.

8.   Professor P.V. Rao Former Director, Centre for Indian Ocean Studies, Osmania University, Hyderabad.

9.   Dr. Anil Kumar P, Assistant Professor, Department of Political Science, University College, Thiruvananthapuram.

10.   Vice Admiral M P Muralidharan, AVSM, Former Director General, Indian Coast Guard.

11.   Dr Rajesh Kunayil, Deputy Project Director, ICSSR, Major Research Project, School of International Relations and Politics, Mahatma Gandhi University, Kottayam.

12.   Miss. Shyna V V and Mr. Khursheed Ahmad Wani, Research Scholars, Centre for Southern Asian Studies, Pondicherry University, Pondicherry.

13.   Dr. Sudhir Singh, Associate Professor, Department of Political Science, Dyal Singh College, University of Delhi, New Delhi.

14.   Dr. C.Vinodan, Assistant Professor & Chair Centre for Strategic and Security Studies, School of International Relations and Politics, Mahatma Gandhi University, Kottayam, Kerala.

15.   Professor V Suryanarayan, Former Director, Centre for South and South East Asian Studies, University of Madras, Chennai.

16.   Dr. S Utham Kumar Jamadhagni, Senior Assistant Professor, Department of Defence and Strategic Studies, University of Madras, Chennai.

17.   Dr. Suresh R, Associate Professor, Department of Political Science, University of Kerala, Thiruvananthapuram, Kerala   & Smt. Rakhee Viswambharan, Assistant Professor, Postgraduate & Research Department of Political Science, Sree Narayana College, Kollam, Kerala.

18.   Mr. Sandeep Menon Nandakumar, Assistant Professor, School of Legal Studies, CUSAT, Kochi, Kerala.

Introduction

The concept of security has various dimensions. In the cold war period threat to security to nation was mainly from the other nation states. However, in the post cold war period the threat to national security emanates mainly from non state actors. There are some non-traditional threats to national security including international terrorism. This new threats can be addressed only with the active support of other nation states as well as people. Similarly in the post cold war period the human security issues assume great significance. Thus it is the responsibility of nation to address both national security and human security simultaneously. Interestingly the coastal security is an area where the national security interests and human security interests converge.

The coastal security of India has become an urgent necessity especially in the context of Mumbai terrorist attack and the threat it poses to the national security. Unlike the attack from state actors the non state actors mode of attack is different. It not only demands a constant vigil throughout the land and maritime borders but also multilateral approach. The Italian Marines issue adds a new dimension to the security of the coastal people engaged in fishing.

India has to step up surveillance and protection of India's vast coastline of 7,516 kms. India's maritime zones, over which it has certain rights and obligations, include a territorial sea up to 12 nm (22 kms) from the baseline, a contiguous zone from 12 to 24 nm (22-44 kms), an Exclusive Economic Zone (EEZ) from 12 to 200 nm (22-370 kms) and a continental shelf up to 200 nm. These zones currently comprise 2.013 million sq km area of sea. India has thousand-plus island territories and offshore installations. Nearly 70 per cent of India's energy requirements of crude oil are currently shipped from abroad, increased focus would be required on the ability to maintain the safety and security of energy shipments and the prevention of any disruption of supply through multilateral cooperation. Another important maritime security interest is the prevention of maritime terrorism through multilateral efforts.

This book focuses on various aspects of maritime security of India. Starting with the changing dimensions of national security, it addresses the issues such as non-traditional threats to security, the threat posed by non state actors, the causes of insecurity and also the imperatives of tackling the human security challenges. The need for a change in the security policy of India is well exposed and certain policy prescriptions are also given. The oceans are generally meant for better inaction among nations, especially in the era of accelerated pace of globalisation. The setting up of an effective global ocean governance mechanism is also sine qua non for smooth international trade and resource management. The multilateral cooperation at the regional and global level is also inevitable for ensuring national security as well as human security. With regard to the coastal security of India the role of coastal community is significant. The needs for inculcating awareness among the coastal community on coastal security matters as well as infrastructure development along the coastal area are also emphasised. It is very important to look into the basic problems of coastal people as they face many human security challenges.

This book is divided into four sections. The first part deals with the National Security: The Changing Dimensions. In this section four articles are incorporated. Professor Nalini Kant Jha in his article entitled Non-Traditional Concept of National Security: A Traditional View address the changing dimensions of national security. He stated that the concept of national security has increasingly come under scrutiny in recent decades from scholars and practitioners alike. It is argued that since the traditional notion of national security put a premium on the security of State and its boundaries, it ignored security of human beings residing within the boundaries of a State. Hence, traditional view of security is regarded as too narrow and militarist view of security. Accordingly, contemporary debate about national security often focuses on transformation of the concept of national security from a narrow prism of territorial security to a wider canvas of human security. It is now argued that while scholars during the Cold War perceived the State as an actor in international politics with a distinct territorial base and sovereign authority without giving much attention to the peoples residing within a State; the end of the Cold War over a decade ago heralded a seminal change about the concept of national security. He had identified the causes of insecurity among the developing countries as the adverse impact global milieu, the regional strategic situation and the internal conflicts within the states.

Dr. Navniit Gandhi, in her paper titled The Changing Dimensions of National Security: The Human Perspective strongly argues that regimes must remember though that the earlier played games of power politics do not guarantee survival any more—neither for the players of the game and nor for the masses. A divided society living in despair will make it impossible even for the rulers to survive in peace. A poor and starved nation cannot boast of an assured sense of security merely on the basis of the deadly weaponry it possesses. A few developing countries have become insecure places to lives in, not because of a lack of a huge defence force but because of overt conflict and violence emanating from chronic poverty, crime, population expansion and an overall deteriorating quality of life.

Professor Mohanan B Pillai argues in his article on India's National Security: Concerns and Strategies that there is a paradigmatic shift in the security discourses, especially a shift from the state centric notion of security to the human security problematic. It also stimulates us to re-visit the security dimensions of India's traditional foreign policy to locate the specificities of strategic autonomy embedded in the precepts of nonalignment. The nonalignment has its own limitations to be rejuvenated as a policy frame work of strategic autonomy as native capital is inclined to have more collaboration with foreign capital. Secondly, in the context of the new social structure of accumulation, translating the concept of human security to implementable policy prescriptions would remain to be elusive. Finally, at a time when integration with the core is further tightened which automatically subordinates the periphery, attempts at multilateralism cannot cross the Rubicon of rhetoric.

Anu Unny in her paper on The Indian Ocean Region and Changing Security Dynamics stated that the issues which threaten the nations' security can no longer be combated within the paradigm of nation states, but they have to be tackled trans-nationally. Security threats such as terrorism, climate change, nuclear proliferation, trafficking of narcotics and human beings are common threats to almost all regional players. In order to combat these long term challenges which affect their national security, more attention need to be placed on developing co-operative security architecture. In this globalized era, only a collective security framework can achieve the goal of regional and national stability. However for that, what we need to re-conceptualize is the idea of security itself. Any analysis on security should be progressed from understanding the concept of human security. Only people centred view of security can ensure sustainable regional, national and global stability. A shift in thinking from national security to human security, more respect for human rights law and principles at national and international level, can actually bolster the efforts directed to enhance Indian Ocean security and stability.

The part two of the book deals with Maritime Security Concerns of India especially in the context of 26/11 Mumbai terrorist attack. Vice Admiral M P Muralidharan AVSM, Former Director General, Indian Coast Guard, is one of the architects of ambitious coastal security scheme. In his well articulated paper entitled Maritime Coastal Security Concerns stated that in the Indian context maritime and coastal stakes are significant. We have a long coastline measuring over 7500 km, studded with vital industrial hubs and a huge EEZ measuring over 2 million square km. Almost 95 per cent of our energy requirements are directly linked with the sea and 90 per cent of our trade by volume is by sea. Threats to India's coastline can therefore have disastrous consequences for our economy. Coastal Security, as we discuss now, emerged only after 26/11. Unfortunately, prior to 26/11, coastal security and any related debate on the subject had remained the exclusive preserve of Indian Navy and the Coast Guard. The task of guarding the vast coastline, unlike our land borders, is a complex phenomenon involving multiple stake holders such as shipping, fisheries, offshore Exploration and Production, tourism, and scientific community. In other words, it's not only about protecting our coastal terrain and territorial waters from direct military or militant attacks, but also safeguarding the interests of all stake holders. Thus, the Coastal Security efforts of today are primarily against: - Infiltration and attack from non-state actors. Illegal economic exploitation of our marine resources both living and non-living, Smuggling of arms, explosives, drugs and other contraband. Piracy, hijacking and other criminal acts including:- Commandeering of fishing boats; and, Presence of unseaworthy ships. The very nature of the maritime environment, it is difficult to achieve fool-proof security. Preventing nefarious activities of pirates at sea or ingress of terrorists from the sea is a challenge. The area required to be monitored is vast and the assets available with security agencies are never enough for surveillance. The problem is compounded by the large numbers of fishing and other boats, which proceed to sea each day, but are not yet fully bound by legal mechanisms that enable effective monitoring and control. While we have made considerable progress since 26/11, there is still some way to go. Synergetic, well coordinated efforts by all the stake holders are the key to ensuring a safe and secure maritime environment.

Dr. Rajesh Kunayil in his paper entitled Coastal Security in India: Challenges and policy concerns after 26/11 Mumbai Terror attacks points out that in the 21st century one of the typical weaknesses of a vibrant and flourishing democracy like India is its vulnerability to attacks on its sovereignty and way of life, by terrorism. The vulnerability increases if the democracy is a multiethnic, secular, and pluralistic one like India with an expanding federal structure that is based on an increasing number of states. There are also greater probabilities of internal fissures and schisms that open up as a result of expressions of dissent and dissatisfaction by ethnic groups, religious extremist forces, and archaic ideological forces. Every terror attack rooted in religious extremism is a calculated attempt to subvert India's secular and vibrant heritage. If you look at the expenditure during the last 60 years, we notice that huge expenditure is incurred on the security of the land borders. Only a fraction of that would have been spent on the security of the coastal waters. The enemy across the land border is visible; the enemy across the land is tangible; the danger is no doubt, real. When the armies stand facing each other across borders, the security concerns are more vitally pressing than anything else. But we must also remember that though unseen, the enemy across the sea is also very real and the unseen enemy ultimately landed on India's coastline on 26/11/2008. That was when many among us woke up and decided that, indeed, coastal security is vital to national security.

Shyna V V and Khursheed Ahmad Wani paper on Five Years Since 26/11: Is India's Coastal Border Really Secure? argued that though coastal and maritime security has been accorded top priority following the Mumbai attacks, the pace of implementation has been extremely slow. Lackadaisical attitude of the state governments, bureaucratic hurdles, stringent laws, turf wars among various agencies, lack of personnel and technical means for implementing projects have all contributed towards the delay. Therefore, the time has, therefore, come for the Government of India to take effective measures to ensure the safety and security of the coastal region. It should be highlighted that India's major ports are located either in or very near cosmopolitan cities like Mumbai, Kolkata and Chennai but India's approach to security still remains heavily land centric and the water front continues to remain open and vulnerable. On the whole, while India has put in place a comprehensive mechanism for securing the country's coasts, great deal to be done in terms of addressing issues relating to perceptions, resources as well as organisational management to ensure effective coastal security. However, coastal Security in India is a very complex issue and the Government will have to put in place measures that address all these threats. Whatever the measures are decided upon, it would need to be implemented as early as possible.

Dr. Sudhir Singh in his article on Chinese Presence in Gwador & Its Impact on India's Maritime Security maintain that Gwadar will provide leverage to Pakistani navy because it is around 500 KM west from Karachi and it will not be an easy task for Indian Navy to block it in case of war. In peacetime too, due to its geo-strategic location, if properly developed will make it conduit of trade hub not for China but also for resource rich Central Asian republics. Chinese presence at Gwadar will be an addition to its open policy since decades of Encircle India within South Asia. In response to China's access to the supposed pearls of Chittagong, HambantotaMarao Atoll and Gwadar, India has no lack of options.

Tracing the ancient Indian wisdom he maintains that Kautilaya has already said that enemy's enemy is friend. We need to extend our mutual cooperation in maritime affairs with likeminded countries. South China Sea is an issue where we could make inroads in the hearts of ASEAN countries. New Delhi has already expressed interest in Iran's Chabahar port, and moving forward, can explore its connections with other countries like Maldives, Mauritius and Seychelles. Still, India should divorce itself from the innate sense of vulnerability that is at times misleading, because of America's and India's firm grasp over China's energy jugular. The reports of conflicting statements by India's External Affairs Minister and Defence Minister as to whether Gwadar is "a serious matter of concern" indicate general confusion in New Delhi. This is not only advantageous to Beijing, which can leverage on this lack of a clear direction to further its national interests rapidly, but also tends to exaggerate fears and therefore encourage unnecessary action. Instead, there is need to assess the true extent to which China's actions are a threat to India. To this end, it is important to keep in mind that, regardless of Beijing's growing ambitions, India will, in conflict situations, have the trump card of force concentration in the IOR. Beside these measures India must register its presence in South China Sea in a comprehensive manner. In December 2012 , Indian Naval Chief, Admiral D.K. Joshi has stated that India will intervene in South China Sea if necessary for the protection of national interests. India must adhere with the Kaultiyan realism and deepen its ties with ASEAN, East Asia and

West Asia and through this process it could ensure its national interests. Gwadar has emerged as a challenge for the promotion and protection of our national interests therefore we must reformulate our strategy to cope with the emerging challenges.

Dr. C. Vinodan, a specialist on energy security studies in his paper entitled Maritime Rivalry and Energy Security: Indian and the South China Sea Dispute maintain that the South China Sea is a strategic waterway providing the key maritime link between the Indian Ocean and East Asia. Sea lines of communication (SLOCs) of the South China Sea are a matter of life and death for the Asia Pacific countries, and SLOC security has been a fundamental factor contributing to regional economic development. The rise of China, as a reckonable power in the global order, is one of the defining features of the 21stcentury world order. China's unprecedented economic growth and modernization have accelerated China's demand for energy resources, especially oil. Recently, China emerged as the world's largest consumer of oil surpassing the United States and now imports over 50 percent of its oil requirement. Concern about energy insecurity has resulted in the establishment of new priorities and objectives for China's international economic interactions, focusing on the search for secure and reliable sources for the long-term. As the global demand for energy rises, China's geo-strategy includes more assertive policies in the vital strategic regions of the world. China's "Go Out" economic policy and its mercantilist approach to controlling energy resources combined with aggressive trade agreements that include weapons, advanced technology, and/or loan deals for oil reflect China's growing energy security dilemma. The South China Sea's vast energy resources in the heavily disputed Spratly and Paracel Island regions stand to raise the stakes of interested parties including the US and India. Given China's rise and its territorial claims to not only the islands, but the vast majority of the South China Sea and its resources, it remains unclear whether such claims will become a platform for cooperation or conflict. China had showed its assertiveness in the South China Sea through a tough posture instead a conciliatory approach of diplomacy and economic integration with its Southeast Asian neighbours. Other South China Sea states are also asserting their own claims and developing their own naval capacity, albeit to a lesser degree than China. As the eastern gateway to the Indian Ocean, South China Sea is India's strategic left flank. And, more than half of India's interests pass through or are located in the South China Sea. Like all other law abiding nations, India is particular about the freedom of navigation in the maritime commons. In her view, it is of paramount importance that status quo be maintained in respect of freedom of access and passage within the South China Sea. How China overcomes its miscalculations in its South China Sea policy will significantly influence Chinas rising profile in the emerging world order. Its handling of sovereignty disputes with some of its neighbors, and differences with the US have already weakened its standing in the Far East and beyond.

The section three focus on Maritime Security of India and the Policy Options. In this section Professor B. Vivekanandan in the article entitled India's Maritime Security: The Policy Options has powerfully argued that the way geography has positioned India in the Indian Ocean, India is destined to be a strong maritime power in the world. Undoubtedly, India should pay more attention to build a strong and well-equipped navy. That apart, the Government of India will have to invest more to strengthen its maritime forces than what it does today, to meet the potential challenge posed by a determined potential enemy, like the expansionist People's Republic of China. Other policy options, before India, are basically political. Instead of making a narrowly defined diplomatic move for "Improving" relations with South Asian – including Pakistan, Nepal, Myanmar, Bangladesh, and Sri Lanka – should strive to pool their destinies approach, and free them from a suspicion based bilateral relationships. Of course, it requires a more generous, humanist, approach, anchored in Solidarity, on the part of India; while dealing with people's problems in the Indian sub-continent. The dynamism embedded in such a policy, would release a lot of new resources for people's welfare, and, at the same time, deny space for outside powers to meddle with, and vitiate, the bilateral relationships between countries of South Asia. It would result in a new cohesive resurgent Indian sub-continent, which can match any power centre in the world, and, at the same time, achieve a high rank in the human development index. He further stressed that the scheme I have in mind in this context is the example of Willy Brandt's Ostpolitik, pursued in West Germany, with a higher level of humanitarian content, which had erased the barriers between the two Germanys, and also changed the perception of international relationship in the whole Europe. India's policy makers often talk about "going an extra-mile" in India's dealings with our neighbouring countries. He stated that such approach is an inadequate framework. The right framework is: "Pooling the destinies" of countries of South Asia. Pakistan should be an integral part of this framework. His optimism in this approach is further strengthened by Nawas Sheriff's return to power in Pakistan. He argues that it would augur well for the promotion of this kind of a relationship in the Indian sub-continent. Another policy option he suggested is that India should support the freedom movement in Tibet, to enable the Tibetan refugees in India to go back to their homes, with dignity. The other policy option is that, India should stop supporting the "One China" policy of the People's Republic of China.

Professor K.R. Singh, in his paper on Maritime Security: An Indian Perspective stated that Article 279 of the Indian Constitution was amended on April 27, 1976 and it defined various maritime zones including the exclusive economic zone (EEZ). Thus, the concept of EEZ was added. That amendment enabled the Parliament to enact the Maritime Zones of India Act, 1976. It fixed the outer limits of territorial waters (12 n.miles from the base line), contiguous zone (24 n. miles), EEZ and continental-shelf (200 n. miles). It also defined India's jurisdiction (not sovereignty) over these zones. However, India has not passed a law that can empower maritime enforcement authorities to neutralize the threat of maritime terrorism beyond the territorial waters of India, despite the events of 26/11 in Mumbai and steps taken in the context of coastal security since 2005-6.

He argues that one can explain the lack of interest in maritime affairs primarily due to two things. The one is the so-called continental mindset of Indian decision makers. It is reflected even in the Indian Constitution when it defines the territory of India. Article 1(3) of Part I of Indian Constitution mentions that the territory of India comprises of the territories of the States, the Union Territories and such other territories as may be acquired. It even ignored mentioning territorial waters that is recognized world over as an extension of state sovereignty. The Indian Penal Code also followed that definition in Chapter II, section 18. After the passing of the MZI Act 1976, Government of India, by a notification extended the provisions of IPC and Cr.P.C. over the entire EEZ of India.

With regard to coastal security he stated that the coastal states can make their contribution to strengthen coastal security in another way. That is in the realm of intelligence. Undoubtedly, maritime security agencies depend upon several modes of intelligence gathering. They are mostly based upon data generated by the satellites, radar network along the coast and various other communication networks. Their input of human intelligence is rather limited. It is here that coastal states and more particularly the fishing community can play a very useful role. To the best of my knowledge there is no organized structure for obtaining intelligence/ information from our fisher folk who operate in India's EEZ further away from the coast. In that context, he made a valuable suggestion for the creation of Marine Guards, maritime version of Home Guards, in coastal states. Regarding its creation he suggested that the cooperation from the Central Government, Marine Police, in coordination with Marine Guards, can provide intelligence that can supplement what is collected from various other sources. In this context, he argues that the fisher folk who own/ operate sea going fishing boats/trawlers can play a meaningful role.

Commodore R.S. Vasan IN (Retd) in his article on Oceanic and Coastal Security Imperatives for India stated that the recalibration of the American maritime strategy with a pivot to the Asia- Pacific reinforces the importance of the Indian Ocean to security safety and well-being of the global maritime activities. This rebalancing has brought in enhanced interest in the Indian Ocean Region. The last decade and the beginning of this decade witnessed both acts of terrorism and increased acts of piracy in the areas of interest to the world and India. Both the acts has the potential to disrupt global trade commerce and development. The terror attacks on the commercial capital of Mumbai in November 2008 brought about key changes in the concept of maritime security in India. Despite many initiatives at both the Centre and the State levels post Mumbai terror attacks, there are still questions about the tools and techniques and their efficacy to prevent another terrorist attack from the seas. While this incident challenged both internal and external security architecture, India as a Regional Power has to also manage its external maritime environment At another level, the acts of piracy in the west Arabian Sea has impacted the maritime Industry in a big way and threatened to disrupt the movement of ships in the arteries of the world. The maritime environment in the Indian Ocean Region is beset with many challenges. India has to take a lead role in managing the maritime domain by combination of cooperative arrangements, technology, procedures, legal support force levels and above all innovative leadership. The list of such initiatives would include: Both long term and short term measures. Drawing up of appropriate contingency plans. Initiation of Collaborative Efforts and Cooperation. Planned induction of newer platforms and shoring up of force levels. Regular drills, exercises, audits and reviews to assess the efficacy of implemented measures. Efforts to have a robust Maritime Security Architecture that caters for the present century challenges. Greater emphasis on Information and system security due to sophisticated cyber threats. Regional initiatives being the most eminent and equipped maritime nation in the region. Working and promoting the concept of "Maritime Clusters" which brings in all the stake holders on the common page and gets them to work together to implement pro-active measures. Bringing about greater awareness through campaigns, media and education at all levels.

Professor P.V. Rao, in his paper entitled Coast Guard and Indian Naval Diplomacy maintains that the maritime security is the protection of a nation's territorial and maritime jurisdiction from foreign invasion by sea. It is necessary against military threats from sea. However, today maritime security denotes more than the armed protection provided by a country's navy. Maritime security has acquired a broader holistic meaning. Twentieth and twenty-first centuries, have added new and non-military dimensions to maritime security, viz; threats from non-state actors (pirates, drug-traffickers, terrorists), maritime pollution and safety of oil and cargo ships. Relief from natural disasters, exploring sea-bed resources, construction of ports and harbours are also covered by contemporary concept of maritime security. The Indian Coast Guard cooperative ventures in varying ways with neighbouring and foreign maritime forces one can conclude that it has gone far beyond the originally mandated responsibilities safeguarding Indian coastal assets and ensuring the overall maritime security in India's EEZ. The Indian Coast Guard services to other coastal security agencies is in a way amounts to offering the Indian maritime soft power endowments to the countries concerned. Rather in a broader sense, ICG is co-opting the Indian Navy's diplomatic roles in advancing the Indian strategic objectives and power projection in Indian Ocean and beyond.

Dr. Anil Kumar P in the paper entitled India's Maritime Security Policy: Issues and Challenges in the 21st Century emphasised that the importance of infrastructure in the maritime domain is underscored by history. During the early twentieth century, Germany was an advanced industrial nation but not a great power since its maritime footprint was small because of low infrastructural capacity. Similarly, today considerable progress has been made by many nations in Asia but, unfortunately, this has not always been matched by a proportional investment in their maritime infrastructure. Hence, it is imperative for Asian littorals that are dependent on the seas for their economic existence to develop their maritime capability. In case of India, he argued that the government should begin by stipulating a change of status of various entities that are part of the maritime domain. To begin with, ports, shipbuilding, ship repair, deep sea shipping, coastal shipping and offshore economic activities need to be grouped together and given the status of an Infrastructure Sector or Strategic Sector, highlighting their importance and placing emphasis on their rapid development.

The part four of the book looks into the Coastal Security of India from a Community as well as Legal Perspective. In this section Professor V Suryanarayan paper entitled Travails of Fishermen in the Palk Bay: A Possible Solution argue that India must project a vision that the Palk Bay constitutes the common heritage of both India and Sri Lanka. Instead of viewing it as a contested territory, joint efforts should be made to enrich the sea. A Palk Bay Authority should be constituted, consisting of the representatives of both countries, fishermen's representatives, marine ecologists and fisheries specialists. The Palk Bay Authority could determine the ideal sustainable catch per year, the type of fishing equipments to be used, the number of days Indian and Sri Lankan fishermen could fish etc. Trawlers must be immediately decommissioned. Joint efforts should be made to enrich the marine resources. What is more, fishermen of both countries should be encouraged to embark upon joint ventures for deep sea fishing. Such endeavour would give a fillip to bilateral and regional co-operation.

Dr. S.Utham Kumar Jamadhagni in has made an empirical study on the topic Coastal Security of Tamil Nadu: An Empirical Study to Elicit a Community Perspective to understand the perception of coastal security according to the people who live across the coast of Tamil Nadu and who primarily depend on the sea, to understand the vulnerabilities in coastal security as understood by these people, the counter measures available and to suggest mechanisms where they are absent and to suggest measures of improvement in coastal security have been completed. He strongly argues that the views of coastal people also have to taken into consideration during the processes of planning and implementation, as the voices from below are as important to effective policy planning as those voices of planning and guidance from above.

Dr Suresh R. & Smt. Rakhee Viswambharan, in their article on Coastal Security of India: The Role of Coastal Community explore into the various aspects of coastal security and role of coastal community. They maintain that the coastal security has become an urgent necessity especially in the context of Mumbai terrorist attack and the threat it poses to the national security. In the post cold war period the threat to the security of nation states emanates mainly from non state actors. Unlike the attack from state actors the non state actors mode of attack is different. It demands a constant vigil throughout the land and maritime borders. The Italian marine issue adds a new dimension to the security of the coastal people engaged in fishing. They also maintain that when we look into the coastal security a convergence of the national security concerns and human security concerns is visible. The overall development of the coastal area would lead to better human security and better human security would result in enlisting the support of the coastal community to ensure national security programme.

Sandeep Menon Nandakumar, in his article on Piracy, Use of Force and Criminal Jurisdiction: An Analysis of Erica Lexie Case in the Light of International Conventions, Guidelines and National Legislations discussed the legal dimension of piracy and related issues. He had stated that the debate ensued as a result of the incident where two Italian marines shot and killed the Indian fishermen on the ground of alleged piracy attack was primarily focused on the jurisdiction that could be exercised by the Indian courts. His paper examines the relevant Kerala High Court Judgment as well as the Supreme Court judgment and analyses the criminal jurisdiction that could be exercised by Indian Courts beyond the territorial waters. His paper also considers whether it is empowered to do so under the national legislations in accordance with International principles. The International Conventions such as UNCLOS of 1982, Territorial Waters, Continental Shelf, Exclusive Economic Zone and other Maritime Zones Act of 1976 (in short Territorial Waters Act, 1976) as well as SUA Convention are carefully analysed and discussed together with the provisions of IPC, CrPC and SUA Act to understand and appreciate the definitions of territorial waters, contiguous zones and Exclusive Economic Zones, to understand as to what constitutes piracy and to examine which state can exercise jurisdiction over this matter. This paper proceeds to prove that Indian Courts do have the jurisdiction and examines whether it is the State or the Union that can exercise jurisdiction over this matter. Most importantly, various guidelines by the IMO, submissions made by different countries before the Maritime Safety Committee and Best Management Practices in case of piracy attack are examined in detail to check whether the use of force by the Italian mariners was proportionate or whether it exceeded than what was necessary. This paper also focuses on various factors that should be taken into consideration during deployment of armed guards on board a ship as per IMO Guidelines. The Italian Regulation on the same is also discussed in detail in this paper.

The above eighteen articles cover a wide spectrum of issues related to maritime security of India. In the maritime security of India, the coastal security concerns assume significance not only from the national security perspective but also from human security.

PART - I

National Security: The Changing Dimensions

Non-Traditional Concept of National Security: A Traditional View

Nalini Kant Jha

The concept of national security has increasingly come under scrutiny in recent decades from scholars and practitioners alike. It is argued that since the traditional notion of national security put a premium on the security of State and its boundaries, it ignored security of human beings residing within the boundaries of a State. Hence, traditional view of security is regarded as too narrow and militarist view of security. Accordingly, contemporary debate about national security often focuses on transformation of the concept of national security from a narrow prism of territorial security to a wider canvas of human security. It is now argued that while scholars during the Cold War perceived the State as an actor in international politics with a distinct territorial base and sovereign authority without giving much attention to the peoples residing within a State; the end of the Cold War over a decade ago heralded a seminal change about the concept of national security.

II

Several factors contributed to the shift in notion of national security. Firstly, the decline in the possibility of global wars, at least among major powers, led to a greater sense of security among the major powers.[1] Secondly, ethnic, linguistic, religious, and communal tensions, which were dormant and overlaid with Cold War rivalries and the earlier colonial dominance over the Third World, got a fillip by the 'decompression' effect of the end of the Cold War. Thirdly, several newer sources of threat to national security such as population explosion, unplanned urbanisation, disparities in economic opportunities; proliferation of small arms, drug trade, international terrorism and money laundering; migration pressures, environment degradation and cyber crimes surfaced after the Cold War.[2] Finally, the shrinking of the globe and explosion of knowledge due to the revolution in information technology and globalisation of economy weakened the boundaries of State and its sovereignty; "ignited identity as a source of conflict" and enhanced sub-State groups and their operations.[3]

Since the traditional concept of security did not address these new dimensions of security, it is further argued; the need of widening the concept of security was felt after the Cold War. Consequently, many scholars began to move away from the State-centric Realist notion of international relations to Liberal view of international relations that stresses on imperatives and possibility of international and regional cooperation. A unilateralist notion of security must give way, in this view, to *cooperative security*.[4] As threat to national security can come not only from other state (s), but also from non-state actors and natural calamities, a much wider notion of security, which broadens the nature and sources of threat and which is may called *composite* or *comprehensive security*, got currency after the Cold War.[5]

Certain critiques of the classical Western notion of security went further to suggest that security cannot be restricted to the well-being of the State, but it must aim at protection and well-being of individuals and citizens residing in a State. This concept of security, which is centred above all on the sanctity of the individual, is known as *human security*. The concept of human security or the security of the individual and humane governance, [6] therefore, gained wide currency, as poverty and deprivation enlarged the problem of human security in the developing world.[7] Accordingly, growing attention is now paid, it is asserted, to human dimensions of security. While the list of threats to human security is long, most can be considered under seven major categories, namely, economic security, food security, health security, environmental security, personal security, community security, and political security. Group identity, security, and recognition are singled out as basic human needs particularly in post-colonial Asia and Africa.[8] It is therefore argued that the shift from the 'national security' to 'human security' paradigm is of historic importance.

III

While the above-discussed transformation of the concept of national security may indeed be revolutionary in the West, as far as India is concerned, the primary strategic objective of security policy has had been, and will remain, the socio-economic development of its people. This has its roots in ancient political tradition, where the ruler's primary duty

(Dharma) was perceived to be the prosperity and happiness of his people.[9] As pointed out by leading expert on Indian culture, kings were expected to nourish their subjects as a father nourishes his offspring.[10]

This is how *Srimadbhagvatam* describes the rule of king Ram: *"Jugop pitravad Ramo manire pitra ch tam"* (King Ram used to protect his subjects like a father and they too treated him as their father).[11] According to the *Valmiki Ramayan*, common people declared during King Ram's rule that the territory beyond Ram's kingdom will be a forest, but if he would reside in a forest that too would be converted into a sovereign nation.[12] This popular faith in King Ram emanated his scrupulous observance of his promise given to people at the time of his coronation, namely, that he would not at all hesitate in scarifying his affection, kindness and personal pleasures including his most beloved wife, Janaki.[13] Not surprisingly, the ancient Indian literature describes *Ramrajya* (the rule of Lord Ram) as full of happiness, where no women became widow, no one got incurable disease or snake bite. There was no question of any theft, robbery or untimely death. Every one followed principles of *dharm* (righteousness) and lived happily. Poet Kalidas, similarly, describes in his *Raghuvansam* how King Dilip protected and cared his subjects like a father.[14]

While above-mentioned description of ancient Indian kingdoms may be exaggerated or many may regard this merely an imagination of poets, these descriptions, however, suggest that foundations of political order or State lie, according to Indian theorists, in people's consent obtained by a king through ensuring their welfare. This is how the *Mahabharat* describes the origin of State and bases of political obligation thus, "Harassed by those who have force, the helpless and the hurt have only the king as their refuge, and their protector." "When the king wipes the tears of the poor, the dispossessed and the old, and creates thereby happiness among the people, that behaviour is called the king's *dharma*."[15] The *Mahabharat* thus prescribes that by its very justification, the State, if is to be itself and not something else, must be an instrument for the protection of people, for protection from violence. And since caring is the essence of protection, the State in all its acts must be caring, as only in a caring nation-State wishes expressed in the *Yujurveda* can be realized.[16]

Commenting on the stress on human security in ancient Indian literature, the famous scholar in this field Professor Kane, observers: "These provisions for the old, the blind, the widows, orphans and helpless persons and for the relief of unemployed Ksatriyas, Vaisyas and Sudras strike one as rather modern in tone.[17]

It was this philosophy and practice of human welfare that influenced modern Indian political thinkers like Mahatma Gandhi, Nehru and others to stood for a people-centred organization of society, economics and politics. The Directive Principles of State Policy enshrined in Part IV of the Indian Constitution that prescribes popular welfare as prime duty of the Indian State reflects this traditional thinking in India. Though it is not mandatory for the Indian State to implement these Directives, successive Governments have taken several steps to realize these popular welfare goals of the Constitution. Indian Judiciary too have joined in implementing this vision of the founding fathers of our Constitution by enlarging, through judicial interpretations, the meaning and ambit of fundamental rights of freedom, life and liberty guaranteed to the people by Art19 and 21 of the Constitution.[18]

One may of course, argue that both ancient and modern Indian political thinkers failed to theorize and explicitly describe popular welfare as an essential pre-condition for national security; systematic and elaborate efforts to define national security in terms of human security have been made only in recent years. What, however, cannot be denied that Indian thinkers and leaders have been fully aware with the significance of people oriented policy as an essential requirement for stability and security of a nation and State.

IV

As the saying goes, "better late than never," it is of course a welcome development that Western scholars too of late now recognize the linkage between development and national security. National security as a concept in the has thus travelled far and wide from the earlier Western notion of physical preservation of a State to a multi-dimensional concern involving military, economic, ecological, ethnic, and political aspects of a nation-State's life. As such, security now subsumes the whole of development in it. The multidimensional approach to security, however, sacrifices precision for inclusiveness, as all threats to human well-being may be regarded as threat to security. Anything and everything 'bad' may be treated as security concern. Squeezing of too many concerns in to security and thereby broadening the concept too much thus involves the risk of blurring distinctions between security and development and security and international relations in general. Neo-realist security analyst therefore argue that lumping together such a disparate set of threats causes the term security to lose all theoretical utility.[19]

Secondly, the concept of human security is attacked also from the policy perspectives. It is argued that by positioning so many different forms of violence there is little hope of framing a coherent response. It is also argued, especially by Realist scholars that inclusion of many and varied aspects of everyday life in to security umbrella may enable the ruling elite and particularly the military rulers in the Third World States to broaden their negative and corrupting influence in the society. Indeed, this has happened to some extent not only in Central America, but also in South Asian States such as Pakistan and Bangladesh.[20]

It is also suspected that the current stress on human security by the Western scholars emanate from their prejudiced view that while the security of Sate though arms race and other military means is the responsibility of the developed nations, security of human beings is the prime responsibility of poor and developing countries. This allegation gets sustenance from the fact the one the one hand the major world powers are not willing to dismantle their weapons of mass destructions and claims right to interfere in any part of the world in pursuance of their military security agenda, they preach, on the other hand, patience, peace and development to Third World countries.

The re-conceptualising of security thus appears to be a double-edged sword in addressing problems of the Third World. In order to rescue this concept from being diluted into nothingness, we need to focus on security policy in relations to crisis. Short of that it is more accurate to assess welfare gains and losses rather than increased security and insecurity. In other words, instead of over-stretching the concept of security to include fundamental concerns of human welfare, it might be enough to recognise the limitations of traditional paradigm in terms of when and where it should be applied. Security policy can then be posited as crisis prevention and crisis management, both with regard to institutional capacity and material capability. Viewed thus the concept of security must be distinguished from the concept of development even while recognising the linkages between the two. It must be recognised that while the latter is a broader concept, which means a process of widening the range of people's choices, the former means that people can exercise these choices safely and freely and that they can be relatively confident that the opportunities they have today are not totally lost tomorrow.

Moreover, even while recognising the need of including these considerations under security concern, the question remains how to maintain conditions under which sustainable development can take place. It is in this context that the security of nation States assumes significance. For, the post-Cold War experience shows the dissolution of States may worsen the cause of human security and development rather than help it. Viewed thus, it may not be difficult to identify the three sets of sources of insecurity, both national and regional, in the Third World in general and South Asia in particular. They are, (i) the adverse implications of global milieu such as unfavourable policies of great powers, conflicts and interventions, economic pressure, technological barriers, informational and ideological penetrations and cultural distortions; (ii) unfavourable regional strategic environment in which nations live. This include, inter-State conflicts and wars on account of boundary disputes, ideological incompatibilities, and economic clash of interests, etc. The erosion of some influence in or some control of the region to the exclusion of others is also viewed as threat to national security; and (iii) internal turmoil and disruption arising from struggle for national liberation, underdevelopment, ethnic, religious and social conflicts; wars of political succession and movements for political transformations, rights and shares in power. While domestic threat to the established regime may be essentially internal, it may also be linked with recognisable external adversaries. The increasing fear of domestic socio-political destabilisation has also brought to the fore the threat to national security emanating from challenges to the core national values the country may have chosen consensually.

V

Needless to say, it may be theoretically absurd and practically misleading to work out a universally applicable matrix to explain security situations in the Third World. Academics depending upon their ideological persuasions, theoretical preconceptions and unspecified biases, have often oscillated between one or sources of threats for identifying the dominant cause of insecurity in the Third World. The reality, however, seems to lie in the fact that all of these sources of threats are inter-meshed in to each other and, therefore, mutually linked and reinforcing. Most of the security crises in the Third World are a curious mix of threats coming from all the three sources.[21] The proportions of each of the components may, of course, vary from one crisis or country to another.

End Notes and References

[1] Barry Buzan, "Rethinking Security after the Cold War," *Cooperation and Conflict* (Sweden), vol. 32, no.1, 1997, pp. 5-8.

[2] See, for example, Nalini Kant Jha, "Comprehensive Security: A view from South India," in V. R. Raghavan, ed., *Comprehensive Security: Perspectives from India's* Regions (New Delhi: Delhi Policy Group, 2002), pp.96-100; and also his, "Security Environment in South Asia in the 1990s and Beyond", in Arun Kumar Bganerji, ed., *Security Issues in South Asia: Domestic and External Sources of Threat to Security* (Calcutta, 1998); and his, Addressing Human Security Concerns in South Asia: The Role of SAARC," in Saurabh and B C Upreti, eds., *Strengthening SAARC*: Exploring Vistas for Expanded Cooperation (New Delhi: Indian Council for World Affairs, 2012), pp 1-9; Lloyd Pettiford, "Changing Conceptions of Security in the Third World" *Third World Quarterly* (London), vol. 17, no, 2, 1996, pp. 289-306; *U N Development Report*, 1994, as reproduced in, *Current History* (Philadelphia, Pa), May, 1995, pp.229-36; Iftekharuzzaman, ed., *South Asian Security: Primacy of Internal Dimension* (Dhaka, 1994); C Thomas, *The Environment in International Relations* (London, 1992); and his, *In Search of Security: The Third World in International Relations* (Brighton, 1987); J F Rweyemamu, *Third World Options: Power, Security and the Hope for Another Development* (Dar e Salaam, 1992); Barry Buzan, *People, States and Fear: An Agenda for Security Studies in the Post Cold War Era* (London, 1991); Stephen Walt, "The Renaissance of Security Studies", *International Studies Quarterly*, June 1991; K Booth, ed., *New Thinking about Strategy and International Security* (London, 1990); T C Sorensen, "Rethinking National Security", *Foreign Affairs* (New York), Summer, 1990; Yezid Sayigh, "Confronting the 1990s: Security of Developing of Countries", *Adelphi Papers*, (London, IISS), no. 151, 1990; Edward Azar and Chung-In Moon, eds., *National Security in the Third World: The Management of Internal and External Threats* (Aldershot. 1988), as also their, "Third World National Security: Towards a New Conceptual Framework" *International Interactions* (Tucson, AZ), vol. 2, no. 2, 1984, pp. 103-35; Robert McNamara, *The Essence of Security* (New York, 1986); E A Kolodziej and R E Harkavy, *Security Policies of Developing Countries* (Lexington, 1982); J Galtung, *Environment and Military Activity: Towards Alternative Security Doctrines*(Oslo, 1982); Dipankar Banerji, ed., *Security Studies in South Asia: Change and Challenges*(New Delhi, 2000); Amarendra Mishra, "Security of State: Theoretical Perspectives", *Journal of Peace Studies* (New Delhi), vol. 8, no. 2, March-April 2001, pp. 3-22; M. Ayoob, *Regional Security in the Third World* (London, 1986); and J G Weiss and M A Kessler, *Third World Security in the Post Cold War Era* (Boulder, Co, 1991).

[3] Victor D. Cha, "Globalisation and the Study of International Security, "*Journal of Peace Research* (Oslo), vol. 37, no. 3, May 2000, pp. 391-403.

4 On Cooperative Security, see Janne Nolan, ed., *Global Engagement: Co-operation and Security in the 21ˢᵗ Century* (Washington D. C, 1994).

5 On composite or comprehensive security, see Muthiah Alagappa, "Asian Practice of Security: Key Features and Explanations," in his, ed., *Asian Security Practice: Material and Ideational Influences* (Stanford, 1998), pp.624-29.

6 The concept of humane governance has been conceptualised in World Bank's "Report on Human Development in South Asia, 1999: The Crisis of Governance", which notices that currently voters only vote, whereas they should be able to "shape their own governance". Humane governance has "three interlocking dimensions – good political governance, good economic governance and good civic governance". Proceeding on the assumption that governance has been captured by easily identifiable special interest groups in a State, the report notes that good political governance requires decentralisation of power to the people, accountability and transparency in public affairs; access to prompt and affordable justice; elimination of discrimination against women and minorities; and, finally, maintenance of peace and social cohesion within States.

7 The best known statements on the contemporary concept of human security are, United Nations Development Programme, "Redefining Security: The Human Dimension," *Current History*, May 1995, pp229-36; and Lloyd Axworthy, "Canada and Human Security: The Need for Leadership," *International Journal* (Toronto), vol. 52, Spring 1997, pp. 183-96. For an assessment of the Canadian view, see Astri Suhrke, "Human Security and Interest of States," *Security Dialogue*, vol. 30, no.3 September 1999, pp.265-276.

8 John W. Burton, *Human Needs Theory* (New York, 1990). In policy terms, the most authoritative treatment of the concept remains the UNDP's *Human Development Report, 1994*, which defined human security according to two main aspects: safety from chronic threats such as political repression and protection from sudden and hurtful disruption in the pattern of daily life.

9 Poet Tulsidas warms a king that if people in his kingdom would be unhappy, he would be condemned to hell. See *Ramcharitmanas*, 2.71/6.

10 Ramji Upadhyaya, *Bharitya Sanskrit Saurabhavam* (Varanasi: Bhartiya Sanskriti Sansthan, 1995), p.26.

11 *Shrimadbhagvatem*, 9/10/51.

12 *Valmiki Ramayan*, 2/37/29

13 *Uttar Ram Charitam*, 1/12.

14 *Raghuvansam*, 1/29.

15 Cited by Chaturvedi Badrinath, "The Dharmic State: Protection of Weak and Oppressed," *Times of India* (Bombay), 20 May 1993; also see his, "The Caring State: Foundations of Social Happiness," *Times of India* (New Delhi), 4 June 1995.

16 The *Yajurved* (22/22) wishes that let peoples in an ideal nation-State belonging to intellectual class possess knowledge; may warriors be brave and own strong weapons for protecting peoples, may there be good and useful animals and noble women; may the common people have brave and powerful sons; may there be rainfall on time and trees

and plants full of fruits; and may all of us prosper and grow.

[17] V Kane, *History of Dharmshastra,* vol. III, pp.59-60.

[18] See, for details, "Fifty Years of Human Rights Jurisprudence in India," in T S N Sastry, ed., *Fifty Years of Indian Independence and the Polity* (New Delhi: A P H Publishing Corporation, 2000), pp.35-40.

[19] See Florini and Simmons, "The New Security Thinking: A Review of the North American Literature," Project on World Security, Rockefeller Brothers Fund, Washington, D.C. and New York, 1998, pp 29-33.

[20] See, Veena Kukreja, *Civil-Military Relations in South Asia* (New Delhi, 1991), pp.236-37; and Pettiford, n.2, p. 303.

[21] Raimo Varrynen, "Regional Conflict Formations: An Intractable Problem of International Relations", *Journal of Peace Research* (Oslo), vol. 21, no. 4, 1984.

Changing Dimensions of National Security: The Human Perspective

Navniit Gandhi

Introduction

The world is witnessing 'change' as never before. Of all the concepts and ideas undergoing a paradigm shift, the notion of 'security' assumes paramount significance in contemporary times. Globally, there is a clamour for acquiring a 'secure' status in as comprehensive a sense as can be possible. Countries, civil society, and the individual at large scramble for realising the cherished goals of peace, security and sustenance.

Threat perceptions have also changed, moving on from the mere defence of territory to identifying other areas of conflict within nations that can explode into threats to national security. The idea of comprehensive security (moving beyond the strategic connotations) has begun to be widely accepted and the importance of deterring existing threats and preventing new threats is being duly recognized.

The concept of National Security needs to be redefined. The gamut of its operations has undergone a paradigm shift. The context against which the policy makers seek to establish national security is undergoing tumultuous changes. The inalienable relationship between national security and human security needs to be recognised and accepted. The former is incomplete without and narrower an objective without the latter.

The concept of human security made its appearance on the world scene in the mid-1990s, a time when new paradigms were being sought to explain the international system and a growing theoretical and practical debate was under way on the traditional concepts of security that drove countries' actions for much of the last century. Academics, certain international organizations and even some states, particularly Canada and Japan, promoted human security as a concept that would provide a better grasp of the new security challenges from the perspective of individuals or citizens.

As Sadako Ogata, (former) United Nations High Commissioner for Refugees aptly said: "Several key elements make up human security. A first essential element is the possibility for all citizens to live in peace and security within their own borders."[1]

According to the findings of a *Participatory Research on Armed Violence and Human Insecurity in Southeast Asia*[2] in 2003:

> *Human security is a human rather than state-based approach to security, which prioritises the freedom from want and freedom from fear as pre-conditions for development. Where small arms availability and misuse constitute a threat to human security, then they also threaten the foundations of development. Understanding how, where and why people are affected, then, becomes central to the task of any intervention. Appropriate policy responses to gauge human insecurity must, therefore, be determined by asking people precisely what makes them "feel" insecure.*

> *Transfer of power to civilian organizations, civilian oversight of the security sector, transparency and responsible governance will be key changes that will help build human security.*

The Changing Dimensions of National Security and the Humane Perspective:

The concept of security has evolved considerably, coming to centre more on individuals, because it has been understood that security does not depend only on the armed forces of each state. International agreements, the opening up of economies to nearby countries, increasing interdependence and inter-connectedness, and even the awareness of mutual vulnerability affect the security of the individuals and the state.

With the increasing complexity of global problems and their repercussions for millions of people, the change in outlook all over the world was inevitable. The threats have not only become multiple, but also multi-dimensional and no threat (and its repercussions) is restricted to any one country. For instance, there are threats very different from those of a military nature on a nation's territory. The threat could be to a nation's eco-system or its economy. Moreover, even if a threat is economic, it has many dimensions and manifestations. The fall out of an economic threat could be on social harmony or political stability. Also, political turmoil or economic slowdown in one nation will no longer remain confined to its own corridors. It will have spill-over effects and set a chain reaction in motion—roping in many countries which will also be trapped in the ripples. Not only is a nation's security position affected by political stability and economic growth within its corridors, but the non-strategic internal domestic realities in its enemy's territory can also send shivers down its spine. The politically and sociallyvolatile situation in Pakistan, for instance, will give migraine attacks to India and she will have to be on constant guard against the spill-over effects. An armed mischief against India during such tumultuous times is likely to suit the jittery rulers of Pakistan very well indeed.

Soft security issues, which do not invoke use of military force, are dominating the security scene for most nation states. Issues related with population, human and drug trafficking, refugees, organized crime, cyber crime; environmental degradation and terrorism are causing tremendous anxiety to policy makers all over the world.

The significant changes and tendencies in the international system are influencing the way we observe and analyse the new security challenges and that have given rise to a conceptualization which highlights the protection of individuals.

Need for Re-prioritizing and Re-interpretation:

'Human security embodies the notion that problems must always be addressed from a broader perspective that encompasses both poverty and issues of equity (social, economic, environmental, or institutional) as it is these issues that often lead to insecurity and conflict.'[3]

The objective of human security is to safeguard the vital core of all human lives from critical pervasive threats, in a way that is consistent with long-term human fulfilment. People and communities are fatally threatened by events well beyond their control: a financial crisis, a violent conflict, AIDS, a national policy that undermines health care, a terrorist attack, water shortages, chronic destitution or Hazardous pollutants. The objective of human security ought to be to create political, economic, social, cultural and environmental conditions in which people live knowing that their vital rights and freedoms are secure.

"We must also broaden our view of what is meant by peace and security. Peace means much more than the absence of war. Human security can no longer be understood in purely military terms. Rather, it must encompass economic development, social justice,environmental protection, democratization, disarmament, and respect for human rights and the rule of law."[4]

Human security is a universal concern. It is relevant to people everywhere in all nations—rich or poor. Human security is people-centered. It is concerned with how people live and breathe in a society, how freely they exercise their many choices, how much access they have to market and social opportunities—and whether they live in conflict or in peace.

Kofi Annan, in his Report to the United Nations gave the following broad description of human security:

'Human Security, in its broadest sense, embraces far more than the absence of violent conflicts. It encompasses human rights, good governance, access to education and health care, and ensuring that each individual has opportunities and choices to fulfill his or her own potential. Every step in this direction is also a step towards reducing poverty, achieving economic growth, and preventing conflict. Freedom from want; freedom from fear; and the freedom of future generations to inherit a healthy natural environment— these are the inter-related building blocks of human and therefore, national security".[5]

The Declaration emphasizes not only the satisfaction of basic material needs of everyone, but also the right to information, and to choose government. The free expression of their choices is as crucial as freedom from squalor and hunger. Another important condition for security is the possibility of peaceful change, both at the domestic and international levels. If the people are dissatisfied and there is no mechanism through which unjust conditions can be detected and corrected, then the erupting violence shall jeopardize the security of states.

The concept of security has evolved considerably, coming to centre more on individuals, because it has been understood that security does not depend only on the armed forces of each state. Soft security issues, which do not invoke use of military force, are dominating the security scene for most nation states. Issues related with population, human and drug trafficking, refugees, organized crime, cyber crime; environmental degradation and terrorism are causing tremendous anxiety to policy makers all over the world.

For instance, not only do policy makers have to focus on conventional threats and conventional weaponry as a means of thwarting them, but also address the newly surfacing dimensions of the threats.

'A Comptroller and Auditor General (CAG) report, tabled in the Kerala Assembly in April 2013, warned in no uncertain terms about the consequences of ignoring or underestimating the dangers posed by lax coastal security. The report painstakingly lists out instances - from haphazard construction of Coastal Police Stations (CPSes) and deployment of untrained police personnel/boat crews to idling Interceptor Boats (IB) that expose the authorities' indifference and could lead to infiltration and attacks from the unguarded sea similar to the Mumbai 26/11 carnage.[6]

Human security may be endangered not only by aggression from outside a country's borders, but also from domestic violence. Crimes against an individual may be committed either for economic gains against the backdrop of a glaringly unequal society, or the threat to an individual's life may emanate from inter-group violence, against the backdrop of a heterogeneous society with conflicting claims over scarce resources. A nation where either of the two is prevalent cannot sustain its sense of security infinitely. National security is meaningless and almost impossible to sustain in the context of human insecurity.

Some of the threats undermining human security at the global level include the continuously altering regional balances, new conflict dynamics among civilizations and new environmental and ecological changes, insurgencies and separatist movements supported by drug trafficking or other crimes, heavily armed criminal gangs and Para-military forces assuming control over substantial areas or enterprises, illegal immigrations and threats to the integrity of national borders, arms trafficking and illegal trade in strategic materials, severe industrial and natural disasters, environmental damage, famine and public health hazards.

Robert Kaplan, in his article in the Atlantic Monthly, envisions a 'worldwide demographic, environmental and societal stress, in which criminal anarchy emerges as the real "strategic" danger. Disease, over-population, unprovoked crime, scarcity of resources, refugee migrations, the increased erosion of nation-states and international borders, and the empowerment of private armies, security firms and international drug cartels…(provide) an appropriate introduction to the issues … that will soon confront our civilization'.[7]

Security through arms build-up exclusively is difficult or almost impossible. The continual overemphasis on just one manifestation (that is, the building of weapons in the nuclear age) will inevitably lead to political repression, economic exhaustion and ecological collapse. And still, countries shall become more insecure. The more nuclear bombs we make and the more advanced delivery systems we deploy, greater shall be the risks of a nuclear war by design, accident, or proliferation. Moreover, the citizens too shall not be able to lead a peaceful or secure life. Undue focus on the military dimension ultimately burdens a nation with enormous political, economic, and environmental insecurities—which are hard to ward off.

The Economic Aspect:

It was hoped and expected that after the end of the cold war, the world will surely become a safer and better place to live in. It was hoped that innocent civilians will no more be slaughtered, intimidated, raped and driven out of their homes due to inter-state or intra-state conflicts—emanating from ideological or political or ethnic and religious grounds. Not only had the fear of an all-out nuclear war between the two superpowers faded, but also the regional conflicts which were hitherto fuelled by the two superpowers would begin to move towards ceasefire. However, this was not to be so.

'In the first twelve years of the post-cold war era (from 1990 to 2001), fifty seven major armed conflicts took place in forty five different countries… Almost all of the deadly conflicts of the post-cold war era have been either intra-state conflicts or intra-state conflicts with regional complications. Only four—the 1991 Gulf War, the 1998-2000 border war between Ethiopia and Eritrea, the 1999 Kargil conflict between India and Pakistan, and the 2003 war in Iraq—could be called conventional interstate conflicts.'[8]

Underdevelopment, chronic poverty, unemployment, and deteriorating living conditions are serious national security concerns. The role of economic factors is crucial because the after-effects of such factors on other national values are extensive. Persistent under-development and absence of economic well being degrade national morale and precipitate social turmoil, thus intensifying internal fragmentation. Such internal crises can trigger hostile actions by potential or actual adversaries.

The then External Affairs Minister Shri Pranab Mukherjee, opined in a Panel Discussion in Dec. 2008 on the theme 'Vision for a New South Asia': "... Security has many dimensions...without economic security can there be freedom? Today, much of South Asia is characterized by high rates of economic growth and yet, it remains as amongst the poorest regions in the world. There are almost 450 million persons who live below US $1 per day. The prevalence of extreme poverty and human deprivation reflects the acute income inequality and disparity prevalent in the region...Unless we can guarantee economic security or development for our people; a 'new' South Asia will not emerge. Indeed, economic security or the freedom from hunger, destitution and poverty is the only path towards dignity and development... Economic Security is the primary focus of our government..."[9]

Greater international economic interdependence can promote either peace or war, depending on how it is structured. Economic development can contribute to peace by making greater resources available for cultivation of people-to-people contacts by encouraging exchange programmes for students, teachers, professionals and the like. Research on how to avoid disputes and mediation efforts can gain momentum if the economic position is advantageous. But, reversely, it has been found that as a country's economy grows, the tendency to accumulate offensive arms is enhanced. Thus, whether economic development contributes to peace or to war is not so much an empirical question as a matter of what goals we choose. Greater wealth offers greater options, which may be used for better or for worse.

However, the reality of the contemporary times is that either the world exists together or perishes together. Consistent efforts at keeping ¾ of the world's population backward and wanting will result in civil wars and global terrorism at its worst.

It is recognized that lives cannot be secure amidst squalor and deprivation. Human security today necessitates the elimination of poverty and scarcity. In fact, conditions of economic backwardness precipitate social fragmentation and political turmoil – which further make the nation and its citizens insecure. The internal crises plaguing several countries are successfully fuelled by antagonistic neighbours primarily because the lives of citizens in the home country are insecure. High levels of inflation, coupled with unemployment and deprivation are the ideal breeding grounds for a plethora of social and political issues such as communalism, terrorism and the like.

If the basic needs of all are met, there is less social tension and less fertile ground for repressive governments. Along with an equitable distribution of wealth, a higher level of literacy and education has the potential to inform itself better, to articulate its needs more clearly, to defend its rights and freedoms more effectively, and to be less easily misled by demagogues. Economic shortages, on the other hand, promote envy and eve, open conflict.

The Socio-political Aspect:

Human security is being increasingly threatened by socio-political conflicts, particularly in societies constituted by people belonging to different religions, ethnic origins, language groups, and/or cultures. Each group may try to impose its way of life and values on another with the immediate objective of gaining political power and an underlying objective of then being able to control the allocation of economic resources.

Fischer, however, extended a note of warning: '...if people belonging to two different socio-economic groups also speak a different language, have a different religion and belong to a different ethnic group, the division between them can become very deep; tensions stemming from various issues tend to accumulate and mutually reinforce one another. In the most acute cases, such polarization may lead to civil war or often genocide'.[10]

National security comes under strain due to such conflicts in society, primarily because the involved parties draw in outside powers and if two foreign powers intervene to support different contending groups, the war escalates.

As such demands are expressed more violently; the other dimensions of security get roped in the imbroglio. Political stability is threatened by such socio-ethnic upheavals and the scarce economic resources have to be diverted to quell violence and restore normalcy. If the inability to handle the situation persists, the involved groups may arm themselves more dangerously and attack civilians in a bid to make those at the helm of affairs accept their demands. Terrorism, which is 'a sort of hybrid between crime and warfare',[11] could come to stay forever in the country and pose a persistent threat to its security system.

In India, for example, the insurgency movements in the states of the North-East have been raging since more than five decades. These states have international borders with neighbouring countries, whose territories are available to be used as training centres for the terrorist groups. The genuine socio-economic and ethnic grievances having been ignored in the initial years, the international vested interests could successfully fuel them along with misperceived grievances. The security of the nation is therefore at stake and the social causes thereof, have been kept alive through moral and material support extended by the neighbouring countries. Insurgency movements are a threat to national security and such threats cannot be tackled by the armed forces alone. Since the threat has a social dimension, the solution too must be socially rooted. While every state in the North-East has its own peculiar set of issues, yet the common grievances include lack of development, poor socio-economic conditions, exploitation of mineral and natural resources without matching benefits reaching the local population, influx of outsiders and their total hold over trade and commerce and most important, the strong feeling of social, economic, and political alienation. Since both China and Pakistan have exploited these causes and continued to fuel insurgency, our national security is endangered

The new biggest threat to India's security is the violence unleashed by the Maoists. On June 22, 2009, the Ministry of Home Affairs (MHA) named the CPI (Maoist) as the 34th terrorist organization under the Unlawful Activities (Prevention) Act, thus making India home to the largest number of domestic terrorist organizations in the world.[12]

The inequalities and injustices that are spiralling in the country give birth to the spree of violence by illegitimate actors like the Maoists. Internal security threats almost always emerge against the context of deprivation, despair, long-standing injustice and repression which have been going on for a long period of time. 'Perhaps this is where return to a focus on the core issue of tribal displacement and habitat, cannot in the circumstances, be delinked from the fate of the Maoist movement. After all the Maoist movement is not only a current problem or a temporary happenstance specific to the present conjuncture. Since 1967, the Naxal movement in its present avatar, the Maoists have stared in the face of the ruling order of the country.[13]

According to Prakash Singh, former Director-General of the Border Security Force (BSF), "I am not surprised that we have so many local terror groups. Since Independence, we have seen the rise of a new terrorist movement in every decade, whether it be the Naxals, militants in Punjab, terrorists in the North East or in J&K. It is failure of governance that has led to this situation".[14]

A recent United Nations Report gave a sombre assessment of a world at peace, but not in peace: 'Civil wars and internal conflicts have become the principal causes of violence, destruction and the displacement of peoples as conflicts between nation-states and rivalries among major military powers subside... During the period 1980-90, there were 33 armed conflicts in the world, only one of which was between nation-states'.[15]

Peace and security conditions are also boosted by the complete provision and protection of political rights. If the rulers and the ruled are at peace, there is no incentive to go to war—even externally. If the redress machinery constituted by the state is effective, discontent can never be taken advantage of, by enemy nations and the nation cannot easily become a breeding ground for terrorism. Also, individual freedom and state security are linked so much so that certain political conditions threaten both simultaneously, viz., unjust laws, abuses of power, excessive state secrecy, absence of constitutional checks and balances and dictatorship. At the same time, conditions such as democracy, basic freedoms, efficient judiciary, and effective mechanisms for conflict-resolution protect both— the individual and the state.

A comprehensive protection of political rights promotes peace in two ways. First, democracies have been found less likely to go to war against each other, and democratic decision making, if fully implemented, restrains a government from starting aggressive war. Second, if people are able to express grievances and have legal means available to redress them, discontent does not explode. Intense frustrations and lack of recourse to obtain justice is often a breeding ground for conflicts, terrorism and for war.

A nation's internal security is inevitably threatened by bad governance marked by incompetence, inefficiency, economic mismanagement, lack of adequate attention to economic and social development, feelings of injustice and alienation among people, corruption and the insensitivity of the administration to the legitimate grievances of the people. All of the above facilitate the exploitation by external powers of the grievances and of the sense of alienation among the people.

The Ecological Aspect:

> *'Traditional perspectives on security have been conceived of primarily in terms of neutralizing military threats to the territorial integrity and political independence of the state. However, in recent years, there has been increased emphasis placed on expanding the traditional conception of security to include so-called non-conventional threats. These include: resource scarcity, rapid population growth, human rights abuses, outbreak of infectious disease, environmental degradation caused by toxic contamination, ozone depletion, global warming, water pollution, soil degradation and the loss of biodiversity. It is now accepted that environmental stress, often the result of global environmental change, coupled with increasingly vulnerable societies, may contribute to insecurity and even conflict'.*[16]

Conflicts in future are most likely to be over food, water, space or energy. Not only will the competition over crucial resources such as oil intensify in the coming years but unequal energy and resource endowments are plausible sources of conflict. Competing national claims, terrorist attacks and growing piracy in the high seas may jeopardize energy supplies and pose grave challenges.

In the pre-Industrial Revolution era, states competed over land and labour because these constituted the primary source of revenue on which states subsisted. When death rates were high and diseases rampant, the demand for labour was greater than that for land. In such contexts, the capture of people as slaves was the primary objective of warfare. Hence extensive slavery was witnessed in tropical Africa, South East Asia, and Latin America and in the Mediterranean too. With rapid growth in population, land became the primary motive for warfare. Some lands were so rich that they were routinely fought over, as for example, Egypt or the Gangetic Plan. If the land was rich in a resource worth warring over—such as oil or water, then the battles intensified.[17]

With the rise in the strategic value of oil as a resource, many wars were fought over it. The best examples are the Pacific War of 1941-45 and the Gulf War of 1991.[18] Environmental changes are more likely to play a significant role in security issues in contemporary times than they have in the past because international competition over crucial resources and hence, ecological pressures are higher than ever before.

Of the utmost concern is the shortage of clean drinking water vis-à-vis the demand for it due to the surging rate of growth in population. Unless the concerned countries sensibly agree to share waters of rivers running between them, the ensuing frictions over supply will cast further burden on other crucial resources. No nation can afford to let water shortage constrain its agricultural development and consequently, economic development—both of which may confine the military potential too.

Similarly, the global demand for energy too will continue to rise despite the developed world cultivating less energy-intensive techniques for boosting economic growth. Perhaps substitutes for oil will emerge in the years to come and we shall see efficiency and conservation in the distribution and use of water too and both these developments will prevent serious conflict. However, environmental considerations will impact upon security of nation-states. And the degradation and disruption that we are causing to the ecological system will endanger human security like never before.

Our decisions and actions which affect the environment do not recognize man made boundaries. Survival of the human race will not just be threatened for the people of the country which is the main culprit of the catastrophe. All countries, irrespective of their contribution to the onset of the greenhouse effect, shall almost equally bear the cost of it.

"There is now overwhelming scientific evidence that the world is now moving towards the point at which irreversible ecological catastrophe becomes unavoidable." [19]

If the natural resources are mismanaged further, not only will every nation's life support system be ruined, but the probability of inter-state war too shall increase. 'There are at least four different ways that natural resource policies can cause or exacerbate international conflicts. Direct competition for resources like oil or water can pit nation against nation. Environmental degradation resulting from resource mismanagement can create global friction. The vulnerability of a resource infrastructure to sabotage or seize can encourage adversary nations or terrorists to attack. And resource mismanagement can mean lost dollars and lost opportunities—that otherwise could strengthen national security'.[20]

The environmental devastation caused by the extraction, consumption and disposal of resources is bound to generate conflicts between nations. Relations between nations are strained when crops, buildings and people are devastated across borders due to say, for example, acid rain. 'Competition over finite resources, including water for human consumption and agriculture, may be a cause of future international frictions'.[21]

The Suggested Measures:

Development must be sustainable so as to improve the prospects for democracy, improve health and economic productivity and alleviate pressure on the global environment. If nations are unable to provide jobs, education, and other services to their citizens, there shall be hunger, malnutrition, economic inequality, migration and social unrest. Citizens must be safeguarded also against diseases such as AIDS and other epidemics that can spread through environmental damage, threaten the health infrastructure of developing countries, disrupt societies and obstruct economic growth.

Civil society—the web of non-governmental groups, organizations and movements that empower citizens to solve their own problems can go a long way in enhancing human security. Associations and/or groups fighting for the rights of the marginalised sections, can release steam from potentially explosive social problems and resolve them through grassroots inventiveness. They can prevent a nation from becoming further vulnerable and insecure. If higher levels of participation within a democracy are encouraged, the degree of self-constraint increases too.

UNESCO has also done important work in promoting this concept, organizing a series of international seminars to promote regional approaches towards a clearer understanding of the needs and the most appropriate modes of action for the joint promotion of human security and conflict prevention in each specific regional and cultural context. In this context, the Chief of the UNESCO Section of Philosophy and Human Sciences, Moufida Goucha, has emphasised the importance of 'preventing conflicts and violence, paying special attention to the combined effect of the risks and threats to citizens and pursuing the eradication of non-armed, non-military threats to peace and security. This means taking the concepts of Human Security and democratic security further, at a time when there is such a clear need to renew the international logic of security'.[22]

Any one exclusive measure can hardly be expected to deliver the desired results in complicated situations which threaten peace in the present times. A carefully planned out and customised combination of measures (with each component in a near-exact proportion) contains the key to address issues. The root causes of conflict have to be understood, faith restored, discipline ensured, governance improved and mediators involved and then there comes a breakthrough! Merely doling out funds in conflict-ridden areas are best avoided because thee insecurity and mistrust persists. There is also every possibility of an assured misappropriation of funds. Similarly, a violent retaliation by the forces of the State to the violence unleashed by the non-state actors too cannot work in isolation, until adequate measures to overcome deprivation, unemployment and poverty are implemented. In addition, political will is also as much necessary as the involvement of non-partisan mediators and the local institutions at the grass root level.

The strategic methods of ensuring security come with grave risks. Nuclear weapons have played an important role in destabilising our sub-continent. There are scholars who remain confident that the leaders of nuclear states in South Asia are rational and will behave responsibly, as they have done in all the years since India and Pakistan have become nuclear weapons capable states. They believe that leaders of both nations will avoid overly provocative actions for fear of triggering a devastating response. However, some others insist that the decade since the South Asian nuclear tests, suggests that a principal risk of nuclear proliferation is not that the leaders of new nuclear states will be irrational or suicidal; the danger is that leaders may weigh their strategic options and reasonably conclude that risky behaviour best serves their interests. [23]

Socio-economic development and good political governance can assuage the wounds of aggrieved groups who are unleashing an array of violent attacks within a nation and also equip the nation to deal with violence sponsored by external forces—with greater focus and strength. In the case of Pakistan, deadly weaponry and sophisticated technology that it has acquired through questionable means have not brought any reprieve from violence for the civil society. The people in Pakistan continue to reel under dangerously unstable and violent conditions. The state of affairs in Pakistan is well expressed by Bennett-Jones:

"The lack of democracy in the country is best seen as a symptom of the problem rather than the problem itself. For as long as millions of Pakistanis remain illiterate, impoverished, and unaware of their rights and responsibilities in society, meaningful democracy will not be achievable..." [24]

Various regimes in Pakistan have tried to integrate the civil society through use of coercion and have tried to exploit the numerous ethno-religious divisions that run through the society. Focus was rarely on assuring a basic minimum provision of food, education, infrastructure, health, and good living conditions to all. [25]

Regimes must remember though that the earlier played games of power politics do not guarantee survival any more—neither for the players of the game and nor for the masses. A divided society living in despair will make it impossible even for the rulers to survive in peace. A poor and starved nation cannot boast of an assured sense of security merely on the basis of the deadly weaponry it possesses. A few developing countries have become insecure places to lives in, not because of a lack of a huge defence force but because of overt conflict and violence emanating from chronic poverty, crime, population expansion and an overall deteriorating quality of life.

Just as at critical moments in life, there are two roads before us and we are exhorted to choose one, a perusal of the history of violence in the world reveals that almost at all times there have been two doors before mankind. Both the doors could never be and cannot be opened at the same time. When one is opened, the other remains automatically shut. **One is the door to justice and the other is the door to violence**. Which door would we like to leave open for the generation to come?

Endnotes and References

1   "Inclusion or Exclusion: Social Development Challenges For Asia and Europe." Statement of Mrs.Sadako Ogata United Nations High Commissioner for Refugees at the Asian Development Bank Seminar, 27 April 1998. <http://www. unhcr.ch/refworld/unhcr/hcspeech/27ap1998.htm> 08/22/01

2   http://www.smallarmssurvey.org/files/sas/publications/co_publi_pdf/2003/2003-southeastasia.pdf

3   http://www.gechs.org/aviso/06/index.html

4 Kofi Annan, "Towards a Culture of Peace", <http://www.unesco.org/opi2/lettres/ TextAnglais/AnnanE.html>08/22/01

5 Kofi Annan, *We the People,* report to the UN, 2000

6 Pradeep Thakur,' CAG report exposes criminal lapse in coastal security', *Times News Network* April 7, 2013.

7 Robert Kaplan,' The Coming Anarchy', *Atlantic Monthly*, (1994), 273 (2) pp.44-75

8 Michael E. Brown, "Security Challenges in the Twenty-First Century", in Grave New World, ed. Michael E. Brown (Georgetown University Press, Washington D.C., 2003) p.3

9 http://meaindia.nic.in/speech/2008/12/20ss01.htm

10 Dietrich Fischer, *Non Military Aspect of Security: A Systems Approach* (UNIDR), 1993, p.19

11 Ibid. p.19

12 http://timesofindia.indiatimes.com/opinion/Editorial/india-has-most-number-of-domestic -terror-groups/articleshow/4694618.cms

13 SarojGiri," Dial M for Maoists", *Tehelka,* Vol. 7, Issue 9, March 6, 2010, New Delhi, p.19

14 http://timesofindia.indiatimes.com/opinion/Editorial/india-has-most-number-of-domestic- terror- groups/articleshow/4694618.cms

15 United Nations Department of Economic and Social Development's: *Report on the World Social Situation* (United Nations, New York, 1993).

16 Read Renner, M., 1989. *National security: the economic and environmental dimensions.* Worldwatch Paper 89. Washington, DC: Worldwatch Institute. Also, Ullman, R.H., 1983. Redefining security.*International Security* 8(1): 129 – 153. And also Westing, A.H., 1989. The environmental component of comprehensive security.*Bulletin of Peace Proposals* 20(2): 129 - 134.

17 Read J. R. McNiell, "Environmental Change and Security" in *Grave New World,* Michael E. Brown, ed. (GeorgetownUniversity Press, WashingtonD.C., 2003)

18 Ibid.

19 http://hdr.undp.org/en/reports/global/hdr2007-2008/

20 Michael H. Shuman and Hal Harvey, *Security without War- A Post Cold War Foreign Policy* (Westview Press, 1993) pp 105-106

21 Dietrich Fischer, *Non Military Aspects of Security: A Systems Approach* (UNIDR 1993), p.21

22 MoufidaGoucha, *Unit for Peace and the New Dimensions of Security*, (UNESCO, December 1999).

23 S.PaulKapur,' South Asia's Unstable Nuclear Decade', *Strategic Analysis*, Vol. 33 (3), May 2009, pp. 393-403

24 See Owen Bennett-Jones,' US Policy Options toward Pakistan: A Principled and Realistic Approach', *Stanley Foundation Policy Analysis Brief Series,* February 2008, at http://www.stanleyfoundation.org/publications/pab/JonesPAB208.pdf.

25 Michael Kraig,' India as a Nuclear-Capable Rising Power in a Multi-polar and Non-Polar World', *Strategic Analysis,* 33 (3), May 2009, pp. 365-380

India's National Security: Concerns and Strategies

Mohanan Bhaskaran Pillai

Introduction

India has always attracted the attention of spectators from all over the world—spectators who are awed by her size, who are surprised by her numbers, who are amazed by the democratic resilience that it has shown over the years. There have been innumerable discussions about *how does India do it?* and there exist ample expert analyses of the same. However, equally large is the literature on *how India could do it better?* And this is where most inter-state dialogues and talks are stalled as the answer to this question, for most part, entails debates over security issues.

Security forms an important component of the way international relations are played out. Though it took some time for India to break out of its *enlightened national interests* cocoon, it has since focussed on its security concerns to a great extent. Internationally, India has been included in the strategic plans of several nations, including the United States of America. It has acquired an important position globally on international matters and issues directly or indirectly affecting it. In fact, it is at the regional level that India faces a number of challenges on the security front.

Being the largest nation in South Asia, India has been timelessly accused of its benevolently despotic attitude and its initiatives in the region have been taken often as attempts to outshine, rather out power the other smaller nations of the region. They feel insecure in the face of India's gigantism. Often likened to a typical South Asian joint family that has broken up, analysts draw attention to the ways in which these broken families are turning to outside help (especially China) in order to protect themselves from India. This has given rise to manifold security concerns within the region and in India in particular and of variegated textures. Terrorism, illegal immigration, trafficking, resource constraints and so on, have all gradually led India to flex its muscles outside South Asia in order to deal with them. This international dimension to India's security policy has infused changes in relations within South Asia. India's security policy and the relation that it shares with the larger world are deeply intertwined where one impacts upon the other and vice versa.

Neo-liberal Globalization and the Security Architecture

The ascendancy of the neoliberal global regime coupled with the demise of Soviet Communism had drastically altered the international power configuration during the closing decades of the twentieth century. The bipolar power structure that ruled the roost in the post-world war governance architecture got replaced by a unipolar (or non-polar ,if we may call so) one, which gave a jostle to the sluice valves of the new security concerns like global terrorism, environmental issues, energy security, food security etc., in addition to the traditional security issues, for the entire world in general and the re-emerging powers like India in particular.

The complexity that surfaced as a by product of the commingling of new and traditional security concerns shook the nations of the global South to think afresh, about the very notion of security so as to cope up with new challenges being thrown open in a non-polar world driven by neo-liberal globalization. In fact the nation-states, in its conventional frame of reference, are not sufficiently attuned to address the new security concerns in a comprehensive manner. In this context, the challenges that confront a reemerging power like India is to formulate its security and strategic policies to address both the conventional security threats as also the new breeds of security concerns that are the creations of the new world order that emerged with the cave-in of the Soviet Union. Therefore, it is the need of the hour to weave a comprehensive strategy to address both the conventional and non-conventional security threats that the country faces both from the domestic theatre and the external setting. The entanglement of the internal situation with a complicated external settings makes it difficult for the policy makers and strategic planners to devise a comprehensive security architecture for India.

It is a fact that the security perceptions of states underwent drastic changes in the post-cold war era. Economic security appears to be the foremost concern of all nations. Though the conventional security perception has not been abandoned outright, it has lost much of its sheen.

The emergence of new forms of threat from the transnational terrorist groups added new dimensions to the security concerns of nations. The operations of these groups have demonstrated that traditional approach to security is redundant. No nation, whatsoever powerful, can single-handedly tackle the threats posed by terrorist groups. This again demands multilateralism in international relations to meet the challenges posed by transnational non- state actors.

The process of globalization- the free flow of financial capital across the world – intertwined every nook and cranny of the world into the logic of global capitalism; it brought together all nations in a common platform. If anything happened in any corner of the world it will have its reverberations felt everywhere. Therefore, the security of a nation is vexed with the security of every other nation. The globalization process has not only brought the nations together at the global platform but also forced nations to have a fresh look at regional cooperation efforts to ensure security and economic growth.

The growth and development of non-state actors in international relations is comparatively a new phenomenon. In the changed situation, domestic and global civil society are gaining prominence particularly as an instrument that constructs consent. The interaction among people as a result of information revolution has contributed substantially for further strengthening of the bonds of universal brotherhood on the other hand. Better understanding among the people, transcending the artificial boundaries would further weaken the role of state as a player in international relations. Today the strength of a nation appears to be based not solely on the possession of destructive weapons but on many other factors including the strength of its economy, democratic institutions and the security that they provide to their people. Thus in the post-cold war period, at least in the analytical plane, the concept of 'human security' has gained grounds.

India's National Security: Concerns and Strategies

After independence India followed a policy of non-alignment that got incubated in the nest of freedom movement. The experiments in diplomacy and foreign policy on a platform of nonalignment with its core value of strategic autonomy were to protect and promote the national interest of the new born nation. Right from the Nehruvian era the recurring theme in

India's foreign policy is "strategic autonomy".The seemingly autonomous space that was carved out of nonalignment policy facilitated the growth of domestic capital in the age of "embedded liberalism".But actually it was not autonomous as it was projected. In fact, foreign policy of a country can never be independent and autonomous. It is the spin-offs from a kind of complex relations that emanate from the domestic theatre and the external milieu.

India's foreign policy during the Nehru era was dominated by the question, how to sustain a full- fledged capitalist development legitimately under state tutelage. Ideologically NAM's argumentation was couched in the fine language of counter- hegemony. But India never delinked itself from the world capitalist system. In fact, Nehru's proclaimed policy of non-alignment was a strategy aimed at augmenting adequate infrastructure facilities from everywhere to accelerate native capitalist development. By adding socialist flavours, the Indian bourgeoisie embarked on a strategy of domestic capital development under state patronage. Import substitution industrialization was ensured under the protectionist umbrella of the state. From a political economy perspective, nonalignment never enjoyed strategic autonomy in the true sense of the term. The objective of nonalignment was to facilitate import substitution strategies to help the growth of domestic capital within the overall framework of welfare state –the dominant paradigm of development of the period. 'Embedded Liberalism' always allowed a bit of flexibility within its extended boundary .Nehru and later Indira Gandhi made use of this extended boundaries of embedded liberalism to promote economic growth and development through import substitution strategies. The world capitalist system has moved out of its welfare capitalist phase to the brand new corporate techno-capitalist phase - a decisive shift from embedded liberalism to neo-liberalism. World capitalist system in its new phase forced the countries of the South to structurally adjust their   economies to the requirements of finance capital. In the present phase of global political economy, the native bourgeoisie is inclined towards more cooperation with foreign capital and the state is attuned to an outward looking growth strategy. The neoliberal reforms in the Indian economy coincided with the formulation of the celebrated Look East Policy (LEP) and strategic partnership with the US.

The post-cold war period witnessed replacement of the bipolar balance of power of embedded liberalism period with the overarching dominance of finance capital controlled by global conglomerates. Side by side, the domestic Indian capital too has grown strong enough to take up roles beyond the territorial limits of India and naturally turned out to be subservient to global finance capital on the domestic front.

During the period of 'embedded liberalism'-precisely during the period of cold war - India's security concerns revolved around the threats emanating primarily from Pakistan. On a conventional analytical frame, China is also perceived as a threat to India's national security. However, the age of neoliberal globalization has added additional dimensions to the conventional threats. In the post-cold war period the major security concern of India emanates from cross border terrorism. All other traditional security concerns are overtaken by economic issues. The challenges posed by international terrorism, global economic meltdown and environmental degradation including climate change are also security concerns that India has to address seriously. The crisis in the energy sector is a major security challenge. On the domestic front India faces many challenges including poverty, illiteracy, social and economic inequality, communalism, regional imbalances and development based displacement, Maoist insurgency etc. The other most important security theatre, that requires a distinct treatment particularly in the aftermath of Mumbai terrorist attack, seems to be the Indian Ocean.

India's national security strategy is required to be dove-tailed with the larger concept of human security.

In a broader sense security of the nation is nothing but the welfare of its people. This is in fact a realization based on the inputs from the nonconventional concept of human security. There appears to be a shift in focus from military security to economic and environment security. The plea for a human security approach is a post-cold war development. The positive as well as negative impacts of globalization process have accelerated the momentum for human security approach. On the positive side, globalization helped the growth of civil society organization at the national and international levels. These organizations make democratic system more participatory and people friendly. With regard to the negative impact of globalization process, the withdrawal of state from welfare activities further worsened the position of poor and marginalized sections in the society.

Tuning the international and domestic situations favourable to India's security architecture is a daunting task. The post-cold war international power structure, is symptomatic of the overarching politico-military dominance of the US which turned out to be the protective shield of the international political economy managed by the Wall Street –WTO-World Bank complex. However, the US initiatives to curb international terrorism and actions against state sponsored terrorism suites to New Delhi's official positions on India's foreign policy objectives which was reformulated in the aftermath of the collapse of the Soviet Union. In official parlance, India's relations with the United States have acquired remarkable maturity and dynamism in the post-cold war period. Many developments created theconducive atmosphere for such a transformation, including the end of the Cold War. India's emergence as a dynamic economic force and an objective assessment of the strategic implications of a world dominated by knowledge-driven societies have also led to the same.

At present the India-US relations are moving beyond a bilateral partnership towards a global partnership, which is anchored not only on common values but also common interests of the dominant sections. The strategic dimension of India's relationship with the US underlines their common interest in combating terrorism, proliferation of weapons of mass destruction and enhancing global peace. There has been a convergence of views on strategic and security issues which extends to cooperation in defense, science and technology, health, trade, space, energy and environment. It is worth noting that the US counts India on its side in the execution of the newly crafted 'rebalancing strategy in the Indo-pacific region'.

On several counts US' rebalancing strategy in the Indo-Pacific region finds strategic convergence with India's "Look East" policy which was drawn up in the 90s to cement further its relations with the countries of South East and East Asia in the context of the disappearance of India's most trusted friend Soviet Union from the political map of planet earth. More than an external economic policy or a political slogan, the look east policy is a strategic shift in India's vision of the world and its place in the evolving global political economy. It is also a manifestation of India's belief that developments in East Asia are of direct consequence to its security and development. Therefore, India is actively engaged in creating a bond of friendship and cooperation with East Asia; and that has a strong economic foundation and a cooperative paradigm of positive inter-connectedness of security interests.The LEP represents a reorientation of India's foreign economic policy in the aftermath of the demise of the Soviet Union and it signaled the end of the era of self-reliant growth strategy. The economic and foreign policy elites of the country facilitate the business class of India to take advantage of the new opportunities thrown open by neoliberalism in the form of international trade and investment. Techno-capitalism manifested its ability to fragment production across borders and reintegrate the process through trade and transnationalisation of production relations. A multi-layered system of transnational governance has emerged under the protective shield of the international political economy managed by the Wall Street –WTO- World Bank complex under the overarching politico-military dominance of the US.

Nature of the state and class configuration in the society and its relations with the world capitalist core are the major determinants of the foreign policy of a nation. In the case of India native capital is inclined to have more cooperation with foreign capital. India's foreign policy establishment is now closely aligned with the interests of business groups and corporates which are exporting capital and welcoming foreign capital.

It is to be noted here that India is part of multilateral interaction with its membership in the four nation grouping called BRIC (Brazil, Russia, India, and China) to strengthen collective relationships. This grouping's political interaction could help to alter the shape of the international financial system and the global economy. One of the objectives of the grouping is democratization of international financial institutions. The joint declaration at the first summit meeting held in Russia focus on global food security. The BRIC countries supported the adoption of a wide range of mid- to long-term measures in order to provide for a solution to the issue of food security. However India's capacity to take forward the momentum of multilateralism is doubtful because of deepening of integration with the capitalism of the globalized age.

India and the Human Security

In the twentieth century, the state centric notion of national security is being replaced with the individual centric notion of security. The classical formulation of security is about how state uses force to manage threat to its territorial integrity, its autonomy and its domestic political order, primarily from other states. Some critiques of classical formulation of security are of the view that the protection and welfare of the individual citizen or human being is central to any security architecture. The conception of human security that talks in terms of the sanctity of the individual and ultimately the security of the entire planet.

According to Human Development Report, Human security means protection of the vital freedoms of the individuals. In other words, protecting the people from critical and pervasive threats and situations, building on their strengths and aspirations are integral part of any conceptualization on Human Security. The report further maintains that creation of systems that provide people the building blocks of survival, dignity and livelihood is components of human security. In fact human security concept strives to connect different types of freedoms - freedom from want, freedom from fear and freedom to take action on one's own behalf. To do this, it offers two general strategies: protection and empowerment. Protection shields people from dangers. It requires concerted efforts to develop norms, processes and institutions that systematically address insecurities. Empowerment enables people to develop their potential to become full participants in decision-making. Protection and empowerment are mutually reinforcing, and both are required in most situations. Human security complements state security, furthers human development and enhances human rights. It complements state security by being people-centered and addressing insecurities that have not been considered as state security threats. By looking at "downside risks", it broadens the human development focus beyond "growth with equity". Respecting human rights are at the core of human security concept. The above discussion naturally takes us to the task of looking at the paradigmatic shift in the security discourses, especially a shift from the state centric notion of security to the human security problematic. It also stimulates us to re-visit   the security dimensions of India's traditional foreign policy to locate the specificities of strategic autonomy embedded in the precepts of nonalignment.

Concluding observations

In the aftermath of the Great Depression and World War II, a new social structure of accumulation came into being in the capitalist world to regulate the macro economy and to provide a set of social programmes under the mixed economy rubric. A world order had been constructed through the Brettonwoods agreements such as UN, World Bank, IMF etc. A blend of state, market and democratic institutions to guarantee peace, inclusion, wellbeing and stability had also been created. As we have noted elsewhere the world capitalist system has undergone a shift from welfare capitalism of the post war II period to the new phase of finance capitalism. The social structure of capital accumulation has simultaneously witnessed a dramatic shift from accumulation through the expansion of wage labour in industry and agriculture to accumulation by dispossession, which in fact entails a very different set of practices. The former form of capital accumulation which dominated the scene during the fifties and sixties was not hostile to the culture of opposition that appeared in the form of trade unions and working class political parties. The contemporary form of capital accumulation on the other hand is fragmented and hostile to oppositional culture.

Viewed thus nonalignment has its own limitations to be rejuvenated as a policy frame work of strategic autonomy as native capital is inclined to have more collaboration with foreign capital. Secondly, in the context of the new social structure of accumulation, translating the concept of human security to implementable policy prescriptions would remain to be elusive. Finally, at a time when integration with the core is further tightened which automatically subordinates the periphery, attempts at multilateralism cannot cross the Rubicon of rhetoric.

The Indian Ocean Region and Changing Security Dynamics

Anu Unny

"Whoever controls the Indian Ocean, dominates Asia. The ocean is the key to seven seas. In the 21st century,the destiny of the world will be decided on its waters."

- Alfred Mahan (US Admiral)

Introduction

The Indian Ocean region (IOR) has emerged as a strategic theatre critical to global trade and energy security. By knitting many Asian, African and Middle East countries together through the extended market networks and commerce, Indian Ocean contributes to their overall prosperity and development. Half of worlds' seaborne trade is now through the Indian Ocean trade routes. It is a strategic area of interest for big powers today,as it contains around 40% of the world's gas and oil reserves. It is argued that most of the conflicts in this region in future would be to gain supremacy over the vast energy resources the region possesses. At present the Indian Ocean region is inhabited by 1/3rd of the world's population and it covers around 20% of the total Earth's sea surface. One thing to be noted that, despite its huge geographic span,Indian Ocean had not been figured prominently in the geo-political interests of global powers for many decades. However the growing population in the region, world's increased dependence on the Persian-Gulf hydrocarbon resources, growing political tensions, destruction of strategic sea lines of communication(SLOCs) and above all the emergence of India and China as key players in the region,is adding a new dimension to its geo-political relevance. In the 21st century, while Indian Ocean opens up vast opportunities to be developed as a potential geo-strategic area, it also presents certain challenges for maritime policy makers, ranging from traditional security threats like piracy and armed robbery, trafficking of narcotics and small arms to new security challenges such as dumping of nuclear waste and environmental challenges. Taking into account these multi facetedchallenges, Ken Booth and William L. Dowdy opined that 'Indian Ocean might be dubbed a kaleidoscope of crisis and not merely an arc'.[1] When we look into the present day challenges that threaten the region's overarching security, we may have to agree with this.

Security Challenges

In the 21st century, concept and meaning of security has undergone a drastic change. Security is no more confined only to military security, but extended to other aspects of security as well including resource security, economic security, environmental security and above all human security. In modern times, security challenges are no longer region specific issues, but they have larger ramifications upon extra regional actors as well. These challenges are interrelated and multi-faceted in nature. When we examine security in the Indian Ocean context, challenges become more and more complex. As Bouchard pointed out, 'challenges in the Indian Ocean Region are distinct, because the region itself is fragmented into number of sub-systems and are characterized by heterogeneity, emergent regionalism and subordination to large regional players'.[2] Therefore what we need to focus is, on developing a new Indian Ocean security paradigm that can address these multidimensional challenges.

Regional conflicts

Today, Indian Ocean Region has turned to become a zone of perennial regional conflicts. So far Indian Ocean Region has witnessed more than half of the world's armed conflicts. Struggle for power and supremacy over the Persian Gulf, recurring tensions in South Asia especially between India and Pakistan, existence of failing and failed regimes in the Indian Ocean littoral states, unrest and civil wars in Southern Africa,competition over marine resources, increased dependence on oil and natural gas all have paved the way for regional disputes and fuelling instability. Apart from this, strong presence of extra regional actors such as United States, European Union states, Japan and China, attempts to possess major SLOCs such as Strait of Malacca, Strait of Hormuz, Bab el-Mansab, huge size of surveillance area and open waters of Indian Ocean etc have complicated the efforts to redress tensions in the region. The increasing concerns about securing SLOCs have given rise to a kind of security dilemma in the region. 'Malacca dilemma' and 'Hormuz dilemma' are the after effects of it.

Extra-regional actors and threat perceptions

Second set of security challenges arise from the power struggle and military presence of extra-regional actors in the region. Though the presence of extra regional actors in the Indian Ocean waters is not a new phenomenon, their military presence is relatively new. The increased interest of great powers especially of United States and China in the Indian Ocean Region has added a new dimension to Indian Ocean security. In the 19th century, if it was Britain which controlled the Indian Ocean waters, with the decline of British naval power, U.S. occupied that position. Now, with the increasing maritime abilities of China in the region, U.S. is facing stiff competition and the region itself has turned to become potential zone of conflict. China's 'String of Pearls' strategy and its attempts to acquire naval bases along important chokepoints have been viewed with much suspicion by regional as well as extra regional states. The 'String of Pearls' strategy which is primarily designed to increase China's access to major ports and airfields, its military modernization programmes, China's increasing involvement in Maldives, Bangladesh, Sri Lanka and Pakistan all are viewed as alarming developments at least by India and United States. Though China has maintained that its Indian Ocean strategy is designed mainly to protect its commercial interests rather than its military interests, this argument has not been taken into account by states like India. It is in this context that U.S's newly formulated Asia-Pacific strategy becomes significant.

U.S, China and 'Pivot to Asia' policy

U.S orchestrated strategic 'pivot to Asia' policy which was articulated in 2011 by the then U.S. Secretary of State Hillari Clinton clearly states that " the 21st century would be America's Pacific century. The U.S would lock in substantially increased investment-diplomatic, economic, strategic and otherwise in the Asia-Pacific region".[3] This U.S. policy shift focusing upon Asia- Pacific Region and attempts to assert its military primacy in the region has been viewed from different security angles by the Indian Ocean community. Some have observed this U.S policy shift as an attempt to rebalance and contain the 'rising China' in the Indian Ocean waters.

China has denounced U.S 'pivot to Asia' policy as a strategic move to contain its booming economic growth. For China, this U.S policy shift is a new version of U.S. cold war containment strategy. It is argued that if U.S. strategy during the cold war was primarily to counter the expansion of Soviet Union and thereby the growth of communism, in the post cold war era its target is primarily containment of China. Chinese foreign policy makers opine that first and foremost the U.S decision to engage in the Indian Ocean waters can be considered only as a strategic move to rebalance and counter China in the region. The 'AIR Sea Battle' strategy developed by U.S Department of Defence, was widely condemned by China. Along with that U.S's increased engagement with India in South Asia Region, also has been perceived with much suspicion by Chinese policy makers.

For United States, Indian Ocean Region has become strategically important because of several reasons. Not only the alarming economic and military rise of China but also the instability factor perpetuated by failed states and non state actors in the region, had drawn U.S. attention to this region. Ongoing conflicts in Afghanistan, concerns about energy security and other vital resources, strong presence of terrorist networks in the region and strategic relevance of SLOCs are some of the determining factors of U.S. policy on Asia-Pacific. Therefore the recent U.S. policy shift articulated by Obama Administration is not a surprise to maritime policy makers. The U.S. decision to increase its naval presence in the Indian Ocean waters was evident from the words of U.S. Secretary of Defense Leon Panetta when he said that "by 2020, 60 % of U.S. naval ships will be in the Pacific, and 40% in the Atlantic, compared with current 50-50 split".[4] Whatever it may be, increased military presence of these extra regional actors especially of China and U.S. in the Indian Ocean Region would be having its effects on Ocean security. At one hand, more military presence and patrolling by the Navies of these extra regional actors would help to combat piracy in the Indian Ocean waters; but on the other hand it would increase the possibility to have more armed conflicts in the region due to mutual struggle for power and intense competition. Nobody can reject the possibility for future wars in this region if these extra regional actors engage in intense struggle to acquire SLOCs aligning with their own traditional defence partners in the region.

Piracy and armed conflicts

Thirdly, Security challenges in the Indian Ocean Region can be broadly classified into two- traditional and non-traditional security challenges. One of the traditional security challenges to maritime security of Indian Ocean is the growing Somali piracy and the repeated hijackings of merchant vessels by the sea pirates. Somali piracy is pausing direct threat both to international maritime security and commerce. By the end of 2011, 237 vessels had been subjected to attack.[5] Most of the time the vessels passing through Gulf of Oman, Southern Red Sea, Gulf of Aden and Arabian Sea become the targets of attack. The lack of maritime security around Horn of Africa is also endangering regional stability. It was in this context of growing piracy and robbery, in order to combat the Piracy Attack Groups (PAGs) from hijacking the vessels, an international naval force was formed called the 'Combined Task Force 151', comprising NATO, European Union and US navy forces and today it has its presence in the Indian Ocean waters. Along with that, deployment of more armed private security teams by merchant vessels also contributes to strengthening security in the region. In recent times though the vessel hijackings have declined in number, piracy and armed robbery continues to be a daunting challenge. In order to find a long term solution for this problem, more concerted action need to be taken at regional, sub-regional and systemic level.

Illicit trafficking

Another long term challenge to be tackled in the Indian Ocean region is the illicit trafficking of narcotics, small arms and people within and via Indian Ocean to some export points located in politically unstable countries. The trafficking of heroin, especially Afghan heroin to Europe via Central Asia or via Arabian Sea shipping route has become quite common in the recent past. Along with this, illicit flow of small arms and light weapons (SALW) including anti-aircraft guns, anti-tank mines and hand guns pause challenges to security. These illicit weapons sometimes reaching into the hands of insurgents can be used for fuelling violence and political instability in the region. For example, the illicit arms trafficking from Iran to Yemen via Suez Canal has facilitated to fuel political instability in Yemen. Coupled with drug trafficking and arms trafficking, trafficking in human beings pause another challenge. The illicit trafficking of people from Southern Red Sea and Somalia to the Southern Arab countries have pushed these countries on many occasions to the extent of even civil war. In some African countries, repeated civil wars and consequent political tensions have been one of the main motivating factors for large scale migration of people to nearby states. This mass migration can actually destabilize the recipient country's economic, political stability.

Maritime Terrorism

Maritime domain with its vast expanse and lucrative targets has subjected to repeated terrorist attacks. Today, Maritime terrorism is an important issue of concern in the Indian Ocean security paradigm. Terrorist attacks carried out by various fundamentalist organizations like Al-Qaeda, Lashkar-e-Taiba, LTTE and Al Shabaab utilizing sea as a medium,is a cause of concern for maritime policy makers. Al-Qaeda's attack on the USS cole in 2000, Lashkar-e-Taiba's terrorist attack on Mumbai in 2008, LTTE attack on Trincomalee naval base in 2000 and again on Dakshina naval base in Galle in 2006 all had used maritime realm as a medium to conduct their terror strikes. Though a number of agreements have been signed by the international community in legal and regulatory framework like SUA and ISPS to counter maritime terrorism, these measures are still not adequate enough to address the diversity of challenges. At present, around 40% of the global trade is through Indian Ocean region.[6] It provides major sea routes connecting Atlantic Ocean with Pacific Ocean and thereby facilitating the entire commerce through the region. Any attempts to destroy the major SLOCs which are located in the Indian Ocean by these fundamentalist organizations would be a huge setback to global seaborne trade. Therefore international community need to be vigilant enough to respond and counter the threats paused by the asymmetric non-state actors which are active in this region.

Environmental challenges

The newly emerging non-traditional security challenges like environmental degradation, over exploitation of resources, marine pollution, over fishing, rising sea temperature and climate change are threatening the future of many littoral states in the region. The existence of communities inhabiting in the low-lying area of the region, especially of East Africa and South Asia, are in danger due to the rising sea level in the Indian Ocean region. In South Asia, Bangladesh and Malidives are the two worst hit areas from climate change. In the case of Bangladesh, even 1m rise in sea level may result in the submergence of 17% of its land mass and it can result in the resettlement of 20 million Bangladeshis by 2050.[7] Malidives being an island country which is just 3 feet above the sea level, a sea level rise of 22 inches may result in the disappearance of the whole country itself.[8] Apart from that, high level pollution causing due to ocean dumping, waste disposal and oil spills are also pausing challenges to the whole marine environment in the region.

Over fishing, depletion of coral reefs and excessive use of marine resources may lead to resource scarcity and later on even to 'resource wars'. When we analyze these new threats we should understand that these issues are no longer domestic security issues, but they have gained a trans-national dimension. Therefore, in this globalized era if we have to combat these challenges,nations need to stick to the idea of 'co-operative security'.

Governance Challenges

There is no doubt that 'governance' related issues can endanger Indian Ocean security. The region has been unable to amicably settle a set of issues including sea laws, maritime boundary disputes and resource distribution. The economic insecurity experiencing by some states in the Indian Ocean region and thereby growing political tensions, absence of good governance and corruption are contributing factors to the regional instability. Efforts aimed at proliferating nuclear weapons raise another set of security challenges. The proliferation of nuclear weapons in the region, have the potential even to lead the states to deliberate or accidental conflicts. Inequality of states in terms of the access to nuclear weapons may endanger the whole global security architecture. The existence of authoritarian regimes in the region, absence of democratization, lack of transparency in the functioning of governments all are daunting challenges to regional governance.

Re-envisioning Security

Indian Ocean region is becoming a potential zone of conflict globally both from a geo-political and geo-economic framework. Emerging powers like India and China strive to establish their supremacy in the strategic Indian Ocean region as they believe that it will contribute to their 'rising power' status. With a strategic shift in U.S. policy –'pivot to Asia policy', United States also has become a decisive player in determining region's politico-security dynamisms. However power struggle among these actors, increased competition to achieve more energy and economic security has the potential today to transform this region to a real zone of conflict. Therefore, to prevent countries from going into an actual state of war, the need of the hour is to construct more security regimes around areas of common interest and concern. The issues which threaten the nations' security can no longer be combated within the paradigm of nation states, but they have to be tackledtrans-nationally. Security threats such as terrorism, climate change, nuclear proliferation, trafficking of narcotics and human beings are common threats to almost all regional players. In order to combat these long term challenges which affect their national security, more attention need to be placed on developing co-operative security architecture. In this globalized era, only a collective security framework can achieve the goal of regional and national stability. However for that,what we need to re-conceptualize is the idea of security itself. Any analysis on security should be progressed from understanding the concept of human security. Only people centred view of security can ensure sustainable regional, national and global stability. A shift in thinking from national security to human security,more respect for human rights law and principles at national and international level, can actually bolster the efforts directed to enhance Indian Ocean security and stability.

Endnotes and References

1 Quoted in Ian W. Porter, "The Indian Ocean Rim," *African Security Review*, Vol.6, No.6, 1997, at P.81.

2 Bouchard, C. (2004), 'Emergence of a new geopolitical era in the Indian Ocean: characteristics, issues and   limitations of the Indianoceanic order', in Rumley and Chaturvedi, op. cit., pp. 84-109.

3 "America's Pacific Century," Remarks by Secretary of State Hillary Rodham Clinton, East-West Center, Honolulu, HI, November 10, 2011.

4 Leon Panetta (speech delivered at the Shangri-La Security Dialogue, Singapore, June 2, 2012) http://www.defense.gov/speeches/speech.aspx?speechid=1681.

5 Annual International Maritime Bureau Piracy Report , 2012 June. 6 The World Factbook. Cia.gov. Retrieved on 2013-07-28

6 INQUA, 2000.The Commission on "Sea level changes and coastal evolution".

7 IPCC Synthesis Report, Observations on Climate Change.in IPCC AR4 SYR 2007

8 Ibid.

PART - II

India's Maritime Security Concerns

Maritime Coastal Security Concerns

M P Muralidharan

Introduction

Broadly speaking, maritime security (and coastal security is a subset of it) may be considered to be the protection of assets and infrastructure that allow a nation to pursue sustainable economic growth through seaborne trade and coastal zone development. This Security of the seas and ocean around our subcontinent must not be seen solely through the prism of military presence and geo-political influence, but must also take into account 'humanistic' considerations.

For littoral nations, the Oceans are a major source of economic sustenance and a number of large coastal communities subsist on its marine resources. Any loss of this sustenance creates problems, including migration of fishermen into illicit/ criminal activities. The prosperity of the Indian Ocean rim states and the economic value of the cargos that ply these seas have prompted various forms of predatory and exploitative behaviour. From human trafficking, drugs smuggling and gun-running to maritime terrorism and piracy, the Indian Ocean has been witnessing many nefarious activities in its waters. There are also serious environmental problems.

The situation is compounded by the lack of understanding between nations on issues concerning 'security' in the littorals, and an asymmetry of influence between established powers and smaller states. While using the high seas for trade and other legitimate economic activities, there is also the need to address environmental and security concerns of nations.

COASTAL SECURITY

Coastal Security in Indian Context

Moving on to the Indian context; our maritime and coastal stakes are significant. We have a long coastline measuring over 7500 km, studded with vital industrial hubs and a huge EEZ measuring over 2 million square km. Almost 95% of our energy requirements are directly linked with the sea and 90% of our trade by volume is by sea. Threats to India's coastline can therefore have disastrous consequences for our economy.

Coastal Security, as we discuss now, emerged only after 26/11. Unfortunately, prior to 26/11, coastal security and any related debate on the subject had remained the exclusive preserve of Indian Navy and the Coast Guard. The task of guarding the vast coastline, unlike our land borders, is a complex phenomenon involving multiple stake holders such as shipping, fisheries, offshore Exploration and Production, tourism, and scientific community. In other words, it's not only about protecting our coastal terrain and territorial waters from direct military or militant attacks, but also safeguarding the interests of all stake holders. Thus, the Coastal Security efforts of today are primarily against: -

- Infiltration and attack from non-state actors.

- Illegal economic exploitation of our marine resources both living and non-living.

- Smuggling of arms, explosives, drugs and other contraband.

- Piracy, hijacking and other criminal acts including:-

  - Commandeering of fishing boats; and,

  - Presence of unseaworthy ships.

Initiatives upto 26/11

Poaching activities in Indian waters were the most visible threat facing us in the seventies and eighties. Fishermen from countries like Taiwan, Thailand, Indonesia and Myanmar, were poaching extensively in our waters, thereby depleting our precious marine wealth. Our conservative economy was also threatened by smuggling syndicates using sea route for trafficking of gold, silver and drugs. The Indian Coast Guard, then in its infancy, tackled both these issues firmly; however, it was the economic reforms of nineties that broke the back of smugglers. Just as the reforms were picking up momentum, came the serial bomb blasts in Mumbai in March 1993 that claimed over 250 valuable lives and injured hundreds of innocents. The sea route was used to smuggle in explosives and land it at various sites along the Gujarat and the Maharashtra coasts.

The reaction to these attacks was enhancing seaward security by the initiation of the three tiered 'Op Swan' along the Maharashtra and Gujarat coast, which saw symbolic involvement of State Police and Customs in coastal security for the first time . Close to coast patrolling was being undertaken by the Navy using hired fishing boats, as Coast Guard, at that time, neither had the manpower nor the wherewithal. These security measures were however not backed by shore based surveillance and there was also lack of coordination amongst intelligence agencies. The origin of Coastal Security really started post Kargil, when the Review Committee of Group of Ministers (GoM) amply addressed the issue. On their recommendations several measures were initiated which included:-

(a) Activation of Border Management (BM) division in MHA.

(b) Setting up of additional Coast Guard stations along the coastline to beef up coastal security.

(c) Setting up of coastal radar chain using existing lighthouses,

(d) Setting up of Marine Police in all coastal States and island territories, police stations were work in hub and spoke concept with CG stations. The GoM also recommended improvement of intelligence mechanism, including setting up of Multi Agency Centres both at Centre and States level (MAC / SMAC) and measures for enhancing the security at sea ports.

Implementation of these plans was however on a slow track and e 26/11 happened.

The Attack of 26/11- Concerns and Complexities

The use of sea route by terrorists for attack on Mumbai on 26/11 once again highlighted the vulnerability of our coastline and the lacunae in our coastal security mechanisms no doubt due to the complicated maritime environment. The seas are vast, and the tens of thousands of fishing boats that go out to sea and return each day to any point on the long coastline, constitute a major threat vector. The identification problem is not limited to fishing vessels alone, but also includes the hundreds of vessels that call at our Ports, or ply the Sea Lines of Communication (SLOCs), which pass close to our shore.

The sea cannot be kept under surveillance on a 24X7 basis. Next, due to inherent complexities and existing Laws, maritime boundaries are often dispute laden. Ethnic similarities and traditional links are utilised by fishermen, and terrorists alike, to cross over boundaries with ease.

COASTAL SECURITY POST 26/11 - EFFORTS AND INITIATIVES

Delineation of Responsibilities

Based on the fact that Maritime Security is not independent of Coastal Security, and none of the security forces have capability to take over the entire responsibility, the new Coastal Security mechanism post 26/11 has been evolved primarily based on coordination of efforts. Major players in the mechanism are the Navy, the Coast Guard and Marine Police, with the Ports, Customs and BSF Marine Wing forming part of the construct with their roles clearly defined in the directives issued by the Government.

The CCS directed Indian Navy to be the authority responsible for **overall maritime security**, which includes coastal security and offshore security. The Indian Navy is assisted by the Coast Guard, State Marine Police and other Central and State agencies for **coastal defence** of the nation.

The CCS additionally designated Indian Coast Guard as the authority responsible for **Coastal Security** in territorial waters, including areas to be patrolled by Coastal Police. The Director General Indian Coast Guard has also been made responsible for overall coordination between Central and State agencies in all matters relating to coastal security.

While the role of Marine Police continues to be the same as envisaged post Kargil; greater emphasis has been laid on strengthening infrastructure for patrolling and surveillance of coastal areas. The role of other stake holders such as Ports in notified port areas, Customs in Contiguous Zone, and BSF in creeks and inland waters are also clearly addressed in the new Coastal Security Mechanism.

The coordination of various operative measures and initiatives at the national level is being overseen by an Apex Committee called the National Committee for Strengthening Maritime and Coastal Security against Threats from Sea. I shall now cover some of the important initiatives taken for enhancing Coastal Security.

Uniform System of Registration of Vessels. National Informatics Centre has developed an online, uniform registration system in the country for implementation of registration of vessels.

Registration of Fishing Boats. Similarly, all fishing boats plying in Indian waters are being registered under a uniform system.

Installation of Transponders. The existing regulatory mechanisms require Merchant vessels above 300 Gross tons to provide their position to concerned authorities through Automatic Identification System and Long Range Identification and Tracking system. However, fishing vessels and other craft are not subject to these regulations. Craft less than 20 m were even beyond the ambit of the registration provisions of the Merchant Shipping Act, 1958. The presence of fishing vessels and craft, many unregistered, in large numbers at sea, who cannot be identified, tracked or monitored by security agencies, poses considerable security threat. Suitable transponders for monitoring such craft are being identified.

National Population Registration in Coastal States. The Cabinet has approved National Population Registration in Coastal areas and Identity Cards are being issued in coastal villages.

Coastal Security Scheme (CSS Phase-I & II). CSS have been implemented in two phases to enhance infrastructure and assets. Significant aspects are setting up of coastal police stations, equipped with Interceptor Boats.

Setting up of Chain of Static Sensors. A chain of static sensors is being set up along the coast in the form of radar stations in areas of high sensitivity and traffic density. The project envisages setting up of Coastal Surveillance radars and Electro Optic sensors at 46 remote sites in Phase-I, which includes 36 in the Mainland, 06 in the Lakshadweep Islands and 04 in A&N Islands. In phase II, 38 additional stations are planned to be setup to further provide gap free surveillance.

Creation of National AIS Chain. National Automatic Identification System (NAIS), which aims at achieving seamless coverage for 04 m high targets up to 25 nm range from the coast, is being steered by Director General of Lighthouses and Lightships (DGLL).

Port Security. The information about vessels, including their crew and cargo arriving and departing Indian Ports, are received by the ICG through the Pre-Arrival Notification of Security (PANS) rendered by all ships entering Indian ports. The ports are responsible for implementation of the measures for the International Ship and Port Facility Security (ISPS) Code.

Security of SPMs. Securing the Single Point Moorings at various ports is the responsibility of the concerned ports. However, close coordination with organizations like Indian Navy, Indian Coast Guard, CISF and Oil companies is much desirable. Deploying CISF for SPM security is being planned.

Formation of State Maritime Boards. An important aspect related to addressing all maritime issues within a state in a synergistic manner is the setting up of State Maritime Boards. Only three coastal states viz. **Gujarat, Maharashtra** and **Tamil Nadu** have established State Maritime Boards.

Activation of Coastal Security Helpline. A toll free Coastal Security Helpline '1093' has been activated in all Coastal States/UTs for obtaining valuable and timely inputs/information.

Key Initiatives by Security Forces. These include enhanced surveillance, regular coastal security exercises and closer coordination between all stakeholders. State wise SOPs have also been evolved. Jointness of operational effort has been infused into the coastal security paradigm in earnest. Capacity building is also being undertaken by all stake holders. Essentially it is a three pronged approach i.e. Capacity Building, Operational initiatives and Inter-agency Coordination.

Capacity Building. Capacity building couldn't be more visible than in the Coast Guard, which shall be doubling its force levels in next five years to numbers that were achieved in the first 35 years. Several new stations have been added along the coastline. Navy is setting up a dedicated force called Sagar Prahari Bal. Customs have inducted nearly 170 boats and CISF is recruiting more manpower. BSF is procuring all terrain vehicles for its water wing. Presence of customs and immigration is also being enhanced in ports.

Along the coast, Village Vigilance Committees, Gram Suraksha Dals and Sagar Suraksha Dals are all active and Community Interaction Programmes with fishermen, first initiated by the Coast Guard in the nineties, has been enhanced and they are now eyes and ears of security agencies.

Challenges and Constraints

Visible end of coastal security is like the proverbial tip of the iceberg. As may be expected in a multi agency setup, there are grey areas, which include **overlapping responsibility, joint accountability and Command and Control** structure. While shortcomings don't exist during high alert situations and exercises, they are evident in day to day functioning. Integration of onshore police organisations into coastal security has been a major gain. However marine police still faces constraints due to lack of trained manpower and resources.

While it's neither economical nor desirable to have our coastal waters under 100% physical surveillance, Surveillance efforts at sea need to be complemented by onshore security mechanisms along landing points, beaches, ports and harbours. Means to establish identity of fishermen and their boats, both at sea and in harbour, are in progress. Lack of stringent laws to prosecute faltering commercial shipping and fishermen is a drawback.

Lastly, the maritime domain in India comes under jurisdiction and lookout of a number of Ministries and departments. It is, indeed, a complex challenge to overcome individual turfs and asymmetry of purpose of different agencies handling sea-based activities, when working to achieve objectives in common national interest in the Maritime Zones of India.

Conclusion

In conclusion, I would like to state that by the very nature of the maritime environment, it is difficult to achieve fool-proof security. Preventing nefarious activities of pirates at sea or ingress of terrorists from the sea is a challenge. The area required to be monitored is vast and the assets available with security agencies are never enough for surveillance. The problem is compounded by the large numbers of fishing and other boats, which proceed to sea each day, but are not yet fully bound by legal mechanisms that enable effective monitoring and control.

While we have made considerable progress since 26/11, there is still some way to go. Synergetic, well coordinated efforts by all the stake holders are the key to ensuring a safe and secure maritime environment.

Coastal Security in India: Challenges and Policy Concerns after 26/11 Mumbai Terror Attacks

Rajesh Kunayil

India faces a combination of indigenous, proxy, and transnational terror threats from both within and outside the country. These constitute what is increasingly being referred to in the west as "hybrid" threats (Hoffman 2010). These threats pose significant challenges to India's attempts to weave together capacities and capabilities to execute an effective Counter-Terrorism (CT) strategy. India has been too late in comprehending the potential dangers to national security from non-state actors and terrorists operating through its maritime territories. The developments such as 26/11 exposed India's vulnerability to such challenges to its security and drastically changed the perceptions of coastal and maritime security. Lack of governance and an ineffective security apparatus in the littorals has resulted in favourable conditions for growth in terrorism, piracy, and other illegal activities. Further, terrorism 'from the sea' is a reality as demonstrated by the Mumbai terror attacks. The sea serves as an easy highway and acts as a catalyst for conducting terrorist attacks on land. In reality, not 'Delhi' but coastal state are the primary targets of criminal activities of NSA and terrorists approaching via adjacent sea apace or its maritime frontier and hence they too need to play an equal role. Contemporary law of the sea, especially the United Nation's Convention on the Law of the Sea UNCLOS-III, also has left its imprint upon the approach towards maritime dimensions of home land security. (Singh 2010: 20) Today's definition of security acknowledges political, economic, environmental, social and human among other strands that impact the concept of security. Maritime security in particular has gained prominence, increasingly in the last two to three decades, largely due to the impact of maritime terrorism which has impinged on coastal security and also threatened trade operations at distant shores. (Loshali 2010: 149)

Terrorist and illegal cross border activities of non-state actors along the coastal region is not new to India. Coastal Security has been a major, vital and critical concern for Kerala and India at least from the time the Portuguese ship under the command of Vasco da Gama bombarded Calicut way back in 1503. But it was almost exactly 500 years later that the Government of India started thinking seriously about the problem. (Tharakan 2010: 87) . The Southern states of India, especially Tamil Nadu and to a lesser extent Kerala were the theatres of illegal activity by the LTTE since 1980s. It was the assassination of Rajiv Gandhi which turned the attention of the Central government towards the emerging danger. But, the latest move by the Government shows their determination to face the challenge with tooth and nail. (Marshal Frank 2010: 189) The infiltration of terrorist into Mumbai through sea route was well planned and executed. It exposed the gaping holes in India's coastal security management.

The criminal gangs in Mumbai split along religious lines, with the Dawood gang posing a significant threat after orchestrating the Mumbai bomb blasts on 12 March 1993. It is believed that after the 1993 attacks, the entire gang escaped from India and found safe havens in Karachi and Dubai where they deepened their strategic alliance with the ISI and established links with the LeT (Rollins, Wyler et al 2010). It is felt that a timely strategy of launching covert attacks by India's intelligence agencies on the Dawood gang in Karachi and Dubai would have sent strong deterrent signals to many global terrorist groups. Synergy among the Indian Navy, the Indian Coast Guard, and other maritime policing forces would also have gone a long way in enhancing littoral and coastal security, preventing the group's ability to exploit India's porous western coastline. Maritime smuggling of weapons of mass destruction and their sub-assemblies components is also a cause for concern and needs to be addressed seriously ((Sakhuja 2009)

India is blessed with a long coastline of 7516.6 kms, which includes 2094 kms, around 1197 islands, and an EEZ of 2.01 million sq. kms. After the delimitation of the Continental Shelf, the area to be covered by the maritime agencies will be 2.9 million sq kms, which is almost equal to the land mass of India. About 50,000 ships visit the Indian ports annually; there are 314,000 registered fishing vessels operating from 300 fishing harbours and a much greater number of unregistered ones. According to informed sources, coastal surveillance was until very recently non-existent. In 2001 the government of India, realizing the gravity of the situation, made a recommendation to upgrade coastal security. (Swaminathan and

Suryanarayan 2010: 83) . The fundamental problem in coastal security today is that anyone can get into any boat and land anywhere he wants. A boat can start from anywhere; it can take you anywhere; one can land on any country's coastline. No country has ever protected its coastline so rigorously and so intensively so as to totally prevent a landing. Jacob Punnoose (2010) puts across a multi- pronged strategy, centered on ensuring the loyalty of the coastal population, for securing the long coastline of the state. Punnoose says that coastal security can never be effectively achieved unless the nation has the loyalty of the coastal population. Presently, the coastal population is marked by high density of population, economic in security, unemployment and social inequality and as such is easy prey to victimization by persons and interest groups who function with ulterior motives.

Barbed fences have become a common feature along transnational land borders, but are a practical impossibility in the area of coastal security. From time immemorial, human communities living along the coast have relied on the sea not only for fishing but also for communication and transport. Sea based commerce is as old as human civilization itself. Shipping conducted through ports and harbours along the coastline account for nearly eighty per cent of the international trade. Drastic measures like shutting off its sea shores to the world at large, if at all practically possible, is not in the interest of the coastal state and no coastal state can afford to do so except at its own peril. At the same time, coastline in an area of enormous security interest to the coastal state since it is a vulnerable frontier through which enemies could infiltrate, thus seriously jeopardizing the state's security. Coastal security thus demands reconciling the genuine interest of the state in safeguarding its security with the equally important interest of keeping open its access to the oceans which are gateways for commerce and economic upliftment. (Kumar 2010: 54). India conducts ninety percent of trade by volume and seventy per cent trade by value through the sea. Majority of people live by the sea side and a large number depends on the sea for their livelihood. We need to holistically view the entire spectrum of activity before arriving at security related conclusions.

The importance of the seas has been well recognized over the years and hence there is an urgent need to maintain stability and protect coastline from the probable use by the non-state actors as a route or passage to reach to its identified destination. The 26/11 event has added an additional fear that sea routes could become safe haven for terrorists' activities in the foreseeable future. Hence, protection of sea coasts for such usage by the terrorists' groups has emerged as a great challenge for India. India has a total length of 7,516.6 km of coastline. There is certainly a growing concern about the safety and security of the overall Indian maritime environment. There is a significant amount of India's industrial and economic activity within 200 km of its 7,516 km long coastline. The existence of India's strategic technologies (nuclear weapons laboratories) within that range adds to the anxieties. Such threat analysis has been done to re-emphasize the vulnerability of India's coastal assets and an urgent requirement to adopt stringent mechanism to guard. (Arvind Kumar 2010: 173)

Current Threats

Terrorist networks from an Indian perspective typically fall under four main categories; transnational terror networks, organized crime syndicates, proxy groups, and indigenous outfits. Transnational threats to India primarily emerge from groups like Al-Qaeda and the Taliban. Their common desire to establish Islamic states in their areas of influence and close linkages with extremist elements and some Madrasas (schools of Islamic learning) in Pakistan and J&K make them particularly potent threats (Rashid 2008). Organized crime syndicates that have threatened India for the last three decades primarily comprise the Dawood Ibrahim gang, also called the D Company. While the syndicate mainly exploits narcotics trafficking, Hawala trading (illegal money transfers), and extortion for profit, it has assumed a threat to India's national security ever since it has been given sanctuary in Pakistan and linked up with the ISI to finance terror strikes in India (Swami 2007). Proxy networks of significance include groups like the Harkat-ul-Ansar, LeT, JeM, and the Harkat-ul-Jihad-Islami (HUJI) (Rashid 2008). All these groups are said to have been financed, armed, and trained by the Pakistani state (Ibid) via the ISI. The Kandahar hijacking in 1999, the Parliament attack in 2001, and the Mumbai terror attacks of 2008 and 2011, have seen very little pro-active and pre-emptive capability being demonstrated by Indian counter-terror mechanisms.

Three prominent Indian leaders, Mahatma Gandhi, Indira Gandhi, and Rajiv Gandhi, were assassinated by extremists or terrorists at various periods of modern Indian history when the threats to their lives were known. All three leaders had spearheaded events that had impacted thousands of lives across the sub-continent and created chain reactions that had some element of trauma, pain, and shock for common and innocent people. It is difficult to imagine that these leaders and the prevailing internal security structures were not alive to the threats that they faced. These three assassinations, spread over four decades, proved that if the Indian state could not protect three of its tallest leaders, how would it be capable of protecting its common citizens and assets from similar attacks? The assassination of Mahatma Gandhi should have sent alarm bells ringing about the possibility of religious extremism emerging as a key driver of terrorism in the years ahead. Similarly, the assassination of Indira Gandhi by her Sikh bodyguards sent out a clear signal of the possibility of ethnic and regional dissent taking the form of terrorism. Finally, Rajiv Gandhi's assassination by the LTTE exposed the porous Indian society and its vulnerability to transnational terrorism. Each subsequent terrorist attack evoked a reactive response from India's strategic community that lacked operational accountability and the capacity to assign responsibility for failures. (Subramaniam 2012)

Coastal Security Post 26/11

India's coastal security remains as vulnerable as ever due to poor human reflexes despite the lessons learnt from the immense tragedy of 26/11, when 10 members of Pakistan's Lashkar-e-Tayiba managed to infiltrate by sea into Mumbai and carried out a well coordinated attack killing over 170 people. In order to enter Indian waters undetected, the terrorists hijacked an Indian fishing boat, 'Kuber', and sailed towards Mumbai. After successfully evading all the security agency patrols, they entered Indian territorial waters, where they abandoned the fishing vessels and used rubber dinghies to reach the Mumbai shore. The scale and intensity of the attack has forced the Indian government in announcing several measures to revamp the coastal security mechanism.

Challenges to Coastal Security

Coastal Security would encompass all maritime issues that impinge on the security of the State arising within 12 NM of coast, i.e., the territorial waters. Also the maritime domain is characterized by 'freedom of navigation' at high seas as well as transit passage rights in territorial waters. This makes the situation rather complex and requires careful scrutiny.

Topography and Location

India's coasts have always been vulnerable to anti-national elements, especially in Gujarat, Maharashtra, Karnataka and Northern Kerala. Numerous cases of smuggling of goods, gold, narcotics, explosives and arms and ammunition through these coasts have been reported over the years. In fact, it has been established that the explosive used in the 1993 serial blasts in Mumbai had been smuggled through the Raigad coast in Maharashtra.

Straying of Fisherman

The straying of Indian fisherman into Pakistan and Sri Lanka and likewise the foreign fishers straying into Indian territorial waters has been a recurrent source of concern. This problem is primarily concentrated along the Gujarat coast, however, such incidences have been reported at Sri Lankan side as well. The arrest of Indian fishermen along with their boats remains a serious security problem. It is important to note that more Indian fisherman stray into Pakistan/Sri Lankan waters and are arrested/exposed to the foreign intelligence agencies. There is the general notion that fishermen trespass into each other's waters since the maritime boundaries are not clearly demarcated and the fishers lack navigational/ communication sets.

Inadequate Littoral Focus

The aftermath of the 1993 Bombay blasts saw most of the terrorists belonging to the Dawood Ibrahim gang escaping to Karachi and Dubai by sea (http://en.wikipedia.org/wiki/1993_Bombay_bombings). This, along with the 26/11 attacks, wherein the terrorists came in from the sea, exposed the porous nature of India's vast coastline and the chinks in the coastal security network. It has been confirmed that for the 26/11 attacks, the group of LeT terrorist hijacked an Indian trawler, landed off the Mumbai coast, and proceeded to attack various sites.[1] With the fencing of the Line of Control in J&K and effective border management by the Indian Army and the Border Security Force on the eastern borders with Bangladesh and Myanmar, it was only a matter of time before the terrorists exploited the vast stretches of the unpatrolled Indian coastline. Adding to this were numerous ambiguities between the Indian Navy and the Indian Coast Guard regarding responsibilities and chain of command, a situation that has now been addressed by the Indian Government by vesting the Indian Navy with overall responsibility for maritime security (Sakhuja 2009)

India's intelligence gathering infrastructure is fragmented, distributed across multiple reporting chains, and plagued by inter-agency turf battles (Cohen and Dasgupta 2010). Till recently, the three ministries that had a significant stake in intelligence gathering were the Ministries of Defence, Home and External Affairs. With India's economic growth gaining momentum, economic intelligence has gained tremendous importance, especially with the role of money laundering and black money in financing terrorism. With so many stakeholders involved, it is inevitable that unless there is a strong, robust, interconnected, and unified intelligence structure, the delays and turf battles are more than likely to occur.

Lack of Photo Identity Card/Smart Card

Another issue of concern is of fishermen going to sea without valid certificates as well as proof of identity. Photo identity cards are issued by the state fisheries department after detailed verification, but the arrest/ interrogation of many fisherman by the Coast Guard bring out the fact that the process of verification either does not exist or is not foolproof.

Upgrading Para-Military and Police Capabilities

The Dantewada massacre in which 74 CRPF personnel were gunned down by left-wing extremists, proved beyond doubt that the state police, central police forces, and para-military forces were not suitably trained and equipped for CT operations. If that is true, their suitability for anti-terrorist operations is in even greater doubt given the complexity of such operations, especially in built-up and densely populated areas. The investigative reports in the aftermath of the 26/11 attacks reveal gross deficiencies in every aspect of the operational capabilities of the Mumbai Police (http://news.rediff.com/report/2009/November/30/mumterror-2611-probe findings-ill-equipped-cops-careless-govt.htm). The only force presently capable of effectively tackling complex terrorist strikes in all their existing manifestations is the National Security Guard (NSG), an elite unit under the Home Ministry.

Post-Mumbai Measures on Coastal Security

Following the Mumbai attacks, the central government announced a slew of measures to tackle these inadequacies and shortcoming in the coastal security mechanism. These include:

a) Entrusting the Coast Guard with the task of guarding the coast right from the shoreline (high tide line) up to territorial water.

b) The Indian Navy to be responsible for overall maritime security

c) Coastal state and union territories to expedite the implementation of the Coastal Security scheme, including the construction of coastal police stations, check posts, outposts and barracks as well as recruitment and training of executive and technical manpower.

d) Coastal state and Union territories to carry out vulnerability/gap analysis of their coasts in consultation with the Coast Guard

e) Ministry of Shipping, Road Transport and highways to streamline the process of registration of all types of vessels and ensure that these boats are fitted with navigational and communication equipment.

f) To bring the entire coastline under seamless radar coverage, the centre has also approved a proposal 'for setting up a static coastal radar chain and a comprehensive automated identification system stations along the entire coast as well as island territories.'

No doubt, these measures will go a long way in ensuring a better functioning of the coastal security mechanism. (Loshali 2010: 168)

One of the typical weaknesses of a vibrant and flourishing democracy like India is its vulnerability to attacks on its sovereignty and way of life, so typical of the targets of terrorism in the 21st century. The vulnerability increases if the democracy is a multi-ethnic, secular, and pluralistic one like India with an expanding federal structure that is based on an increasing number of states. There are also greater probabilities of internal fissures and schisms that open up as a result of expressions of dissent and dissatisfaction by ethnic groups, religious extremist forces, and archaic ideological forces. Every terror attack rooted in religious extremism is a calculated attempt to subvert India's secular and vibrant heritage. If you look at the expenditure during the last 60 years, we notice that huge expenditure is incurred on the security of the land borders. Only a fraction of that would have been spent on the security of the coastal waters. The enemy across the land border is visible; the enemy across the land is tangible; the danger is no doubt, real. When the armies stand facing each other across borders, the security concerns are more vitally pressing than anything else. But we must also remember that though unseen, the enemy across the sea is also very real and the unseen enemy ultimately landed on India's coastline on 26/11/2008.

That was when many among us woke up and decided that, indeed, coastal security is vital to national security.

Endnotes

1 This can be confirmed from the confession of Ajmal Kasab, the lone terrorist who was captured and now stands sentenced to death by the Bombay High court for his role in the terrorist attacks.

References

"A Leap of faith," Times of India, February 2010, p. 1.

Cohen, Stephen, P. and Sunil Dasgupta (2010): *Arming without Aiming: India's Military Modernization*, New Delhi: Penguin.

Hoffman, Frank, G. (2010): "Further Thoughts on the Hybrid Threats," Small Wars Journal, available at http://www.smallwarsjournal (accessed 24 December 2010.).

http://en.wikipedia.org/wiki/1993_Bombay_bombings (accessed 12 April 2013.)

http://news.rediff.com/report/2009/November/30/mumterror-2611--   probe-findings-ill-equipped-cops-careless-govt.htm (accessed 02 June 2013.).

Kumar, Akhilesh, T.P. (2010): "Coastal Security: Needed for Synergy", in K. R. Singh and K.M. Seethi, (eds) Coastal Security: Needed a New Look, K.P.S. Menon Chair, DC Press: Kottayam.

Kumar, Aravind (2010): " Role of Technology in Maintaining Coastal Security", in K. R. Singh and K.M. Seethi, (eds) Coastal Security: Needed a New Look, K.P.S. Menon Chair, DC Press: Kottayam.

Loshali, B.K. (2010): "Coastal Security: Post 26/11, A Reelok", in K. R. Singh and K.M. Seethi, (eds) Coastal Security: Needed a New Look, K.P.S. Menon Chair, DC Press: Kottayam.

Marshal, Frank (2010): "Fishing Community and Coastal Security", in K. R. Singh and K.M. Seethi, (eds) Coastal Security: Needed a New Look, K.P.S. Menon Chair, DC Press: Kottayam.

Punnoose, Jacob (2010): "Coastal Security Challenge in Kerala", in K. R. Singh and K.M. Seethi, (eds) Coastal Security: Needed a New Look, K.P.S. Menon Chair, DC Press: Kottayam.

Rashid, Ahmed (2008): *Descent Into Chaos,* London: Allen Lane.

Rollins, John, Liana Sun Wyler, and Seth Rosen (2010): "International Terrorism and Transnational Crime: Security Threats, US Policy and Considerations," Congressional Research Service Paper, January 5 , pp. 15–16, available at http://fpc.state.gov/documents/organization/134960.pdf.

Sahni, Ajai (2011): "Covertly Does It," *Times of India*, New Delhi edition, 04 May , p. 18.

Sakhuja, V. (2009): "Securing India's Littorals," *Journal of Defence Studies*, 13: 2.

Sandhya, R. (2010): "Role of the State Fisheries Department in Ensuring Coastal Security", in K. R. Singh and K.M. Seethi, (eds) Coastal Security: Needed a New Look, K.P.S. Menon Chair, DC Press: Kottayam.

Singh, K. R. (2010): "Coastel Security: Position Paper", in K. R. Singh and K.M. Seethi, (eds) Coastal Security: Needed a New Look, K.P.S. Menon Chair, DC Press: Kottayam.

Swami, Praveen (2007): *India, Pakistan and the Secret Jihad*, New York: Routledge.

Swaminathan, R. and V. Suryanarayan (2010): "Reflections on Coastal Security", in K. R. Singh and K.M. Seethi, (eds) Coastal Security: Needed a New Look, K.P.S. Menon Chair, DC Press: Kottayam.

Syam Kumar V.M.(2010): "Castel State's Security Concerns and Transnational Norms Governing Freedom of Navigation", in K. R. Singh and K.M. Seethi, (eds) Coastal Security: Needed a New Look, K.P.S. Menon Chair, DC Press: Kottayam.

Tharakan, Hormis (2010): "Building Institutional Coherence in India's Coastal Security Architecture", in K. R. Singh and K.M. Seethi, (eds) Coastal Security: Needed a New Look, K.P.S. Menon Chair, DC Press: Kottayam.

Five Years Since 26/11: Is India's Coastal Border Really Secure?

Shyna V V & Khursheed Ahmad Wani

The coastal areas are given special attention, due to the increasing importance that they have assumed in the global context of present economic development but the coastal security remains as vulnerable as ever due to poor human reflexes despite the lessons learnt from the immense tragedy of 26/11. India, with vast coastal border of 7516 kms covering nine coastal States and four Union Territories, poses serious security issues and challenges. About 20 per cent of the population of India live in coastal areas, a larger percentage of this being in coastal cities like Mumbai, Chennai and Kolkata. However, the vast coastal belt should be reckoned as a "border" and needed to be protected much the same way as the landlocked frontier is taken care of. It is vital to the security of India and will continue to occupy a prominent position in national security matrix. The degree of threat to national security posed by smuggling and refugee flows through the Indian coast was not considered grave enough to merit much attention. It was only after the terrorist onslaught on Mumbai that national consciousness awoke to the need for revitalising the existing coastal security system and have highlighted vividly the links between maritime security and terrorism and drew into sharp focus the need to understand and counter the threat of international terrorism.

The awareness about the vulnerability of the country's coasts first arose in the wake of the 1993 Mumbai serial blasts, when it was established that the explosives used were smuggled in through the coast at Raigad in Maharashtra. This led to the launch of 'Operation Swan' with the aim of preventing the landing of contraband and infiltration along the Maharashtra and Gujarat coasts. Further attention to coastal security was once again highlighted by the Task Force on Border Management as a part of the Kargil Review Committee recommendations. The Task Force recommended, inter alia, the setting up of a specialised marine police in the form of coastal police stations, augmentation of the strength of the Coast Guard in terms of personnel and material, the formation of fishermen watch groups, and the establishment of an apex body for management of maritime affairs. On the recommendation of the Task Force, the central government launched the Coastal Security Scheme in 2005-06

The coastal security mechanism has been fine tuned for optimum response to maritime threats through regular exercises & operations. But there was public outrage after each of the major tragic incidents like serial blasts in Mumbai in 1993, 26/11 attacks in Mumbai and the incidents of beaching of MVs Wisdom and Pavit on Juhu beach as well as the sinking of MV Rak off the coast of Mumbai.[1] On each occasion, public perception pointed a finger at the Indian Navy (IN). Notwithstanding the clear jurisdictional demarcation of responsibilities, the media also held the Navy guilty of dereliction of duty. But the government did not make any attempt to correct this flare-impression.

Initiatives after 26/11

Even though, many threat occurred in the coastal border, it is necessary look at the measures adopted by the Government after 26/11. Experience from across the world shows us that terrorism may be contained or reduced but not completely eradicated. Nonetheless, India have succeeded in controlling terrorist attacks based on our own experience in handling terrorist activities in our respective territories, have adopted diverse strategies and different measures to counter maritime terrorist threats. However, after the Mumbai terror attacks of 26/11, the entire coastal security scenario of the country has been thoroughly reviewed by the Government at various levels.

While there have been numerous attempt at securing the Indian coastline during the last five years, the Government has made concerted efforts to build a robust coastal security mechanism. To begin with, the existing multi-layered patrolling and surveillance arrangement have been furthered strengthened and also various other measures were announced, including additional patrolling by the Indian Navy and Indian Coast Guard (ICG) aircraft and ships. Therefore, a three level Coastal Security Scheme (CSS) is being implemented in full swing to safe guard the Indian coast. They are:-

- Marine Police to patrol up to 12 nautical miles from the coast.

- Indian Coast Guard to patrol from 12 to 200 nautical miles.

- Indian Navy to patrol beyond 200 nautical miles.

However, the overall responsibility for coastal defence is with the Indian Navy.[2] It has been brought into the folds of the coastal security mechanism and entrusted with the overall responsibility of maritime security including coastal and offshore security. The Indian Coast Guard has been assigned the additional responsibility of patrolling the territorial waters as well as coordinating between the central and state agencies. Another achievement has been the integration of all maritime stakeholders, including several State and Central agencies into the new coastal security mechanism. The Government has set up a multi-agency mechanism to share information from intelligence agencies on a daily basis, streamlining the nation's intelligence system through the creation of joint operation centres like, Mumbai, Visakhapatnam, Kochi and Port Blair. As a result of this there is good coordination, synergy and understanding between all agencies. All coastal security operations are now coordinated from the Joint Operations Centre, which are manned round the clock by Naval and Coast Guard teams. In addition, the State Marine Police and other agencies such as Customs, Intelligence Bureau and Ports etc. are also networked with these centres.

The awareness campaigns have been carried out in coastal villages across the country since 2009 for the purpose to integrate the fishermen community into the coastal security structure, Navy, Coast Guard and State Police teams have visited coastal villages and fishermen have been made aware of possible threats from the sea and their important role towards strengthening coastal security.[3] Furthermore, the introduction of Surveillance patrols is a major step to ensure coastal security. There has been a significant increase in the coastal surveillance patrols by Naval and Coast Guard ships and aircraft. Patrols by the Indian Navy and Coast guard are closely coordinated so as to optimise their efforts and keep the entire coast under surveillance. For achieving near gapless surveillance of the entire coastline as well as preventing the intrusion of undetected vessels, the Coastal Surveillance Network project is being implemented. It aims at providing real time surveillance up to 25 nm into the sea and involves the installation of 46 Coastal Static Radars (36 in the mainland and 10 on islands) which would help in identifying and monitoring maritime traffic.[4]

To review the readiness of the security agencies, the Indian Navy has taken the lead in conducting coastal security exercises in every coastal states and in the Island territories in conjunction with the Coast Guard, Marine Police, Customs and Immigration and Port Authorities etc. During these exercises several contingency scenarios are simulated, including hijacking of fishing crafts, landing of terrorists on the coast, stowaways on ships etc.[5] Moreover a coastal radar chain was to be set up to detect ships at 30 to 50 nm by getting "instant" details about their crew, cargo, movement, last port of call, next port of call, etc. through the Automatic Identification System (AIS), which is triggered by radar pulses from coastal, ship-borne or airborne radars. In addition, the coastal radar chain was to have an optronic sensor which would enable the display of TV-like images of ships and fishing vessels in India's territorial waters. Any vessel not triggering an AIS response on the radar screen would be immediately stopped and searched.[6]

This project is supplemented by the National Automatic Identification System (NAIS) chain, inaugurated in August 2012, to track and monitor vessels by receiving feeds from AIS transponders installed in sailing vessels. The data generated by the static radar chain and the AIS sensors are being integrated with the data from the Vessel Traffic Management System (VTMS) installed in all major ports as well as in the Gulfs of Kutch and Khambhat and these are being shared with all agencies through the centralized National Command Communication Control and Intelligence Network (NC3I).[7]

Additionally, Distress Alert Transmitters (DATs) are being provided to fishermen so that they can alert the Coast Guard if they are distress at sea. For identification of fishermen at sea, a scheme for issuing identity cards has been launched and till date the biometric data of 16 lakh (90 per cent) fishermen have been captured. The data generated will be fed into a single centralised database (NC3I), thus creating a composite picture for Maritime Domain Awareness. And, most importantly, to supervise the implementation of these measures, the National Committee to Strengthen Coastal and Maritime Security (NCSMCS) under the chairmanship of the Cabinet Secretary was constituted in August 2009. It was chaired by the Cabinet Secretary and its members are all stakeholders such as the Indian Navy, the Indian Coast Guard, the Ministry of Home Affairs (MHA)/ Fisheries/Shipping /Surface Transport/Agriculture, DG Light House/ Ships and Chief Secretaries of Coastal States. The first meeting was held on

September 04, 2009.[8]

Nevertheless the task of securing India's vast coastline is immense. The proposal of the Coastal Security Scheme (Phase-II), formulated on the basis of vulnerability/gap analysis carried out by the coastal States and UTs in consultation with the Coast Guard was approved by the Government on 24 September 2010 for implementation from 1 April 2011 for a period of five years. The Scheme is expected to provide support to coastal States/ Union Territories to upgrade their coastal security apparatus.

Continues to be a formidable challenge

Despite these measures, it has not been possible to prevent the entry of Non-state actors across the coastal borders because of various reasons. In an era of heightened coastal security concerns, Indian Coast Guard (ICG) remains ill-equipped to discharge its enhanced role and meet the challenges of today. The most coastal State Governments remained unenthusiastic about the important security initiative. While some states cited financial constraints, others wanted the Centre to shoulder the entire responsibility for coastal security. In the aftermath of the Mumbai attack, the Home Ministry officials came out with the statement that short, medium and long term measures would be implemented to beef up coastal security. But then, given its poor and dismal track record in formulating and implementing measures, no one is sure as to how it will go about in strengthening coastline security in an effective and time bound manner.[9] Lack of 'actionable' intelligence has been widely attributed as the main reason for this failure. But there are certain inherent inadequacies in the coastal security mechanism, making it incapable of preventing infiltration through the coast. These deficiencies are:

Absence of physical barriers on the coast and presence of vital industrial and defence installations near the coast enhance the vulnerability of the coasts to illegal cross border activities. Moreover, the threat posed by organised gangs carrying out smuggling of narcotics, arms and explosives led to a serious domestic security concerns by their networking with terrorists and providing logistical support for terror operations ashore. For example, in the case of 1993 serial bomb blasts in Mumbai when the explosives used were smuggled the Raigad coast of Maharashtra with the active involvement of the Indian customs officials. Another important challenges of the coastal security is illegal inflow of migrants and refugees from Bangladesh and Sri Lanka, especially along the Odisha and Tamil Nadu coats. Though such people do not pose direct security threat but they could be diverted and used for smuggling of arms, ammunition and infiltrators.[10]

One of the main shortcomings is the lack of coordination between various agencies engaged in coastal security. There are too many agencies dealing with security and several joint coastal security exercise have been conducted and also Standard Operating Procedures (SOPs) formulated to create awareness about sea-borne threats and thus achieve coordination among the relevant agencies but still there is complete lack of integration, coordination and exchange information between state and central agencies and also there is turf war between these agencies. For example, several breaches – such as the drifting of ships like MV Pavit and MV Freedom into Indian waters – highlight certain inherent inadequacies and shortcomings of the system, which in turn have impaired the effectiveness of the system.

Another factor undermining the effectiveness of the coastal security mechanism is differing perceptions among various stakeholders about their roles in ensuring coastal security. Every agency that is engaged in coastal security feels that the task is an additional responsibility that has been thrust upon it. The problem is that there is no clarity of the role and functions of these agencies and also inadequacy of inter-agency cooperation and sharing of information. However, the indifferent attitude towards coastal security percolates down to the district and sub-division levels resulting in their poor participation in various coastal security coordination meetings and thereby adversely affecting information sharing and coordination at the ground level.

The other hurdle is lack of proper training. Presently, most of the police stations in the coastal region either do not have any trained marine police personnel or have only a few. An adequately trained marine police force is an important area of concern and also the short training programmes and those actually available on the job have all contributed to the discontent of the marine police. Because of these, the police are unwilling to shoulder additional responsibilities of coastal security.[11] Additionally, growing discontent among fishermen is also an area of concern. The villagers and fisherman in almost every coastal village have been sensitised to threats from the sea and the measures they could take to contribute to coastal security. They could provide valuable information of any out-of-the ordinary happenings. But the perceived highhanded behaviour of the security agencies coupled with the loss of traditional fishing harbours to security and strategic establishments have generated a sense of disaffection among fishermen communities. This trend could hinder the flow of vital information from fishermen to the security and intelligence agencies.[12]

In addition to that, the lack of a large pool of trained manpower and the associated training of personnel employed for coastal security duties is another hurdle that needs to be overcome.

	Officers	Enrolled Personnel	Civilian Staff	Total
Sanctioned Strength	1,841	9,793	1,619	**13,253**
Personnel (Coast Guard)	1,234	7,345	1,030	**9,609**
Personnel on Deputation	93	186	04	**283**
Total Strength	1,327	7,531	1,034	**9,892**
Shortage	514	2,262	585	**3,361**

The issue of shortage of manpower in the coast guard, too, didn't escape the PAC's scrutiny. The data showed that the force is short of 514 officers, 2,262 enrolled personnel and 585 civilian staff as on March 31, 2013.[13]

Another area of concern is inadequate infrastructure and equipment. A series of coastal police stations have been operationalized, with some having adequate manpower and interceptor boats. Still these police stations have been unable to function effectively which was evident during the MV Pavit incident. The major reasons behind that the sufficient attention has not been paid to provide these police stations with essential requirements such as proper training to their personnel for sea operations, adequate fuel and funds for the running and maintenance of the boats, buildings for police stations, etc.[14]

State/UT	Nos. of sanctioned coastal Police stations	Operationa-lization of nos. of coastal PSs in current Year 2011-12	Identifica-tion of land/site	Land ac-quisition process started	Whether land ac-quired
Gujarat	12	12	11	3	8
Maharashtra	7	-	5	1	4
Goa	4	-	4	-	1
Karnataka	4	4	4	1	3
Kerala	10	-	10	9	-
Tamil Nadu	30	-	30	9	21
Andhra Pradesh	15	15	15	5	10
Odisha	13	-	4	2	2
West Bengal	8	-	8	7	1
Daman & Diu	2	-	2	-	-
Puducherry	3	3	3	-	3
Lakshadweep	3	-	-	-	-
A&N Islands	20	20	20		20
Total	131	54	116	37	73

Coastal Police Stations, 2013-14 outcome Budget, www.mha.co.in

The above table shows the lack of infrastructure facilities for coastal police stations. Because of funding delay and slow implementation of the project, it is very difficult to enhance the functioning of costal police stations. Sadly, dozens of landing points for fishing boats in some coastal areas don't have police posts, and ships entering the 12 nautical mile (nm) territorial waters outside the Mumbai port are not strictly monitored even though the media has highlighted the dangers. Even the newly inducted vessels lack critical equipment including guns and identification radar. The new vessels are not fully operational because of lack of crucial equipment such as super rapid gun mount, CRN 91 guns and identification of friend or foe system. It is important to reiterate that the problem lies not in the measures adopted but in the inadequate attention paid to the functioning of the system at the ground level where the actual action takes place.[15]

The Lack of governmental sensitivity to the importance of the coastal security is another challenge. A performance audit of the Indian Coast Guard (ICG) carried out by the Comptroller and Auditor General (CAG) shows that besides various shortcomings related to acquisitions and expenditure, the lackadaisical approach of the Coast Guard has led to the Mumbai terror attack becoming possible. The CAG report says that in respect to Maharashtra and Gujarat for the period leading to 26/11, the Coast Guard did not conduct a single boarding operation on any suspicious vessels that they spotted on the high seas before the attack took place. Moreover, the Coast Guard even tried to mislead the auditors by fudging their official reports. The CAG figured out that the Coast Guard tried to project more boarding operations when, in reality, it did not do any in the days preceding the attack. In fact, the Coast Guard vessels on patrol duty did not undertake the prescribed boarding operations per quarter for identification and investigation of fishing boats/ships.[16]

The inability of the entire international maritime community to suppress the piracy menace originating from Somalia in spite of all its resources, is a pointer to the dilemma. The media report indicated that in mid-2011, when several incidents of ships drifting on to Mumbai beach took place, but there was no action from the Government side. Moreover, there were reports of boats tied up alongside, unable to undertake any patrolling due to lack of fuel supply and inadequate technical manpower.[17] In spite of all the public outrage at the time of the series of episodes, it clearly illustrates the apathy displayed by the state authorities. Furthermore, Phase II of the coastal police scheme was launched in 2011, but some state has failed to start the projects under this phase even after two years. The Ministry of Defence stated that "The Indian Coast Guard requires 150 ships/boats and 100 aircraft for securing the coast and maritime interests of India to reasonable levels. It is anticipated that this force level would be achieved by 2018. The fully desired level of 154 ships, 126 boats and 139 aircraft is planned to be achieved by 2027."[18] But these initiative are only in paper because the delay of implementing measures is a biggest hurdle for any initiatives.

Imperative Action Sought!

There still are many loopholes in our coastal security in several areas that need to be plugged urgently and time bound actions should be taken for ensuring a full proof coastal security system. Faced with a virtual onslaught of criticism for inept handling of coastal security matters, the Government and its various departments, as well as the India Navy, adopted a multi-pronged approach to tackle coastal security at various levels.[19] It would be worthwhile for a joint team comprising the Indian Navy, ICG, IMP, the Customs Department, the Department of fisheries and above all the people living in coastal areas will have to work together. However, all the stakeholders should work with unified purpose and ensure that there are no gaps in the Coastal Security framework. For this the central government needs to clearly spell out areas of jurisdiction of different agencies engaged in coastal security and ensure coordination among all agencies by establishing a central command system. Furthermore, it is high time that all the agencies involved in coastal and maritime security make a sustained and extensive use of data available through satellites, for which the ongoing processes should be stepped up. The Central and state governments should expedite funding and implementation of projects to ensure Zero Tolerance for encroachment of India's maritime interests.[20]

An effective counter- terrorism strategy based on domestic, regional and global threat perception is vital. Such a strategy should be articulated in clear terms to avoid mis-interpretations by stakeholders at the federal as well as at the state levels. The strategy should incorporate multi-dimensional threats and lay out comprehensive national objectives. A regular review of the strategy should become part of the strategy itself. In addition to this, the Navy will be strengthened with additional submarines, surveillance helicopters and amphibious vessels because of the growing Chinese maritime presence in the Indian Ocean and also the construction of additional bases and naval air stations in Andaman & Nicobar Islands and Lakshadweep & Minicoy Islands is necessary to further extend our operational reach. Inspite of this, there should be more ships and long-range maritime patrol aircraft, along with additional dedicated maritime surveillance-cum-communications satellites.[21]

Besides the development of infrastructure, it is imperative to address the grey areas that hamper the effective functioning of the security forces. However, better coordination between various security agencies has to be ensured. At present, whatever coordination or information sharing takes place between the three agencies is largely based on personal rapport between the concerned officers. So this rapport has to be institutionalised.

An institutionalised system needs to be put in place within the Ministry of Defence to monitor periodically, the efficacy and continuity of, coastal security measures. Further, corruption in the implementation of security schemes is rampant, and their implementation needs to be closely monitored.

The Coast Guard is the primary agency for ensuring coastal security under the overall direction of the Indian Navy. There is an immediate need for ICG to evolve norms for patrolling in maritime/coastal zones, based on available resources. Annual/ periodic achievements against the norms should be reported to the Ministry of Defence. However, the expansion and strengthening of the Coast Guard will be necessary for the security. Further, incentives such as special allowance and insurance could be considered for police personnel engaged in coastal security. In addition to this, the intelligence gathering process both human and electronic should be made effective and rationalised and also manpower shortage could be addressed by recruiting retired Coast Guard and Navy personnel. Likewise, people from the coastal villages could be enlisted in the coastal police force. There is need for improving police infrastructure and also specialised training should be given for the Coastal Police.[22]

Homeland security should be the pivot of an effective counter terrorism strategy. It not only needs an extraordinary coordination among intelligence agencies but also should incorporate security forces as well as investigating agencies of non-security wings of the government. Another valuable measure is the establishment of marine version of home guard- the sea guard or sea wing of the home guard. Its members can operate from local fishing boats and besides some financial incentives can be provided with GPS and mobile to communicate with designated authorities on matters relating to suspicious movement of foreigners and anti-national elements. However, it will promote people's involvement in matters concerning coastal security and a solution at from below has greater chances of success rather than solution imposed from above. Such a goal can be accomplished only if we consider the surrounding sea as a common heritage and not as a contested territory.[23]

Another important thing is that at present no Indian port is Container Security Initiative (CSI) compliant. A CSI compliant port requires large numbers of special electronic and X-ray machines to quickly scan hundreds of containers being offloaded from ships onto trucks before they are driven to major cities inland. This prevents explosives or "dirty nuclear bombs" being smuggled into cities by terrorists. And also network coordination essential to security build-up because Technology, Speed and Strength will play an effective role. A seamless and integrated approach is essential for a strong coastal security, for this to encourage fishing community in the coastal security programme because they were the "eyes and ears" for overall coastal security. It is vital in strengthening of coastal security mechanism. Community interaction programmes to be given impetus in order to sensitize the fishing community on the prevailing security situation and to develop them to be the eyes and ears for intelligence gathering.

Another measure to enhance security is Cooperation between Inter-Governmental Organizations in the region. Most governmental organizations are unwilling to share any actionable information with "outside" organizations. This xenophobic attitude is always cloaked under the excuse of "compromising security" and must be shed to overcome challenges and threats of transnational nature. And also cooperation with Central and State Government is an unavoidable factor. It is well known that priorities associated with Central Governmental initiatives/projects are often disregarded by state governments in consonance with the prevailing local politics. The earlier attempts at coastal security were unsuccessful due to a various reasons, including lack of financial sustenance and political will.[24]

The Coast Guard has taken a number of steps but more needs to be done. This has the potential to elevate the maritime status of a nation among littoral states. However, an integrated public private security partnership will be essential to ensure critical gaps in coastal security. For this, Nations must cooperate with each other to ensure everlasting peace and security. Finally, Governments and law enforcement agencies must implement national and international laws that can act as a deterrent for unscrupulous elements. Since maritime security has emerged as a vital subject of national importance, it may be desirable to have a new subject under Concurrent List. It will provide functional flexibility both for the central and state governments in discharging their burdensome duties. And also will pave the way for better Centre-State relations based on cooperative basis. Of course, Parliament needs to pass a comprehensive law, plugging all loopholes in our national and coastal security system. However, the Governments should take swift policy decisions and top priority must be accorded to the creation of safe and secure oceans looking at the current maritime environment and also the state governments to be equal partners in this important National Security Issue.

Conclusion

We live in an age of globalization and it is now accepted wisdom that the risks we face are more catastrophic than those of the past because they are global. However, countering threats and challenges require consistent cooperation between the states affected and the associated maritime agencies. Though coastal and maritime security has been accorded top priority following the Mumbai attacks, the pace of implementation has been extremely slow. Lackadaisical attitude of the state governments, bureaucratic hurdles, stringent laws, turf wars among various agencies, lack of personnel and technical means for implementing projects have all contributed towards the delay. Therefore, the time has, therefore, come for the Government of India to take effective measures to ensure the safety and security of the coastal region. It should be highlighted that India's major ports are located either in or very near cosmopolitan cities like Mumbai, Kolkata and Chennai but India's approach to security still remains heavily land centric and the water front continues to remain open and vulnerable. On the whole, while India has put in place a comprehensive mechanism for securing the country's coasts, great deal to be done in terms of addressing issues relating to perceptions, resources as well as organisational management to ensure effective coastal security. However, coastal Security in India is a very complex issue and the Government will have to put in place measures that address all these threats. Whatever the measures are decided upon, it would need to be implemented as early as possible.

Endnotes

1 Pushpita Das, "Four Years Hence: A Review of the Coastal Security Mechanism", *IDSA Working Paper,* 26 November, 2012.

2 "Coastal Security Group: Marine Police Station in Tamil Nadu," 13 April, 2009. Available at   http://www.marinebuzz.com/2009/04/13/coastal-security-group-marine-police-stations- in-tamil-naduAccessed on 27 July, 2013

3 "Coastal Maritime Security Initiatives," Available at http://indiannavy.nic.in/operations/coastal-maritime-security-initiatives.Accessed on27 July, 2013

4 http://indiannavy.nic.in/operations/coastal-maritime-security-initiatives. Accessed on 29 July, 2013

5 "Coastal maritime Security Initiatives," available at http://indiannavy.nic.in/operations/ coastal-maritime-security-initiatives, Accessed on 28 October 2013

6 http://maritimeindia.org/article/coastal-security-deep-water. Accessed on 28 July, 2013

7 Pushpita Das, "Four Years Hence: A Review of the Coastal Security Mechanism", *IDSA Working Paper,* 26 November, 2012.

8 Rear Adm AP Revi , "Coastal Security Paradox", *Indian Defence Review,* Vol. 27, No.1, Mar 2012, p.4

9 RadakrishnaRao, "India's Coastal Security," *India Strategic,* December 2008.Available at http://www.indiastrategic.in/topstories231.htm.Accessed on 29 July, 2013

10 P K Gosh, "India's Coastal Security : Challenges and Policy Recommendations,"*Issue Brief 22,* August, 2010, p.2

11 Pushpita Das, "Securing the Andaman and Nicobar Island", *Strategic Analysis,* Vol.35, No.3, May 2011, p.473.

12 Saurab Joshi, "Coastal Security: Navy's Report Card", Available at http://www.merinews. com/article/navy-sagar-prahari-bal-to-secure-indias-coastline/15714400.html. Accessed on 26 July 2013

13 "CAG savages Coast Guard over lax coastal security," Available at http://www.dailymail. co.uk/indiahome/indianews/article-2372677/CAG-savages-Coast-Guard-lax-coastal-security.htmlAccessed on 29 October, 2013

14 Pushpita Das, "Why India's Coastal Security Arrangement Falters?", *IDSA Working Paper,* August 26, 2011,

15 http://www.dailymail.co.uk/indiahome/indianews/article-2372677/CAG-savages-Coast-Guard-lax-coastal-security.htmlAccessed on 27 July, 2013

16 "CAG Report Expose Gaping Holes in Coast Guard's Operations and Maritime Preparedness". Available at http://www.defencenow.com/news/263/cag-report-exposes-gaping-holes-in-coast-guards-operations-and-maritime-preparedness.htmlAccessed on 28 July, 2013

17 Rear Adm AP Revi, op.cit. Available at http://www.indiandefencereview.com/spotlights/ coastal-security-paradox/Accessed on 30 July, 2013

18 Kartikeya Sharma, "CAG savages Coast Guard over lax coastal security," July 21, 2013. Available at http://www.dailymail.co.uk/indiahome/indianews/article-2372677/CAG-savages-Coast-Guard-lax-coastal-security.htmlAccessed on 2 August, 2013

19 P K Gosh,op.cit. p.3

20 Pushpita Das, "Coastal Security Arrangement in Maharashtra: An Assessment", *IDSA Working Paper,* May 15, 2009

21 "India to Add Navy Bases, Expand Coastline Security Sensors," May 14, 2013, http:// www.defensenews.com/article/20130514/DEFREG03/30514001Accessed on 29 July, 2013

22 http://www.dnaindia.com/india/1264792/report-navy-initiates-coastal-campaign-on-

securityAccessed on 2 August, 2013

23 V.Suryanarayan, "Challenges of Coastal Security: Tamil Nadu's Case," Paper No.3565, *South Asian Analysis Group,* December 24, 2009, pp.3-5

24 P.K.Gosh, op.cit.

Chinese Presence in Gwadar & Its Impact on India's Maritime Security

Sudhir Singh

Gwadar is situated in the western most part of Baluchistan and close to Iran. Baluchistan had a different tale during freedom struggle. They were ruled by the Khan of Kalat. Mohhamad Ali Jinnah was legal adviser of Khan of Kalat. One part of Bluchistan was occupied by Iran and a small part is in Afghanistan too. The Khan of Kalat collaborated with the British but periodically demanded that all Baluchlands someday must be returned to his domain. When Great Britain withdrew from the Subcontinent in August 1947, the Khan refused to join the newly created Pakistan, declaring an independent Baluchistan. Under military pressure, the Kalat state was compelled to sign on an instrument of accession with Pakistan on 27 March 1948. The struggle for independence for the Baluch started from this date in recent times. The agreement between M.A. Jinnah and the Khan of Kalat had promised full autonomy to the Baluch tribe, but the Instrument of Accession was not honored after Jinnah's death. This breach of trust proved to be a turning point in Baluchistan's history. However when Pakistan came into being, Gwadar was not its part.

Gwadar is altogether a different story. It was purchased by Pakistan from Oman in 1958 by a civilian government — a reminder that a civilian government added new territories to Pakistan instead of losing any — and has since then been part of mainstream Pakistan.[1] Even after its merger with Pakistan, Baluchistan remains a turbulent place since then. In 1973, Prime Minister, Zulifikar Ali Bhutto dismissed elected provincial government of NAP resulted into the bloody war which had consumed around 7,000 people including more than 3,000 Pakistani soldiers. Baluchistan is the largest province of Pakistan in terms of territory with sparsely habited population. Previous PPP government led by Asif Ali Zardari (2008-2013) gave Hoqqok-A- Baluchistan. This government has ensured provincial autonomy including fiscal one with the passage of 18th constitutional amendment in April 2010, first time in history, real federal structure has been put in place in Pakistan. But due to prevailing insurgency propelled by the assassination of Baluch leader, Akbar Bugti in August 2006 by the Pakistani army, violence is sustainable. It has consumed thousand of human lives and is still going on. The U.N human rights agencies have sent a delegation in 2012 to investigate the prevalence of disappearance and torture of Baluchs in police custody. Supreme Court of Pakistan has also stressed that security agencies are behind the disappearance of Baluch people. These things are going on and keeping the province volatile. It is the largest number of natural asset producer province as well but due to Hobssian state of nature these things have not been duly developed.

In the backdrop of this kind of situation Pakistan has handed over the management and development works of Gwadar port to China in the beginning of 2013. Earlier it was with a Singapore company.

China and Pakistan has concluded an agreement in February 2013 under which Gwadar port's infrastructure developments work will be furnished by the Chinese. Before that Singapore was doing this job but due to prevailing unrest in Gwadar in particular and rest parts of Baluchistan in general it was not able to complete it within the stipulated time. Gwadar is strategically located for energy security and commerce as well not for South and South West Asia but other adjoining parts as well. China has grown rapidly in recent years and slated to be an important and dominant global power due to changing global security architecture. In the year of 2012, the Chinese military budget was over $ 115 billion but India had hardly $ 39 billion dollar. In the changing contours of power configuration China is willing to dominate Asia-Pacific.

According to Mearchiemer, if China becomes an economic powerhouse it will almost certainly translate its economic might into military might. Thus, Chinese military power will appear more dangerous to its neighbors and complicating America's commitments in the region. China has developed its Navy (PLAN) to dominate the high seas. It has been said by the scholars that domination of Seas are necessary for the establishment of a strong nation. China has virtually declared South China Sea as its own lake and dispute with Vietnam, Malaysia and the Philippines on this issue is prevalent. China has perceived that India and Japan have emerged challenger in Asia and undermining Chinese aspirations. It is reason which has promoted China to encircle India within South Asia.

Chinese naval presence is mushrooming though out South Asia.

Similarly, China also resents the hegemonic designs of India towards the Indian Ocean and has always exhibited her opposition to such Indian attempts. China also suspects India of supporting superpower presence in the Indian Ocean as a means of countering China. The most serious challenge is that the US military presence in Central, South and South-East Asia may undermine Chinese influence in these regions and make it more difficult for China to achieve its security, economic and energy objectives in the future.

The Chinese are well aware of the geostrategic realities and have been engaged in diplomatic, economic and military activities to build a maritime infrastructure to safeguard their maritime interests around South Asia. Present Chinese commitment to build-up infrastructure is impressive as it is probably the start of long-term Chinese intent in the Indian Ocean. The same is also evident from her assistance for construction of the Gwadar Port at the northern most tip of the Indian Ocean.

Xinjiang Province lies 4,500 kilometers from China's east coast but just 2,500 kilometers from Gwadar. This will make it possible for China to route some of its external trade through the Gwadar port.

The Persian Gulf is an important trade route in the strategic northern reaches of the Indian Ocean. Some 80 % of the world's oil tankers leave the shores of the Persian Gulf destined to other parts of the world.

India is perhaps the only country on the Indian Ocean that has the economic potential, military strength and the political will to dominate this vast expanse of water. Indian strategic doctrine revolves around the protection of its maritime resources/assets, such as offshore oil platforms/rigs and sea-lanes of communication, tonsure smooth flow of trade. There are up to 30 Indian ships at sea in Indian waters at any given time and a much larger number of ships of other nations engaged in trade toad from Indian ports, in addition to 8-10 tankers carrying crude oil to India daily. India is working on the strategy of building up a viable maritime force to deter any potential aggressor and to protect her SLOCs. Joseph S. Nye, Jr., in his book "The Paradox of American Power", writes that India's military capabilities are impressive in South Asia but not in the larger Asian context. However, its strategic interests extend way beyond that and tend to enter the domain of regional hegemony, which dictates her relations with other countries.

In the late 1990s, the United States began to tilt toward India, as Washington and New Delhi turned from 'estranged democracies' of the Cold War to 'engaged democracies' in the post-Cold War era.

The importance of the Indian Ocean to the Japanese cannot be exaggerated; it would not be wrong to state that the Indian Ocean is a lifeline of Japan. Japan averaged 3.9 million bbl/d of net oil imports from the Persian Gulf during 2002. The need to protect her economic interest may one day invoke deeper involvement of her "Self Defense Maritime Forces."

Most recently, the 'String of Pearls' garnered renewed attention through Pakistan's official transfer of operational rights of the deep-sea Gwadar port in its Baluchistan province to the state-run China Overseas Port Holding Company. Dubbed as the crowning jewel in the string, Gwadar's geographic advantages – a mere 400 kilometers away from the Straits of Hormuz – certainly suggest the possibility of investing it with great strategic and military importance. In the light of the Chinese proposal to the United States Pacific Fleet Commander in 2009 that "the Indian Ocean should be recognized as a Chinese sphere of influence", of Pearls, and specifically the acquisition of Gwadar port, is a genuine strategic plan aimed at undermining India's maritime security in the IOR.

Gwadar as Strategic Hub

Pakistan is blessed with a sea boundary of 1100 kms, stretching to West and Southeast axis. With a population of 2,27,984 having 12,637 sq kms area, Gwadar Port yields of its vitality for regional and extra regional key players. Gwadar has the potential to acquire the status of a center piece as a gate to Strait of Hurmoz; it can compete with the UAE ports by improving the exiting links to Caspian Region, and thus providing a better trade for route to land locked Caspian Region. Gwadar has the potential to be developed into a full-fledged regional hub and a trans-shipment port in the future. Pakistan has very little strategic depth from east to west; Gwadar will increase this strategic depth considerably, as a strategic port being further away from India. The additional distance of 460 Kms away from India will decrease the vulnerability of Pakistan. Gwadar will help Pakistan to monitor the Sea Lines of Communications (SLOCs) originating from the Persian Gulf and bottle neck at Strait of Hormuz. Strategically, considering the establishment of Naval Bases at Gwadar and Ormara by Pakistan, presence of Chinese Naval assets, domination of Arabian Sea at Persian Gulf by US 5th Naval Fleet and Indian aspiration to emerge as a Blue Water Navy will be checked. This will also establish Pak-China naval nexus to deny maneuver space to Indian Navy in Indian Ocean. Gwadar caught the attention of Pakistani and Chinese policymakers due to its pivotal location near the entrance to the Gulf through which one third of the world's oil supplies pass and for its potential as a terminal for North-South transportation of oil and gas from the landlocked Central Asian countries and western parts of China.[2] Since the early 1990s, Pakistan has considered Gwadar a cornerstone of its strategy to increase its economic and military clout in the Middle East and Southwest Asia. US$ 248 Million were spent in building the first phase of *Gwadar Deep Water Port Project* with technical and financial assistance from China (Government of Pakistan 2005).[3] The first phase of Gwadar Port was completed in 2007 and its operation and maintenance were handed over to the Port Authority of Singapore (PSA) through an open international bidding process.

There is little doubt about the highly strategic situation of Gwadar, due to its close proximity to the important Straits of Hormuz chokepoint, and its general location in the IOR which has a high density of the world's oil-shipping traffic. Given China's geographical location, Gwadar presents access to the Indian Ocean through Pakistan, and a favorable alternative for the China-bound tankers to offload Persian Gulf oil without having to navigate through East Asian waters.

Although external threats always weigh in heavily on strategic decision-making, Beijing may perhaps be interested in a secure and stable internal situation in both Pakistan and China. The threats to Gwadar are both from within and without. To supply the port with resources, there have been plans to connect the Karakoram Highway to Gwadar over land, as well as lay oil and gas pipelines linking the port to China's restive Xinjiang province. Yet, these are cast with many uncertainties as Baluchistan is troubled by insurgency and separatism. This has obstructed development in the past, when the Chinese withdrew grand plans for oil refineries, citing security reasons.

Development of the region is also further hindered by the cautious and "hard-nosed" business approach that Beijing has adopted. It had previously demonstrated reluctance to be engaged in Gwadar in order to avoid raising hackles in New Delhi and Washington as well as over concerns of stability in Baluchistan. Now that it has made the decision to acquire the Gwadar port, it remains unclear how far and how rapidly the Chinese would see its development through, given the current socio-political circumstances. While this is not evidence to conclude that Gwadar has no strategic value, its military potential is greatly constrained in the short-term.

Energy Security, Chinese Games & Gwadar

Pakistani policy makers and metropolitan publics came to see Baluchistan as a 'golden land', and considered Gwadar as the jewel in their crown. As veteran journalist Amir Mateen puts it:

"The dream was that the sight of Gwadar's emerald green waters would make us shake our shoes off to stroll on its white sands. It was supposed to fulfill our longing for the beaches of Bahamas, the skyscrapers of Shanghai and the lifestyle of Dubai. It was meant to be a strategic deep water port that would snatch away trans-shipping business from regional giants like Dubai and Muscat; outsmart Iran's upcoming Chahbahar port in unlocking the gateway to the central Asian markets, and in turn transport their oil and gas to the 'warm waters' of the Persian Gulf. Itwas designed to be a tax-free trade and industrial hub that would link China's western regions to the outside world through the ancient Silk Route. [4]"

Pakistani plans for constructing a deep water port at Gwadar were part of an evolving regional competition for oil and gas resources in Southwest Asia. This contemporary quest for the control of territory in the Persian Gulf and Central Asia is animated, in large part, by the phantom of factories in Europe, USA, and China grinding to a halt due to declining oil and gas resources around the world. Persian Gulf has the world's largest reserves of proven oil (40%) and Central Asia is seen as the future of world oil due to the presence of unexplored oil reserves around the Caspian Sea Basin. This anxiety over energy security has incited a 'gold rush' for Central Asia's oil and gas resources since the 1990s, turning much of Southwest Asia into a virtual *Pipeline-istan*.

Baluch Insurgency & Gwadar

One of the biggest hurdle of the Gwadar as another Dubai is ongoing insurgency in Baluchistan. Being the biggest province in terms of territory it has huge natural assets including all important sea shores. The magnitudes of the Baluch insurgency have been sustainable since the inception of the country. Baluchi people have been complaining their discrimination by dominant Punjabi elite since decades.

It is one of the bravest ethnic groups of the contemporary world. It could be compared only with the Kurds sandwiched among Iran, Iraq, Turkey and Syria seeking independence has sustained insurgency since last many decades. Since second world war, Kurds have lost more than 50,000 people in their fight of self determination. A Baluch aspiration for self determinations is not a different saga. In the 1970s having reached its peak led to an open war with the Pakistani military. In the rebellion more than 55,000 Baluchis took part, and the number of the Pakistani troops, leading military actions against the Baluchis, reached 77,000. Even the Shah of Iran, being worried about Baluchi separatism, sent several helicopters to Pakistan. In this violence more than 7,000 people from both the sides were killed. There are different propelling factors of insurgency but it is sustainable in Baluchistan till date. However, local Baluch political leadership in general, and the local fishermen of Gwadar in particular, have been largely excluded from key decisions over the development and future use of Gwadar Port. As a result, the Port has become an important site of contestation between Baluch fishermen and political activists, and the Pakistani government.

Baluch people are a minority ethnic group within Pakistan whose territory is divided between the sovereign states of Pakistan, Iran, and Afghanistan. The Baluch in Pakistan have maintained historical grievances against the state since the country's inception in 1947, giving rise to four armed insurgencies in the last 66 years. Within this context, the displacement of local agriculturalists and fishermen from their lands and fishing waters and the threat of the influx of labor migrants from the dominant Punjabi and Mohajir ethnic groups into Gwadar have increasingly fed local people's disillusionment with the Gwadar Port Project. Baluch apprehensions are very acute that if Gwadar will develop as claimed it would change the demography of Baluchistan and will put Baluchis as minority within their own province. These processes have also contributed to a growing separatist insurgency which has claimed hundreds of lives. This backdrop has propelled the insurgent activities in entire Baluchistan and of course, Gwadar is not aloof from this wave. The sustainability of Karzai regime in Afghanistan since last 12 years has provided sanctuary to Baluch insurgents. Major Baluch groups leaders are based in Afghanistan and coordinating the insurgency. In September 2013 there was an earthquake in Baluchistan near Iran border in which more than 400 people were killed. During the rescue operation all high voltage visits to earthquake hit areas were greeted by missiles, rockets and landmines. Even in September 2013 when Pakistani Prime Minister, Nawaz Sharif met his Indian counterpart, Dr. Manmohan Singh at New York in the sidelines of UN General Assembly meeting in September 2013 , Pakistan alleged Indian intervention in Baluchistan.[5]The government of Pakistan since General Musahrraf (1999-2008) period keep telling Baluch people that all round development of Gwadar will change their life positively. Sometimes they keep threatening them as well. General Mushrraf threatened Baluch insurgents with dire consequences in 2006 if they will derail the development process of Gwadar. Baloch nationalist leaders and activists, however, were not deterred by Musharraf's threats. His warning to the Baluch nationalist leadership provoked an equally strong riposte from the octogenarian chief of the Bugti tribe and the Chairman of *JamhooriWatan Party* (JWP), Nawab Akbar Khan Bugti: he stated "The general [Musharraf] has promised to hit us in such a way that we will not know what hit us. In one sense, it is quick death that he is promising us. He could do this to me, and to a few other Baluch leaders, but not to the entire Baluch nation." [6]Nawab Bugti was assassinated by the Pakistan military in August 2006 in his hideout mountains. He was an ageing leader but his departure gave new ferment to the Baluch insurgents and since then till today the fire is sustainable despite many lucrative commitments and awards by the government of Pakistan. Since March 2008, civilian regimes are ruling in Pakistan and has been positive for Baluchistan but Baluch's have not believed in their generosity and sustained the insurgency. This prevailing insurgency in Baluchistan has the capability to undermine all pipeline dreams to be realized and beside that it has the capability to prevent the emergence of Gwadar. It could only be resolved when government of Pakistan will address the genuine aspirations as per their demand or at least at the middle path. Till date government of Pakistan seems to adapt military mode of the resolution but the problem is political and going out from the reaches of the government by every passing weeks and months. Baluch insurgents have been openly saying that they seek separation from Pakistan not the resolution of the problem.

Concluding Remarks

Gwadar port handling by China has certainly put a new threat to India. During our previous wars with Pakistan, we were easily blocking Karachi and thus compelling Pakistan from at least sea side to accept Indian conditionality. Gwadar will provide leverage to Pakistani navy because it is around 500 KM west from Karachi and it will not be an easy task for Indian Navy to block it in case of war. In peacetime too, due to its geo-strategic location, if properly developed will make it conduit of trade hub not for China but also for resource rich Central Asian republics. Chinese presence at Gwadar will be an addition to its open policy since decades of Encircle India within South Asia. In response to China's access to the supposed pearls of Chittagong, HambantotaMarao Atoll and Gwadar, India has no lack of options.

Kautilaya has already said that enemy's enemy is friend. We need to extend our mutual cooperation in maritime affairs with like minded countries. South China Sea is an issue where we could make inroads in the hearts of ASEAN countries. New Delhi has already expressed interest in Iran's Chahbahar port, and moving forward, can explore its connections with other countries like Maldives, Mauritius and Seychelles. Still, India should divorce itself from the innate sense of vulnerability that is at times misleading, because of America's and India's firm grasp over China's energy jugular. The reports of conflicting statements by India's External Affairs Minister and Defense Minister as to whether Gwadar is "a serious matter of concern" indicate general confusion in New Delhi. This is not only advantageous to Beijing, which can leverage on this lack of a clear direction to further its national interests rapidly, but also tends to exaggerate fears and therefore encourage unnecessary action. Instead, there is need to assess the true extent to which China's actions are a threat to India. To this end, it is important to keep in mind that, regardless of Beijing's growing ambitions, India will, in conflict situations, have the trump card of force concentration in the IOR. Beside these measures India must register its presence in South China Sea in a comprehensive manner. In December 2012 , Indian Naval Chief, Admiral D.K. Joshi has stated that India will intervene in South China Sea if necessary for the protection of national interests. India must adhere with the Kautilyan realism and deepen its ties with ASEAN, East Asia and West Asia and through this process it could ensure its national interests. Gwadar has emerged as a challenge for the promotion and protection of our national interests therefore we must reformulate our strategy to cope with the emerging challenges.

Endnotes

1 *Dawn,*Karachi, 17 August 2013.

2 While the relative significance of the Central Asian oil resources and the various doomsday scenarios portrayed by security and energy sector analysts are debatable, the power of these visions is very concrete and real.

3 Phase II of Gwadar Port is to be constructed at estimated costs of US$ 524 Million. Detailed figures were retrieved from Board of Investment, Government of Pakistan, *Gwadar.* Accessed onlinehttp://www.pakboi.gv.pk/News_Event/Gwadar.htm on November 12, 2007.

4 Mateen, A. (2010): *The Agonizing Contrast of Gwadar Dream.* Amir Mateen Dot Com. Retrieved fromhttp://amirmateen.com/?p=307 on March 31, 2011.

5 Dawn.Com; Pakistan says evidence of Balochistan interference shared with India, *Dawn,* Karachi, 5 October 2013.

6 Mir, A. (2011):*Balochistan Caught in a Spiral of Violence.*Asia Times Online. August 12. Retrieved from http://www.atimes.com/atimes/South_Asia/MH12Df03.html . Hong Kong: Asia Times Online HoldingsPvt.) Limited.

Maritime Rivalry And Energy Security: India And The South China Sea Dispute

C. Vinodan

Energy security has become one of the world's foremost concerns and a potent source of international conflict. While potentially rich oil and gas resources lie within national maritime zones, they are inaccessible for exploitation so long as the hundreds of overlapping offshore boundary claims remain in dispute. This paper examines the energy security dimensions of the maritime disputes in the South China Sea. The thrust of the paper will be India's maritime concerns in the dispute. The South China Sea has recently become the locus of disputes that have the potential of escalating into serious international conflicts. It is a critical region among the disputing countries because of its geographic position in major oceanic routes used by crude oil tankers from the Persian Gulf to Asia and for transporting goods to the rest of the world. It is important, as well, for its promising offshore oil and gas reserves, other undersea resources, and rich marine life. The rise of China and India as major global economic powers, the continued growth in Western energy demand, challenges of global climate change and instability in key oil-exporting regions are dramatically transforming global energy landscape. Prospects for stable production are increasingly linked to internal political issues and the regional ambitions of major suppliers. These dynamics will affect the global balance of power, as energy security is becoming a more important factor in countries' national security and economic development calculations. Without adequate and affordable energy to underpin the economic growth of a country, its sustenance and indeed its very survival is at risk. Given the fact that energy is simultaneously (either implicitly or explicitly) linked to maintaining social cohesion, the economic well-being of a country and the military might of a state, it is considered to be the *sine qua non* of national security. To that extent therefore, all states, whether developed or developing, rising or declining, energy producing/exporting or energy importing, need energy to survive. Energy therefore is an incredibly important component of national security, understood here both in the traditional and non-traditional sense, where the state and the individual are referents, respectively. This paper examines China's behaviour in the South China Sea disputes through the lens of its new energy security strategy. The South China Sea, potentially rich in energy resources and straddled by international waterways, is beset with territorial and maritime disputes. The strategic and economic significance of the South China Sea has led to a contest over features dotting the semi-enclosed sea. With shipping routes potentially endangered by maritime border disputes, freedom of navigation is therefore a main concern of countries that use vital shipping lanes in the South China Sea. The risk of conflict in the South China Sea is significant not only for regional security but also invite global ramifications. The paper argues that China is exhibiting a more assertive posture to bolster its strategic position in the South China Sea. China, Taiwan, Vietnam, Malaysia, Brunei, and the Philippines have competing territorial and jurisdictional claims, particularly over rights to exploit the region's possibly extensive reserves of oil and gas. Freedom of navigation in the region is also a contentious issue, especially between the United States and China over the right of U.S. military vessels to operate in China's two-hundred-mile exclusive economic zone (EEZ). These tensions are shaping—and being shaped by—rising apprehensions about the growth of China's military power and its regional intentions. This paper also examines the dimensions of maritime security interests of various actors in the South China Sea. It finds that multiple stakeholders pursuing diverse interests have yet to close the gap between goals and means of achieving maritime security.

The rise of China and India as major global economic powers, the continued growth in Western energy demand, challenges of global climate change and instability in key oil-exporting regions are dramatically transforming global energy landscape. Prospects for stable production are increasingly linked to internal political issues and the regional ambitions of major suppliers. These dynamics will affect the global balance of power, as energy security is becoming a more important factor in countries' national security and economic development calculations. Without adequate and affordable energy to underpin the economic growth of a country, its sustenance and indeed its very survival is at risk. Given the fact that energy is simultaneously (either implicitly or explicitly) linked to maintaining social cohesion, the economic well-being of a country and the military might of a state, it is considered to be the *sine qua non* of national security. To that extent therefore, all states, whether developed or developing, rising or declining, energy producing/exporting or energy importing, need energy to survive. Energy therefore is an incredibly important component of national security, understood here both in the traditional and non-traditional sense, where the state and the individual are referents, respectively. This paper examines China's behaviour in the South China Sea disputes through the lens of its new energy security strategy. The South China Sea, potentially rich in energy resources and straddled by international waterways, is beset with territorial and maritime disputes. The strategic and economic significance of the South China Sea has led to a contest over features dotting the semi-enclosed sea. With shipping routes potentially endangered by maritime border disputes, freedom of navigation is therefore a main concern of countries that use vital shipping lanes in the South China Sea. The risk of conflict in the South China Sea is significant not only for regional security but also invite global ramifications. The paper argues that China is exhibiting a more assertive posture to bolster its strategic position in the South China Sea. China, Taiwan, Vietnam, Malaysia, Brunei, and the Philippines have competing territorial and jurisdictional claims, particularly over rights to exploit the region's possibly extensive reserves of oil and gas. Freedom of navigation in the region is also a contentious issue, especially between the United States and China over the right of U.S. military vessels to operate in China's two-hundred-mile exclusive economic zone (EEZ). These tensions are shaping—and being shaped by—rising apprehensions about the growth of China's military power and its regional intentions. This paper also examines the dimensions of maritime security interests of various actors in the South China Sea. It finds that multiple stakeholders pursuing diverse interests have yet to close the gap between goals and means of achieving maritime security.

Maritime strategy and Energy Security

Energy security can be defined as a condition in which a nation and all (or most) of its citizens and industries have access to adequate energy resources at reasonable prices for the foreseeable future, free from serious risks of major disruption of service (Hancher and Janssen 2004). Insecurity can arise from various causes, such as geopolitical instability, natural disasters, terrorism, poor regularity designs, or a lack of investments (Redgwell 2004).

The literature on energy security suggests that different countries have developed different strategies for securing their energy supply. The UN-mandated and US-led coalition's campaign to secure Kuwaiti sovereignty in 1990 and 1991 can be understood within this context. The US and others prevented Iraq from becoming the second-largest oil producer in the world, controlling the Persian Gulf transit and threatening Saudi Arabia, the largest oil producer, militarily. It is also argued that the US and UK's military intervention in Iraq in 2003 can be evaluated in this context. As the argument goes, especially after the 9/11 attacks, the nature of US–Saudi relations has become ambiguous in ways that might have led the US and UK to unlock the Iraqi oil potential for world markets by removing the Baath regime.

Many aspects of modern life, economies, and the relations between states are shaped by the development of energy resources and technologies. The reliance on energy in every field of life has made energy security tremendously important for states and societies. Especially for modern militaries, securing energy resources has become of utmost importance since the beginning of the twentieth century. Therefore, "second only to national defense," energy security has become a primary concern for the survival and wellbeing of both developed and developing nations (Hamilton 2005:xxi). History proved that First and Second World Wars in the twentieth century were also linked with energy use. Winston Churchill's decision to use petroleum by replacing coal for the British Navy to maintain its hegemony before World War I shaped the course of the war; it also led the Allies to invade the oil-rich territories in the Middle East. Energy resources were even more important in World War II. One of the major reasons that Japan attacked the US was the latter's oil embargo against the former's empire. The Axis powers, lacking substantial energy resources, based their strategies on first gaining access to energy-rich areas, such as Romania and the Caspian Sea. The Allies, on the other hand, "floated to victory on a sea of oil" and used nuclear power for the first time to conclude the war (Barton et al. 2004:3). The modern concern with energy security began with the Arab–Israeli war of 1973 – 4 and the Organization of Arab Petroleum Exporting Countries (OAPEC) and Organization of Petroleum Exporting Countries (OPEC)'s use of the "oil weapon." OPEC's boycott of major energy-importing countries in Europe and the US has shown how important it is for modern societies to secure their supply of energy; it became clear that an energy crisis can hurt everyone in society, including government, business, and individuals. Consequently, securing energy resources has become a key aspect of foreign policy making of major powers since the 1970s. With the collapse of the Soviet Union in 1991, the concerns for energy security acquired a new dimension: The newly independent energy-rich ex-Soviet republics in the Caspian basin have become a playground for great-power rivalry. The US and EU, both having suffered from dependency on Middle Eastern energy in the 1970s, have begun increasing their political and economic influence on the region to gain access to energy resources. "The New Great Game" was coined as a term to describe the rivalry between the Western powers and a weakened Russia for the control of the Eurasia region and its energy resources (Kleveman 2003). Since energy-hungry China has begun pursuing aggressive foreign policies to secure the supply of energy to its growing market, this rivalry has taken a "tripolar" shape.

China's search for energy security has come under close international scrutiny in recent years. This is partly because of the economic impact on other countries – most notably changes in the price and availability of some energy resources. But there are also important political dimensions to these debates. For example, supporters of a liberal global order are concerned that China is undermining attempts to pressure authoritarian states to reform. If such states don't like the conditions that accompany aid and economic relations with the West (or more correctly, some in the West), then -if they have things that the Chinese want they can deal with them instead. They might insist that you don't have political relations with Taiwan, and want guarantees that their investments are safe, but they won't pressure you to liberalize your political or economic systems. And as an added bonus, the repayment terms of Chinese development loans are often cheaper than those offered by places like the World Bank.

Chinas New Energy Strategy and the South China Sea Dispute

The world has entered a new era of more of dramatic transition, heralding a century of serious energy uncertainty. Major powers are moving from a position of relative energy independence to one of significant dependence on imports. Security for Asia's major energy sea-lanes—running from the Hormuz Strait, into the Indian Ocean, through the Malacca Strait to Singapore, and into the South China Sea—currently lags behind the growing criticality of these waterways. Key economic powers in the region depend on sea-lane transport for the vast majority of their oil supplies, which in turn help to fuel their economic growth. The growing mismatch between the importance of the sea-lanes and the stress on and vulnerability of the system has contributed to rising energy insecurity in the region. The majority of the world's rising consumption of energy, and oil in particular, is occurring in Asia. Limited regional oil production means that Asia increasingly relies on imported oil, primarily from the Middle East. Close to 90 percent of the energy that China, Japan, and South Korea import must pass through the Southeast Asian sea-lanes (Storey, 2009a, p. 36). Continual access to these energy supplies is critical for sustained economic growth in Asia, which has been a source of stability in the region.　In the last two decades, Asia's economic growth has diverged from that of other developing regions. Since the mid-1980s, economic growth in emerging Asia (including China and India) has been much stronger than elsewhere. Such growth has benefited from economic integration with the global economy. From the mid-1990s, China and India started to make their mark in the world economy. In 2009, according to World Bank, the Asia and Pacific region accounted for almost one-third of global GDP, while 54 percent of the region's GDP comes from just China and India.[1] China has experienced rapid economic growth over past decades. In total economic size, China has quickly caught up with other large economies. In 2008, it overtook Germany to be the second largest economy in the world, and in 2010 it surpassed Japan to be the second largest economy. China has enjoyed rapid economic growth ever since it embarked on reform and opening up to the world in 1979, although the speed has varied from time to time. The surge forward was particularly impressive from the start of twenty-first century until the financial crisis, with the economy zipping along at a double-digit growth rate. In recent years, its economy has turned into a driving locomotive for the entire Asian continent. Undoubtedly, the country has become an important factor in global politics and economics with a tremendous impact on the political, social and economic development of all other states on our planet. Today's emerging new world order is unimaginable without China playing a crucial role in it. (Hauser and Kernic 2009).China has achieved remarkable economic growth during the past three decades, with Real Gross Domestic Product increasing at an average annual rate of over 10% between 1978 and 2008 (World Bank 2009). China's rapid growth since 1978 has been highly dependent on energy. As its economy has expanded, energy use has increased by over 200 percent and by nearly 150 percent per capita, with over half of this growth occurring in the years since 2001. This tight connection between growing energy use and economic development means that energy policy is a central concern of the government. Following its economic development, China's demand for energy, particularly oil, has skyrocketed. According to IEA research, almost half of global oil demand growth in the next five years will come from China. Looking farther ahead, the scenarios in the IEA's *World Energy Outlook 2010* (IEA, 2010a) show China importing 79% of the oil it consumes by 2030, and accounting for a larger increment in oil demand than any other country.

Maritime security in the South China Sea faces a number of challenges, ranging from lower-level nontraditional threats to traditional politico-strategic considerations, including the potential for conflict between regional states over territory or marine resources and the possibility of conflict between major powers. At the highest level of the threat spectrum, the possibility of conflict between major powers is also rarely absent from such an important sea area, which involves some of the world's busiest and most important sea lines of communication (SLOC). There are many reasons, why efforts to address and ameliorate challenges to order, security, and well-being in a semi-enclosed sea area, within which many of those challenges are transnational, ought to be shared cooperatively between littoral states. However, the political sensitivities involved in Southeast Asia, where national interests often clash, or at least diverge, as much as they are shared, make the achievement of a "stable maritime regime," extremely unlikely.[2] The South China Sea is a large space linking southern China and Taiwan to peninsular and archipelagic Southeast Asia and peninsular and continental Southeast Asia to archipelagic Southeast Asia. The South China Sea is categorized as semi-enclosed sea under the United Nations Convention on the Law of the Sea (the LOS Convention).[3] It is surrounded by six countries—China, Vietnam, the Philippines, Brunei, Malaysia, and Indonesia—and has an area of 648,000 square nautical miles, twice the area of the Sea of Japan.[4] The South China Sea also constitutes a vital section of the seaborne trade route linking: both Europe and the Middle East to Northeast Asia; Southeast Asia to Northeast Asia; and much of Southeast Asia to the Pacific Ocean and North America.[5] The geography of the South China Sea area is an important factor in a strategic analysis. Its central location in East Asia ensures its importance for trade and strategic communications. Its complexity ensures both physical dangers for the safety of navigation and political dangers as a source of international dispute. The South China Sea is semi-enclosed by eight littoral polities:

Brunei, China, Indonesia, Malaysia, the Philippines, Singapore, Taiwan, and Vietnam as well as Cambodia and Thailand within the   Gulf of Thailand. The geographic limits of the South China Sea are poorly defined and to some extent contested.[6] Such contested claims and counter claims led to the regional actors to engage in militarization especially in naval modernization. A leading factor in the South China Sea has been the disputes over the territorial features and, as a consequence, the potential maritime jurisdiction to which such features may be entitled, including the related living and nonliving marine resources. Questions exist over the extent of possible hydrocarbon resources in the central South China Sea. Another factor often overlooked is the South China Sea's importance as a fishing ground, accounting for 10% of the global catch,[7] with the annual harvest of around 5 million tonnes representing the fourth largest of the world's 19 major fishing areas.[8] The centrality of China's role as a claimant state, and the linkages between its interests in the South China Sea and the development of Chinese maritime power and its overall ambitions for regional hegemony, make the disputes important beyond the limited face value of a few small, scattered islands, rocks, and reefs—or even potential energy resources. China has long been wary of the strategic presence of opposing hegemonic powers in Southeast Asia, who might exploit Chinese weaknesses at sea to apply pressure on China from its southern maritime periphery. China's strategic ambitions in the South China Sea therefore involve the extension of its defensive perimeter, countering the presence of other major powers, countering threats to its territorial and maritime interests by other claimants, and, ultimately, seeking some measure of maritime command over the area to enforce its hegemonic pretensions. Furthermore, China also has an interest in being able to exert control over East Asian sea-lanes, both to safeguard its own oil supplies and to threaten the economic lifelines of Taiwan and Japan if necessary. A permanent strategic presence in the South China Sea, particularly if it can successfully enforce its territorial claims, might conceivably provide China with such an ability in the future. The establishment of bases, staging, and surveillance posts along the vital sea-lanes has been described as China's "string of pearls" strategy. [9] China has over a period of more than three decades slowly built up its military facilities throughout the South China Sea, including in the Spratlys. In recent years, it has significantly enhanced bases, in particular, on Hainan Island and in the Paracel archipelago. There have also been reports that the People's Liberation Army (PLA) Navy intends to bolster its forces in the area, with a senior PLA officer suggesting that the security situation was "very grim," requiring China to deploy more ships to the disputed region, and to enhance the militarization of occupied features in the Spratlys, including constructing a port for naval vessels and an airport on Mischief Reef, a Chinese occupied reef that lies inside the EEZ claimed by the Philippines.[10] Chinese strategists also noted the geopolitical importance of controlling Taiwan and the Taiwanese-occupied islands in the Spratlys if China is to establish a dominating position into the "southernmost reaches of the South China Sea." Another driver of naval modernization is the likelihood that these factors have led to a degree of hedging by the Southeast Asian littoral states against strategic uncertainty or the possibility of a significant conflict. Although rarely stated by the regional states, it is fair to suggest that the most likely contingencies that might directly affect the South China Sea area involve China. The possibilities include a conflict over Taiwan, with Japan *or* the United States, Chinese moves in the Spratlys or against Vietnam, or the external consequences of internal instability within China itself. Although less likely to lead to armed conflict, the region is also rife with longstanding local rivalries.[11] Naval modernization in the South China Sea states thus cannot be attributed to any single factor. While each individual state may have its own priorities, all of the issues discussed above influence most of the littoral states of the South China Sea to a greater or lesser extent. However, the fluid state of great power relations and the rise of China should not be discounted as a leading driver of at least some of the higher end war fighting capabilities being procured, such as submarines.

India and the South China Sea Dispute

The South China Sea is a strategic waterway providing the key maritime link between the Indian Ocean and East Asia. Sea lines of communication (SLOCs) of the South China Sea are a matter of life and death for the Asia Pacific countries, and SLOC security has been a fundamental factor contributing to regional economic development. As the eastern gateway to the Indian Ocean (IO), South China Sea (SCS) is India's strategic left flank. And, more than half of India's interests pass through or are located in the South China Sea. India has had civilizational contacts and relations, predating the middle ages, with most of the South China Sea littoral nations. The geostrategic significance of the South China Sea lies in the fact that it is the eastern access to the Indian Ocean. India established a presence in the South China Sea in the early days of the "Look East" policy, conducting its first-ever joint naval exercises with Indonesia (1991), Malaysia (1991), and Singapore (1993). In 2001, India held separate bilateral exercises in the South China Sea with the Vietnamese and South Korean navies. Singapore, which during the Cold War had considered the Indian navy to be a threat, reversed course in 1996 and signed an agreement on military cooperation with India. The Indian navy now conducts exercises regularly with Singapore. Thailand has developed a complementary "Look West" policy and has become an increasingly close ally of New Delhi. Coordinated naval patrols are an element of this closer relationship. India's ties to Vietnam were greatly strengthened in 2000 following the visit of the Indian defense minister to Vietnam.[12] India has entered into bilateral defense cooperation agreements with Malaysia, Singapore, Laos, and Indonesia. It has also provided military aid to the armed forces of Myanmar and Thailand. India's current maritime doctrine states that "the Indian maritime vision for the first quarter of the 21st century must look at the arc from the Persian Gulf to the Straits of Malacca as a legitimate area of interest."[13] While India's naval chief, Admiral Arun Prakash, indicated in 2005 that India had no intention of patrolling the Malacca Strait, this view changed in 2006 when New Delhi signaled its willingness to help patrol the strait subject to an invitation from the littoral states.[14] India's rapid rise to strategic prominence in the region has been aided by its absence of any history of disputes in the region. It has no territorial claims in the region. Unlike Japan, China, or the United States, India is perceived as having no strategic ambitions in the region. It is seen as a power that could balance China's rise without posing a direct threat. However, as its trade with ASEAN and China grows, India has an increasing economic incentive to keep regional SLOCs open for international shipping. India is now embarking on Phase II of its "Look East" policy, expanding its scope to include Australia, China, Japan, and South Korea. More emphasis will be placed on security cooperation, including joint operations to protect sea-lanes and the pooling of resources against common threats. The military contacts and joint exercises that India launched with ASEAN states on a low-key basis in the early 1990s are now expanding into full-fledged defense cooperation.[15] Bilaterally, India regularly engages in naval exercises with the US, French, British, Russian and Singapore navies and on an opportunity basis with the Indonesian, Japanese, Philippines, Vietnamese, Saudi Arabian, German, Omani, Iranian and PLA navies. It is noteworthy that India's policy of bilateral naval engagement with a power such as the US is no different at all from that with the regional or other powers. India is also distancing from the emerging rivalry of the US and China over South China Sea. The challenge is for India to become a responsible balancer within the international order by effectively partnering with the key players to manage an increasingly insecure world.

As a resident power in the Indian Ocean region which is still growing, India has new responsibilities in the 21st century. These relate not only to defending her own national interests but also to ensuring security and order in her maritime neighborhood. The Indian Maritime Military Strategy identifies the South China Sea and the Pacific Ocean as 'secondary areas' of operational interest for the Indian Navy. It elaborates "Areas of secondary interest will come in where there is a direct connection with areas of primary interest, or where they impinge on the deployment of future maritime forces". Around 55% of India's trade in the Asia Pacific transits through the South China Sea region. For India, the South China Sea region serves as a strategic link between the Pacific and the Indian Oceans whose security is vital for the smooth flow of her sea borne trade. India's new energy foreign policy also gives priority for active engagement with the South China Sea littorals to commercially participate in exploration of the vital energy resources. Any attempt by China or any other external actors to unilaterally seek to change the status quo will have the potential to impinge upon India's commercial interests relating to energy security and the navigational prerogative to freely use the South China Sea as provided for by the international law. India should also play a proactive role both strategically and diplomatically to ensure peace and order in this vital region. India's policy towards the nations involved in the South China Sea imbroglio would be to respect their viewpoints and persuade them to resolve their issues bilaterally. While not interfering in the ongoing bilateral or regional dialogues is the right policy for India, she should also hedge her bets and be ready to safeguard her own national interests. India should, therefore, extend full support to reducing friction in the region. This would be best done through principled negotiation and peaceful resolution of all potential conflicts under a defined set of rules.

Conclusion

The South China Sea is a strategic waterway providing the key maritime link between the Indian Ocean and East Asia. Sea lines of communication (SLOCs) of the South China Sea are a matter of life and death for the Asia Pacific countries, and SLOC security has been a fundamental factor contributing to regional economic development. The rise of China, as a reckonable power in the global order, is one of the defining features of the 21st century world order. China's unprecedented economic growth and modernization have accelerated China's demand for energy resources, especially oil. Recently, China emerged as the world's largest consumer of oil surpassing the United States and now imports over 50 percent of its oil requirement. Concern about energy insecurity has resulted in the establishment of new priorities and objectives for China's international economic interactions, focusing on the search for secure and reliable sources for the long-term. As the global demand for energy rises, China's geo-strategy includes more assertive policies in the vital strategic regions of the world. China's "Go Out" economic policy and its mercantilist approach to controlling energy resources combined with aggressive trade agreements that include weapons, advanced technology, and/or loan deals for oil reflect China's growing energy security dilemma. The South China Sea's vast energy resources in the heavily disputed Spratly and Paracel Island regions stand to raise the stakes of interested parties including the US and India. Given China's rise and its territorial claims to not only the islands, but the vast majority of the South China Sea and its resources, it remains unclear whether such claims will become a platform for cooperation or conflict. China had showed its assertiveness in the South China Sea through a tough posture instead a conciliatory approach of diplomacy and economic integration with its Southeast Asian neighbours. Other South China Sea states are also asserting their own claims and developing their own naval capacity, albeit to a lesser degree than China. As the eastern gateway to the Indian Ocean, South China Sea is India's strategic left flank. And, more than half of India's interests pass through or are located in the South China Sea. Like all other law abiding nations, India is particular about the freedom of navigation in the maritime commons. In her view, it is of paramount importance that status quo be maintained in respect of freedom of access and passage within the South China Sea. How China overcomes its miscalculations in its South China Sea policy will significantly influence Chinas rising profile in the emerging world order. Its handling of sovereignty disputes with some of its neighbours, and differences with the US have already weakened its standing in the Far East and beyond.

Endnotes and **References**

1. Gross domestic product (GDP) is the sum of gross value added by all resident producers in the economy plus any product taxes and minus any subsidies not included in the value of the products (World Bank, *World Development Indicators Online, 2010*).

2. Michael Leifer, "The Maritime Regime and Regional Security in East Asia," *Pacific Review* 4 (1991): 126–136. See also, more recently, Sam Bateman, "Building Good Order at Sea in Southeast Asia: The Promise of International Regimes" in *Maritime Security in Southeast Asia*, eds. Kwa Chong Guan and John K. Skogan (London: Routledge, 2007), 97–116.

3. United Nations Convention on the Law of the Sea, 1833 *U.N.T.S.* 397, Article 122.

4. J. R. V. Prescott, *TheMaritime Political Boundaries of theWorld* (London: Methuen, 1985),209.

5. John H. Noer,withDavid Gregory, *Chokepoints: Maritime Economic Concerns in Southeast Asia* (Washington, DC: NDU Press, 1996), Figures 17–20, 63–66.

6. For example, the International Hydrographic Organization (IHO) has been trying to revise its published 1953 South China Sea limits for over 20 years. The revised 2002 edition of its *Limits of Oceans and Seas* publication remains in draft form only. The 2002 draft edition excludes significant areas incorporated within the 1953 edition: the Natuna Sea in the south (this revision seems to approximate Indonesia's archipelagic baselines); the Gulf of Tonkin in the west (in addition to the already excluded Gulf of Thailand); and the Taiwan Strait in the north. This article takes no position on the limits of the South China Sea, simply noting the problematic nature of definition. Nevertheless, no matter where exactly the limits are drawn, it is a large body of water encompassing a surface area of approximately 2.7 million to 3 million square kilometers. For a discussion on the geographical scope of the South China Sea, See Nien- Tsu Alfred Hu, "Semi-enclosed Troubled Water: A New Thinking on the Application of the 1982 UNCLOS Article 123 to the South China Sea," OceanDevelopment&International Law 41(3), 2010, pp. 281–314, at 299–301.

7. Clive Schofield, "Dangerous Ground: A Geopolitical Overview of the South China Sea" in *Security and International Politics in the South China Sea: Towards a Cooperative Management Regime*, eds. Sam Bateman and Ralf Emmers (London: Routledge, 2009), 14 18.

8. United Nations Environment Programme (UNEP), *Global InternationalWaters Assessment. South China Sea: Regional Assessment 54* (Kalmar, Sweden: University of Kalmar, 2005), 40–41.

9. This term was coined by a U.S. report, *Energy Futures in Asia*, produced by consultants Booz Allen Hamilton for the Office of the Secretary of Defense. A string of ports, bases, and listening posts stretching from the entrance to the Persian Gulf through to the South China Sea constitute the so-called "pearls." The report was first publicised by Bill Gertz, "China Builds Up Strategic Sea Lanes," *Washington Times*, 18 January 2005.

10. L. C. Russell Hsiao, "In a Fortnight: PLA General Advises Building Bases in the South China Sea," Jamestown Foundation, *China Brief* , 24 June 2009, 1–2.

11. Some of these are historically based, such as between Singapore and Malaysia; related to territorial or maritime disputes, such as that between Indonesia and Malaysia over the Ambalat offshore development area on the east coast of Borneo; or both, such as the nascent Philippine claim to Sabah or the long-standing enmity and distrust between Vietnam and China. Religious and ethnic factors may also play a role in some rivalries. Even though many of the rival states would never admit to it, such relationships are factors in military modernization.

12. Faizal Yahya, "India and Southeast Asia Revisited," *Contemporary Southeast Asia* 25 (2003): 7.

13. Integrated Headquarters, Ministry of Defence (Navy), *Indian Maritime Doctrine. INBR 8* (New Delhi: Integrated Headquarters, Ministry of Defence, 2004), 56.

14. "India Has No Intention of Patrolling Malacca Straits," *Daily Times,* 23 July 2005.

15. India-ASEAN Summit, *India-ASEAN Summit Declaration, 30 November 2004* (New Delhi:

References:

Barton, B., Redgwell, C., Ronne, A., and Zillman, D.N. (eds.) (2004) *Energy Security: Managing Risk in a Dynamic Legal and Regulatory Environment.* Oxford: Oxford University Press.

Hamilton, L.H. (2005) Foreword. In J.H. Kalicki and D.L. Goldwyn (eds.) *Energy and Security:Toward a New Foreign Policy Strategy.* Washington: Woodrow Wilson Center Press, p. xxi.

Hancher, L., and Janssen, S. (2004) Shared Competences and Multi-Faceted Concepts – European Legal Framework for Security of Supply. In B. Barton, C. Redgwell, A. Ronne, and D.N. Zillman (eds.) *Energy Security: Managing Risk in a Dynamic Legal and Regulatory Environment.* Oxford: Oxford University Press, pp. 85 – 119.

International Energy Agency. (2007), *Toward a Clean, Clever and Competitive Energy Future – IEA Report to G8 Summit in Heiligendamm, Germany 2007.* Available at: www.iea.org/Textbase/ publications/free_new_Desc.asp?PUBS_ID=1920, accessed July 2, 2009.

Klare, M.T. (2008) *Rising Powers, Shrinking Planet: The New Geopolitics of Energy.* New York: Metropolitan Books.

Kleveman, L. (2003) *The New Great Game: Blood and Oil in Central Asia.* New York: Grove Press.

Redgwell, C. (2004) International Energy Security. In B. Barton, C. Redgwell, A. Ronne, and D.N. Zillman (eds.) *Energy Security: Managing Risk in a Dynamic Legal and Regulatory Environment.* Oxford: Oxford University Press, pp. 17 – 46.

Nye, J. (2005) *Understanding International Conflicts: an Introduction to Theory and History.* New York: Pearson/Longman.

Hauser, Gunther / Kernic, Franz (eds.), China: The Rising Power Frankfurt am Main, Berlin, Bern, Bruxelles, New York, Oxford, Wien, 2009. 215 pp., 1).

Yunchang Jeffrey Bor and ZhongXiang Zhang(2010), Energy Economics: Asian Energy in the Context of growing Security and Environmental Concerns., Amsterdam.

Zweig, David, and Jianhai Bi. (2005) China's Global Hunt for Energy. Foreign Affairs 84 (5): 25–38.

David Rosenberg a & Christopher Chung, Maritime Security in the South China Sea: Coordinating Coastal and User State Priorities, Ocean Development & International Law, 39:51–68, 2008.

Vijay Sakhuja, "Maritime Power of People's Republic of China: The EconomicDimension," *Strategic Analysis* 24 (2001): 2024.

PART - III

India's Maritime Security: The Policy Options

India's Maritime Security: The Policy Options

B. Vivekanandan

1. If we look at the geo-strategic and geo-political map of the world, the Indian Ocean occupies a prominent position.

    • In the Indian Ocean setting, India's geo-political location is also very prominent.

    • The way geography has positioned India in the Indian Ocean, India is destined to be a strong maritime power in the world.

2. India has an old seafaring tradition, which, apart from mercantile goods, took Indian scholars and missionaries across the Ocean, and to South – east Asia, Japan, China, Indonesia, Sri Lanka, etc. to spread the message of peace and goodwill, embedded in the Indian cultural tradition, the footprints of which are visible in those countries even today.

    • That tradition was broken with the advent of the Mughal rule in India, followed by the British colonial rule.

3. During the British colonial rule in India, the Indian Ocean was virtually made a British lake.

    • Barring a minor passage through the Indonesian Archipelage, the Royal Indian Navy controlled all entry points of the Indian Ocean – the Suez Canal, the Cape of Goodhope, Singapore, and the passages around Australia.

    • The only occasion in which this British supremacy of the Indian Ocean was challenged occurred in 1942, when Britain temporarily lost Singapore to Japan during the Second World War.

4. India's independence in 1947 did not bring much change in the British dominance of the Indian Ocean.

    •   Britain maintained its dominance with a reduced size of the Royal Navy, until, in a bid to reduce the public expenditure, the British Government came out with an announcement in January 1968, that Britain would withdraw its forces from the East of Suez by the end of 1971.

5. Although the Indian Ocean is rightly named after India, independent India did not pay much attention to build up a strong naval force to safeguard its long-term security interests.

    •   More attention was paid to build up the Army and the Air Force.

6. But, in early 1970s, India was provided with an opportunity to start building a strong blue-water navy.

    •   But the Indian leadership had wasted it.

7. The opportunity came to India when, in the aftermath of Britain's decision to withdraw its forces from the East of Suez, the Americans put pressure on Britain to permit the US to build a naval base in Diego Garcia.

    •   But Britain was not willing to oblige US.

    •   Britain thought that it would be better to have a security arrangement for the Indian Ocean, involving the littoral states under India's leadership.

    •   To explore that possibility, Britain's Foreign Secretary, Sir Alec Douglas – Home, came to New Delhi, and met Prime Minister, Indira Gandhi and External Affairs Minister,Swaran Singh, in February 1972, and discussed the matter.

    •   During their discussions, Douglas-Home told Indira Gandhi and Swaran Singh that if India was willing to play a larger role in the Indian Ocean, including the maintenance of the safety and security of Sea-lanes in the Indian Ocean, Britain would help India to build a strong navy for the purpose.

- The British perception was that, if India emerged as a strong naval power between South African and Australia, and played a strategic role of a Sea-Power, that would not only guarantee free navigation through the Indian Ocean, but also would provide an incentive for super powers to refrain from sending their strong naval fleets to the Indian Ocean.

- Moreover, Douglas-Homes proposal clearly implied Britain's acceptance of India as its true successor in the Indian Ocean.

- But Indira Gandhi and Swaran Singh declined Sir Alec Douglas-Home's offer.

- These details of discussions were told to me by Douglas-Home himself when I met him in London.

- From a long-term perspective, Indira Gandhi's rejection of the British offer was a grave mistake.

- If India had seized that opportunity and accepted the British offer in 1972, the Indian Navy today would have been a World Class Navy.

- However, India missed that opportunity.

- It was after India's rejection of the British offer that Britain allowed the Americans to build a naval base in Diego Garcia.

8. Although 1960s, 1980s and 1990s saw the presence of the Super Power navies and the navies of other big powers like Britain, France and Germany, India did not feel any threat to its security from them mainly because none of these powers had entertained any basic hostility towards India.

9. But, today India is faced with new security challenges developing in the Indian Ocean.

- The foremost challenge to India's maritime security emanates from the growing naval activities of China, which nurses a deep-seated evil design against India.

- As part of its defence modernization programme, China is now building up an Ocean-going blue-water navy which now has an aircraft carrier.

- It has strengthened its submarine fleet as well.

10. For India, China is not like any other big power.

- Way back in 1950, SardarVallabhai Patel had assessed it as India's national enemy.

- It is a country whose expansionist ambitions have no end.

- The first thing China did after the Revolution in 1949, was to put its expansionist agenda into action, and, within a year, launched an attack on the neighbouring Tibet, in 1950, and occupied that country, and forced the Dalai Lama to flee from Tibet in 1959.

- Then, it raised territorial disputes with all its other neighbours – India, Japan, Vietnam and USSR.

- It has refused to accept the MacMahon Line as India's border with Tibet.

- In 1962, it invaded India and annexed about 38,000 Sq.Kms. of Indian territory.

- In recent years China has built up a huge logistic network in Tibet, including roads, railways, airfields, missile launching sites, etc. to be used against India when need comes.

- It is making a claim on Arunachal Pradesh and refuses to issue Chinese Visas to Indian citizens living there.

- It has raised objection to Indian Prime Minister's and Defence Minister's visit to Arunachal Pradesh.

- It has occupied the Aksai – Chin in Jammu & Kashmir.

- China does not recognize Jammu & Kashmir as part of India, and distributes Indian maps, without J & K and Arunachal Pradesh in it.

- For the people of J & K. it issues only stapled Visas.

- It has built up a highway connecting Xinjiang with Gwadar port in

Pakistan, thereby made a direct entry into the Arabian Sea.

- Similarly, China is trying to make another direct entry into the Bay of Bengal, through the Chittagong port in Bangladesh.

- It has bolstered up Pakistan against India, by clandestinely helping Pakistan to become a nuclear weapon state, and uses Pakistani leaderships as its pawns to checkmate India everywhere in the international arena.

- After building up all these, land – based infrastructure against India, and stirring up considerable anti-India feeling among India's neighbouring countries, China is now trying to complement its 'encirclement of India process by building up a maritime set up in the Indian Ocean to sand witch India, from both land and the Ocean.

- Obviously, the Chinese intentions behind all these multi-pronged moves against India are just evil, no less.

11. Simultaneously, China engages India in phony talks on border issues, in a boomerang style, without conceding anything.

- No wonder, that after 15 rounds of border talks between officials of both countries, the negotiators have not yet touched the core issue- the demarcation of the border.

- However, it seems that, the on-going boomerang game China plays with the Indian negotiators on the border issue, along with intermittent. Chinese acrobatics in the form of LAC violations may culminate in another serious conflict, for which China seems to be preparing, to force the border issue, and settle it in Chinese terms.

- The present Chinese move in the Indian Ocean, and in the India Ocean littoral states, seems to be part of that preparation.

- Therefore, the real challenge to India's maritime security and its security in general, emanates from the growing Chinese activities in the Indian Ocean, and from the hostile diplomacy China is carrying on with India's neighbouring littoral states of the Indian Ocean.

- Port constructions in Sri Lanka, Pakistan, and Bangladesh, and the military base China is seeking from Seychelles, etc. are parts of it.

12. Other challenges are basically coastal security challenges.

   - Piracy is one, which is not new.

   - Terrorism is another.

   - The large-scale flow of counterfeit Indian currencies of high denominations to destabilize the Indian economy is the third.

   - But, all these challenges can be contained by efficient naval patrolling and coastal-guard activities.

13. Finally, what are the policy options? For India?

   (a) Undoubtedly, India should pay more attention to build a strong and well-equipped navy.

      - The addition of a 3rd aircraft carrier is laudable.

      - That apart, the Government of India will have to invest more to strengthen its maritime forces than what it does today, to meet the potential challenge posed by a determined potential enemy, like the expansionist People's Republic of China.

   (b) Other policy options, before India, are basically political.

      - 30 years ago, at an International Conference on Indian Ocean Studies, held in 1984, in Perth in Australia, I made a proposal that, instead of making a narrowly defined diplomatic move for "Improving" relations with South Asian – including Pakistan, Nepal, Myanmar, Bangladesh, and Sri Lanka – should strive to pool their destinies together – i.e. 'a sink or sail together' approach, and free them from a suspicion based bilateral relationships.

      - Of course, it requires a more generous, humanist, approach, anchored in Solidarity, on the part of India; while dealing with people's problems in the Indian sub-continent.

      - The dynamism embedded in such a policy, would release a lot of new resources for people's welfare, and, at the same time, deny space for outside powers to meddle with, and vitiate, the bilateral relationships between countries of South Asia.

- It would result in a new resurgent cohesive Indian sub-continent, which can match any power centre in the world, and, at the same time, achieve a high rank in the human development index.

- The scheme I have in mind in this context is the example of Willy Brandt's Ostpolitik, pursued in West Germany, with a higher level of humanitarian content, which had erased the barriers between the two Germanys, and also changed the perception of international relationship in the whole Europe.

- India's policy makers often talk about "going an extra-mile" in India's dealings with our neighbouring countries.

- To my mind, this is an inadequate framework.

- The right framework is: "Pooling the destinies" of countries of South Asia.

- Pakistan should be an integral part of this framework.

- Nawas Sheriff's return to power in Pakistan augurs well for the promotion of this kind of a relationship in the Indian sub-continent.

- Another policy option is that, India should support the freedom movement in Tibet, to enable the Tibetan refugees in India to go back to their homes, with dignity.

- The other policy option is that, India should stop supporting the "One China" policy of the People's Republic of China.

Maritime Security: An Indian Perspective

K. R. Singh

Even though Indians claim to be a maritime nation yet there is a reluctance to learn about maritime affairs. Over the decades, Indians have started overcoming their so-called continental mindset. The strategic location of India in the Indian Ocean and new maritime challenges posed to India has contributed to it. Seas do not know any frontier. Hence, whatever happens in one part of the ocean affects sooner or later everyone else. Therefore, Indians need to be aware of global dimensions of maritime affairs so that they are not left behind as had happened in the past.

This seminar focuses on maritime security and more particularly upon coastal security. The subject involves study of multiple variables like correct understanding of the term maritime and security, nature and extent of state's jurisdiction over waters adjacent to its coast, international law and conventions dealing with maritime affairs as also acts and ordinances passed by the government to protect and promote its maritime interests, maritime enforcement agencies etc. Of late, the issue of maritime terrorism has become a new source of threat particularly to the coastal states and its people.

Issue of jurisdiction

The term maritime is derived from Latin word *mare* meaning sea. The question as to who owns it and what is the extent of state jurisdiction in waters adjacent to its coast has been a hotly debated issue since late fifteenth century. Bartholomo Diaz rounded the Cape of Good Hope in 1488 thus opening a new way to the East. Columbus reached the shores of America in 1492. Pope Alexander VI, in 1493, through a Papal Bull distributed the world among the two Catholic Kings. Spain got the western half and Portugal the eastern half. Thus, for the first time in history, a non-regional power extended sovereignty over Indian Ocean. Portugal imposed its sovereignty by employing ships armed with guns.

Regional powers tried to challenge the Portuguese but failed because they lacked naval power that could deny the sea to the Portuguese. Portuguese claims of *mare clausum* were challenged legally by Hugo Grotius who propounded the doctrine *mare labarum* (open sea). The Dutch Navy and the British Navy imposed the new doctrine. Since then, freedom of the high seas has been a basic principle of maritime law.

The concept of open sea clashed with the concept of state sovereignty over its adjacent wasters. After a great deal of debate a 3 n. mile sea was designated as the territorial sea. The 3 n. mile limit was allegedly based upon the range of the cannon fired from the coast. The 3 n. mile limit continued to be the norm till the end of World War II. Since then, over the years, state's jurisdiction over adjacent sea space began to expand, largely because of economic reasons and rapid evolution in technology. USA was the first state to advance its claims. It discovered vast deposits of oil in offshore waters in the Gulf of Mexico that could be exploited by advances in drilling technology. USA, thus, introduced the concept of continental-shelf in 1945. The Geneva Convention of 1958 accepted the concept of state jurisdiction over sub-soil resources in the continental-shelf but without defining any limit to it.

During the same period, many coastal states began complaining of fishing vessels from far off areas fishing in waters near their coast thereby hurting the economic interests of their fishermen. During that period, undersea exploration in deep waters discovered vast deposits of manganese nodules in mid-ocean. Right to exploit them became a major issue of international debate.

United Nations Conference on the Law of the Sea (UNCLOS-III) was convened in mid-seventies to discuss all these issues dealing with maritime affairs. After a great deal of debate some consensus was reached in 1982. Provisions of UNCLOS-III sought to balance two basic questions; freedom of navigation on the high seas and expanding jurisdiction of coasted states in their adjacent waters. Ocean space was broadly demarcated under following zones; territorial sea, contiguous zone, exclusive economic zone/ continental shelf and the high seas. UNCLOS-III defines the jurisdiction of coastal state in relation to these zones while reaffirming the principles of freedom of the high seas beyond the outer limit of territorial waters.

India had participated actively in the deliberations of UNCLOS-III and had signed it in 1982. It ratified it only in 1995. India has as yet not passed an act of the Parliament that would give legal status in Indian courts to the provisions of UNCLOS-III. In the meanwhile India had passed ordinances, acts of the Parliament and amendments to the Constitution to frame its own maritime zones. Hence, these would have preference over provisions of UNCLOS-III if there is a clash between them in the court of law.

India's Expanding Maritime Zones

India extended the outer limit of its territorial waters from 3 n. miles to 6 n. miles through a Presidential Ordinance in 1956. The same year, it also introduced the concept of contiguous zone by a Presidential Ordinance. It extended 6 n. miles beyond the outer limit of territorial waters. India amended Article 297 of the Constitution in 1963 and added the concept of continental-shelf. The amended article said that sea-based resources within the territorial waters or the continental-shelf vest in the Union. That concept was already accepted in the Geneva Convention of 1958. That amendment legalized the exploration and exploitation of oil and gas resources in the Bombay High.

Article 279 was once again amended on April 27, 1976. It defined various maritime zones including the exclusive economic zone (EEZ). Thus, the concept of EEZ was added. That amendment enabled the Parliament to enact the Maritime Zones of India Act, 1976. It fixed the outer limits of territorial waters (12 n.miles from the base line), contiguous zone (24 n. miles), EEZ and continental-shelf (200 n. miles). It also defined India's jurisdiction (not sovereignty) over these zones. It also took care not to violate the concept of freedom of navigation on the high seas.

Maritime security: legal gaps

It must be underlined that the MZA Act predated UNCLOS-III of 1982. Though India had taken active part in the deliberations of UNCLOS-III and had signed it in 1982 and ratified it in 1995, it has not enacted a law that will give legal sanction to provisions of UNCLOS-III. Another thing that needs to be underlined is that UNCLOS-III does not deal with matters of security (except acts of piracy). MZI Act does under section 5 and sections A (a). However, framers of MZI Act, 1976 also did not provide for arrest, trial and punishment of persons apprehended for violating its provisions. Parliament had to enact specific laws in that context. India had enacted the Customs Act, 1962. It was periodically updated. India also enacted the MZI (Regulation of Fishing by Foreign Vessels) Act, 1981. The Coast Guard is entrusted with implementing it. India has, to my knowledge, not enacted any law specific to maritime terrorism, except for the SUA Act of 2002 under which the Parliament legalized the provisions of the SUA Convention of 1988. It also passed the Piracy Act in 2012. But to the best of any knowledge it has not passed a law that can empower maritime enforcement authorities to neutralize the threat of maritime terrorism beyond the territorial waters of India, despite the events of 26/11 in Mumbai and steps taken in the context of coastal security since 2005-6.

Before the Government of India enacts a new act in that context it can take advantage of the provisions of MZI Act. As noted, section 5, sub-section 4(a) that deals with India's jurisdiction over its contiguous zone, empowers the Union Government to take measures in relation to the security of India. Some experts object to this clause by arguing that it denies freedom of navigation. But it is not true. In that context I would like to differentiate between defence of India and security of India. Defence is *vis-à-vis* state actors. Security is *vis-a-vis* nsa/terrorists. If India has the jurisdiction in the contiguous zone over economy-related criminal activities of NSA, can it be denied jurisdiction over criminal activities that target its population and property?

The framers of the MZI Act had made their intention very clear. The Statement of Objects and Reasons, appended to the act, asserted in the context of that section that any enactment made in that context shall have the effect as if the same was a part of the territory of India. It is most unfortunate that despite the events of 26/11 and the new emphasis on coastal security, no enactment was made or ordinance promulgated to give legal effect to security-related provisions of section 5, sub-section 4(a) of the MZI Act. If done, all the maritime enforcement agencies of the Union like the Navy, the Coast Guard and the Customs (Marine Wing) will be empowered to take action against suspected vessels/ persons even in sea space 12 n. miles beyond the territorial waters limit. Thus, even under the present enactment (MZI Act), the security zone of India can be extended upto 24 n. miles from the coast without violating the norms of national and even international law.

Though India has not enacted laws specific to maritime terrorism, it did pass SUA Act, 2002, to give legal effect to the provisions of SUA

Convention of 1988. Though the Convention as also the SUA Act do not use the term terrorism, yet the crimes committed on board a ship or on oil/gas platforms in the continental-shelf cover acts of terrorism without specifically using that term. That act gives details of arrest, trial and punishment for various criminal activities. India, however, needs a comprehensive act that takes cognizance of specific legal nature of its jurisdiction over multiple maritime zones, to apprehend and even preempt action of criminals who target the security of India *via* the adjacent sea space.

Enforcement Agencies

Maritime security, in the context of coastal security, has been entrusted to four enforcement agencies, the Navy, the Customs (Marine), the Coast Guard and the Marine Police. Except the Marine Police the rest are under the Union Government. Also, except the Marine Police none of them were established to meet challenges of coastal security, especially in the context of terrorism.

The Navy is primarily entrusted with the defence of India *vis-a-vis* threats posed by state actors. Hence, it is equipped with large and sophisticated warships like the aircraft carrier, destroyer, frigate, submarine etc that are not suitable for the needs of coastal security. The Navy is forming a new wing, Sagar Prahari Bal, for that purpose. However, being the senior most agency, it has been entrusted with the leadership role in relation to coastal security. It is a classical example of rule of seniority determining the leader. One wonders how appropriate that will prove in actual practice.

The second maritime security agency, the Customs (Marine), was strengthened since the mid-sixties to check smuggling. It was given adequate support till the end of the seventies when its role was shared by the Coast Guard after it was formed. One can well say that the Coast Guard grew at the expense of the Customs (Marine). Also, one does not see the Customs (Marine) discussed as an important part of coastal security set up. Does it reflect inter-ministerial turf war?

The Coast Guard was formed in 1977-78 to implement the provisions of MZI Act, 1976, especially preventing unauthorized foreign fishing boats from poaching on India's EEZ. It was also entrusted with tasks like checking smuggling, protecting fishermen, search and rescue operations, pollution control, anti-piracy role etc. There is no doubt that since 1978, the Coast Guard has expanded into a large and well equipped force but it can divert only a part of its resources to coastal security. It is being expanded keeping the new role in mind. Yet the Indian coastline is so vast and its island territories so dispersed that Coast Guard alone cannot deploy enough resources to effectively take care of requirements of coastal security.

In that context the new thinking in the Government of India of promoting coastal states to play a more proactive role in coastal security needs to be welcomed. Though the concept was accepted unfortunately the coastal states are not given the role that they really deserve. It cannot be forgotten that the coastal states are the prime targets of terrorists arriving *via* the sea. Also, unless the terrorists are intercepted on the sea away from the coast *per se* they have to be located and intercepted in the adjacent coastal belt. Thus, the state police, including the Marine Police, will have to play a crucial role. It is unfortunate that provisions of Indian Constitution do not provide for coastal state's role in coastal security.

Even though the framework of coastal security provides for synergy among these enforcement agencies, yet that concept is new to India where seniority claims leadership position. I hope that the younger elements among the maritime security agencies will interact in a more cooperative mode. Also, some way needs to be found to actively involve the Customs (Marine) in this synergy since it is entrusted with economic security in the contiguous zone under section 5, subsection 4 of MZI Act.

Coastal states can make their contribution to strengthen coastal security in another way. That is in the realm of intelligence. Undoubtedly, maritime security agencies depend upon several modes of intelligence gathering. They are mostly based upon data generated by the satellites, radar network along the coast and various other communication networks. Their input of human intelligence is rather limited. It is here that coastal states and more particularly the fishing community can play a very useful role. To the best of my knowledge there is no organized structure for obtaining intelligence/information from our fisher folk who operate in India's EEZ further away from the coast.

In that context, I am suggesting the creation of Marine Guards, maritime version of Home Guards, in coastal states. This will need cooperation from the Central Government, Marine Police, in coordination with Marine Guards, can provide intelligence that can supplement what is collected from various other sources. In this context, fisher folk who own/ operate sea going fishing boats/trawlers can play a meaningful role.

If the concept is accepted, a coastal state can seek volunteers from suitable candidates spread along its coast to join as Sea Guard. Since they are trained seamen and have access to sea going vessels, time and finances to create such an organization can be greatly reduced. They can be trained in navigation through the use of GPS as well as to operate radio for communication with the designated authority, mostly the Marine Police, who would then share the information with appropriate authorities. The state will have to equip their vessels with GPS and radio communication system. These volunteers can also be given a suitable honorarium and an identity.

If a coastal state recruits, as an experiment, even 300 Sea Guards, it will need to spend a sum of about two to three crore rupees as honorarium per year and invest some money for GPS and radio. Even if one third of the Sea Guards are on the sea in their boats every day, the coastal state will have 100 pairs of trained eyes at all times in its adjacent sea space at an affordable cost shared between the State and the Central Government. Trained eyes, who know the waters, the coast and local fisherfolk, can see and report more quickly if they find something unusual happening around them. I hope that coastal states give this concept a try and not only benefit in practical terms but also induct coastal fishing community in a more organized and meaningful way in matters related to coastal security, be it in search and rescue, pollution control, presence of foreign (unknown) fishing vessels, or even suspicious behaviour of some local boat.

Maritime security and inadequacy of sea governance

One can explain the lack of interest in maritime affairs primarily due to two things. The one is the so-called continental mindset of Indian decision makers. It is reflected even in the Indian Constitution when it defines the territory of India. Article 1(3) of Part I of Indian Constitution mentions that the territory of India comprises of the territories of the States, the Union Territories and such other territories as may be acquired. It even ignored mentioning territorial waters that is recognized world over as an extension of state sovereignty. The Indian Penal Code also followed that definition in Chapter II, section 18. After the passing of the MZI Act 1976,

Government of India, by a notification extended the provisions of IPC and Cr.P.C. over the entire EEZ of India.

The term territorial waters was mentioned only twice but only in the context of Centre-State relations. Under article 297, the Union Government was given the right to exploit minerals and other items of value in territorial waters. Item 57 of Union List of VIIth Schedule (List I) gave the Union Government exclusive jurisdiction over fishery resources beyond territorial waters. Thus, coastal states whose fishermen operate in those waters have no jurisdiction over them beyond the narrow territorial waters.

The second important factor that puts constraints on the evolution of robust mechanism for sea governance is the fact that the Constitution makers had placed all matters dealing with maritime affairs under the Union. They included shipping, major ports, marine fishery and maritime security. While some concession was made in the context of coastal shipping and non-major ports, marine fishery and maritime security were placed exclusively under the Union Government.

As seen earlier, item 57 of List I of VII Schedule gives the Union Government exclusive jurisdiction over fishery in sea space beyond the territotrial waters. Though constitutionally the coastal states have not been given explicit jurisdiction over fishery in territorial waters adjacent to its coast yet, by interpreting item 57 of List I, the coastal states were able to acquire jurisdiction over fishery in those waters. These coastal states passed laws to regulate fishing in those waters. However, the Union Government, that was given exclusive jurisdiction over fishery in waters beyond territorial sea, did not frame laws regulating fishing by Indians. The Coast Guard has powers to regulate fishing by foreign vessels but not by Indian vessels. The result was near anarchy. Some effort was made in 2009 by presenting the Fishery Bill. But it created more confusion.

Maritime fishery, smuggling and maritime security are often closely interrelated. Marine fishery cannot be fully regulated unless coastal states are fully integrated in that process. But the Constitution acts as a constrain. It needs to be overcome because one cannot think of coastal security without some robust mechanism to regulate marine fishery as a whole.

The legal question of coastal security is also influenced by the constitutional constraint. Item 1 and 2 of List II (State List) mention public order (item 1) and police (item 2) under the state jurisdiction. It also needs to be noted that the Indian Constitution treats all states as equal while defining their 'territory'. Thus, territory of the coastal state is also restricted to the land space and at best, to inland waters. As yet there is no constitutional amendment or even an ordinance that gives the coastal state criminal jurisdiction over its territorial waters though by default it is allowed to exercise that power. This grey area or legal lacuna needs to be corrected as early as possible now that the Marine Police has been formally constituted to act against criminal elements in the territorial waters. The only saving grace is that provisions of IPC and Cr.PC apply up to the outer limits of EEZ.

Another facet of Centre-State relations that is becoming important in the context of coastal security deals with foreign policy issues. The Constitution grants the power to formulate and conduct foreign policy to the Union Government. No one will dispute that. But, there needs a mechanism that will enable the state to discuss matters of foreign policy or relations that directly affect it or interests of a section of its people with the Central Government. Otherwise, such issues might not only affect Centre-State relations but also the foreign policy *per se*. Tamil question in Sri Lanka has become a matter of domestic policy in Tamil Nadu and has started adversely affecting relations between India and Sri Lanka. This is equally true of relations between Bengal and Bangladesh, between the North-East and Myanmar etc. Hence, it is time that while one discusses foreign policy of India one also gives due attention to the internal dimension of that policy as it might affect the states.

If we apply that principle to maritime affairs, one has to look at regional maritime affairs not only in the context of interaction between sovereign, independent states in the region but also of the coastal states that are directly affected by developments in that region. In this context, I will like to draw the attention to a maritime region that has been neglected so far. That region comprises of sea space bound by Maldives, Sri Lanka and India. In India, two coastal states, Tamil Nadu and Kerala, and the Union Territory of Laceadives play a direct role in this maritime region. This water space comprises of the adjacent EEZs of all these states thereby promoting prospects of cooperation in fishery-related activities. The relatively narrow sea space also provides the opportunity for joint project on building relatively small ports, as also ships, increased intra-regional trade and travel, as well as a coordinated approach to monitor shipping in the busy international sea routes that pass through these waters. Cooperation at the level of Maldives, Sri Lanka and India (MASLIND), with added inputs from Tamil Nadu, Kerala and the Laceadives, can also strengthen regional maritime security. This theme needs greater indepth study.

Coastal Security: Need to update Legal System

Though the country has been facing threat of maritime terrorism Indian Parliament has not passed an act specific to maritime terrorism. Indeed it has enacted SUA Act, 2002 to give legal status to the SUA Convention of 1988. But, it is inadequate in its scope. Parliament also enacted Piracy Act in 2012. That act could have been expanded to cover other aspects of maritime crimes but India's Piracy Act confines itself to the definition of piracy as given under UNCLOS-III. Thus, India, as of today, does not have a comprehensive law covering different facets of maritime security including maritime terrorism.

In that context I would like to reiterate the significance of section 5, sub-section 4 (a) of MZI Act. As discussed earlier, it has provisions that cover maintaining security of India up to the outer limit of the contiguous zone. For some reasons that section, which under an act of Parliament, extends India's maritime security frontier up to a maximum of 24 n. miles from the coast, has been ignored by decision makers. As act of the Parliament empowering agencies to take action under that section can provide for interception of vessels that are allegedly involved in acts of terrorism even on the high seas *i.e.* 12 n. miles beyond the outer limit of the territorial waters of India. I want to underline the fact that Indian court will take cognizance of an Indian act like the MZI Act even though it might go beyond, not against the provisions of UNCLOS-III.

The second point that I wish to emphasize in this context is that coastal security can be best ensured only with full and active cooperation of coastal states. In that context, I would like to suggest minor amendments to the Concurrent List (List III) of the VIIth Schedule that deals with subjects that are common to both; the Union and the State. I suggest that two new items be added to the Concurrent List: marine fishery and maritime security. That will not erode the powers of the Central Government. Rather, by involving coastal states that will facilitate better sea governance and thus strengthen the overall structure of coastal security.

Oceanic and Coastal Security Imperatives for India

R. S. Vasan

Abstract. The recalibration of the American maritime strategy with a pivot to the Asia- Pacific reinforces the importance of the Indian Ocean to security safety and well-being of the global maritime activities. The traditional terminology of Asia Pacific has given way to an "Indo Pacific" one for obvious reasons. This rebalancing has brought in enhanced interest in the Indian Ocean Region. The last decade and the beginning of this decade witnessed both acts of terrorism and increased acts of piracy in the areas of interest to the world and India. Both the acts has the potential to disrupt global trade commerce and development.

The terror attacks on the commercial capital of Mumbai in November 2008 brought about key changes in the concept of maritime security in India. The use of the seas from across the border for transporting ten well trained terrorists to subsequently launch commando type attacks highlighted the porosity of our coasts and exposed the chinks in our armour. The daring attacks on iconic symbols of a modern growing India in Mumbai that brought death and destruction exposed the hollow claims of the security and intelligence establishment in being prepared to thwart such plots. Despite many initiatives at both the Centre and the State levels post Mumbai terror attacks, there are still questions about the tools and techniques and their efficacy to prevent another terrorist attack from the seas.

While this incident challenged both internal and external security architecture, India as a Regional Power has to also manage its external maritime environment. This involves active engagement with the maritime neighbours on both flanks. The maritime strategy is undergoing rapid transformation due to the presence and initiative of China which is increasingly looking to expand the sphere of its activity in India's traditional areas of influence. This is another inclusive challenge that needs to be taken up based on the long term multi-dimensional impact in the coming decades. These challenges would be examined in the context of oceanic security in the IOR.

At another level, the acts of piracy in the west Arabian Sea has impacted the maritime Industry in a big way and threatened to disrupt the movement of ships in the arteries of the world. The psychological trauma faced by the crew held hostage and their families has affected the morale of the industry and seafarers. The increased incidents of piracy compelled the IMO and the navies of the world to rush to the area to protect vital maritime interests of trade and commerce. While maritime terrorism and piracy have taken center stage, there are other issues of equal importance both to the maritime states of India and also the Central Government. These include non-traditional forms of maritime security such as fisheries, livelihood, marine pollution and other issues of maintaining law and order at sea.

The paper seeks to examine all the related issues that impinge on Oceanic and coastal security in the Indian context. Based on case studies, recommendations would be made on the way ahead for India to acquire that Maritime Power Potential that would place it at the apex in the Indian Ocean Security architecture.

The Big Picture. There has been a paradigm shift in the very concept of Oceanic and coastal Security in the Indian Ocean Region. It is evident that the global happenings and the action of the major powers impinges on the regional and sub-regional maritime environment and the nature of transactions amongst maritime nations and other stake holders. While there seems to be hardly any doubt that this century belongs to Asia with the growth and integration of Asian economies with the global economy, there is a sense of imbalance due to the astronomical growth of China both as a economic and military power.

The last few decades has witnessed a great degree of consistency in China's meteoric rise[1] in all spheres, though China claims that is not aimed at any other country. The economic dividend has resulted in greater allocation towards military modernization and Science and Technology initiatives. The availability of large funds for investment in far corners of the world has not only enhanced the economic power potential but also has paved the way for enhancing the sphere of influence in Africa, Middle East, Asia, Latin America and other parts of the world. The growth has been viewed suspiciously particularly by the neighbours in the Pacific region. The incidents in South and East China Sea have demonstrated that China does not hesitate to flex its muscles to settle outstanding disputes. The conversion of Woody Island in to a military garrison is a case in example. The events in SCS and ECS do have the potential to influence the events in the Indian Ocean Region as both India and China have displayed interest in the neighbourhood of each other's country.

Thus the long standing association of India with Vietnam for joint exploration of energy resources has been challenged by China which feels that South China Sea is its backyard. The littoral countries are not comfortable with the stance of China which seems to be only interested in settling disputes on its terms. The increasing cooperative initiatives between Japan and India are also being viewed suspiciously by China which appears convinced that the rest of the so called democracies are ganging up to counter the influence of China. The formation of such alliances or cooperative arrangements are largely due to the fears of the Pacific nations who feel that it is only through such cooperative collective resistance can one tame China and compel it to deal with disputes based on international norms. It is here that USA seems to have taken it up itself to position US forces and interest in areas close to China from which response can be orchestrated. While China has no qualms about considering South China Sea as its own lake and considers it as one of the core interests, when it comes to Indian Ocean, it has through its officials has indicated that Indian Ocean is not India's Ocean. This stance is supported by its engagement with various smaller maritime neighbours of India which are looking for investments and to a degree playing the China -India card as warranted to meet their own domestic compulsions.

The Pivot to Asia Pacific[2]. The developments in Asia Pacific with an increasingly assertive China have been a source of concern for USA which does not want to hand over any leadership role in the region. With its traditional relations with Japan, Australia, Philippines, South Korea, Vietnam,New Zealand and other countries in the region, US feels that it has to reorient its position to remain relevant and effective . This has become even more important particularly with the impending pull out from Afghanistan in 2014. It can also be said that it is not that the USA had pulled out altogether from the Asia Pacific. It continued to maintain its presence due to various obligations with Japan post the World War and also due to the military and strategic relations with other countries. So when one talks about the change of pivot, it is obviously to be in a happening part of the world which is increasingly being referred to as Indo Pacific.

Energy Security Imperatives. Both India and China are heavily dependent on the energy supplies from various countries of the world. They are scouting around the world for petroleum products, gas and coal [3] to meet their energy demands. These countries include oil and gas rich Middle East, Iran, Africa and other countries. The Sea Lines of Communication in the Indian Ocean Region are the life lines supporting the carriage of energy products. The import in both the cases is upwards of 80 percent of their requirement. The quest for energy has taken both India and China to far corners of the globe and it is the sea lines when land routes are not available that is resorted to bring in large volumes of energy products.

At another level, the detection of Shale gas in America has the potential to change the global energy scenario[4]. It has been forecasted that US may overtake Saudi Arabia in oil production due to the new technologies to extract energy sources from greater depths. The expectation is that energy independent US may not have a need for clinging to the Carter Doctrine[5] and hence may create a vacuum in the Straits of Hormuz and Middle East. China doubtlessly would like to fill the gap as it is now in the same state that US was in at the time promulgation of the Carter Doctrine. In that, Oil and Gas have become the drivers of China's energy policy. China has not given up any chances to invest in the maritime neighbourhood of India. So Gwadar in Pakistan, Investments in Maldives, Hambanthota in Sri Lanka, Sittwe in Myanmar and Chittagong in Bangladesh are future potential investments not just for economic engagement but also for ensuring that there are enough staging posts or even naval bases in the Indian Ocean in times of need. While this may not happen in the immediate future, in the long term it has the potential to be used as strategic leverage by using the economic tools with the smaller developing nations of the IOR.

The geographical advantage enjoyed by India which is jutting in to the Indian Ocean with outposts on both flanks is a matter of concern for China which feels that its shipping and energy routes through the watchful eyes of India are vulnerable. Doubtlessly, this is a great advantage for India which can monitor the traffic exiting from or entering the Malacca Straits on the East and likewise, monitor the .,two way traffic from the Straits of

Hormuz, Gulf of Aden and even South of Africa that is headed to or from China.

The situation off the Somali coast is again a factor that has brought Chinese naval forces to the Indian Ocean. The PLA-Navy[6] has maintained a presence since January 2009 when it deployed two ships in rotation to protect ships against piracy. In addition to the deployment of combined maritime forces from the West, individual navies from different parts of the world are patrolling the High Risk Areas.

India's Maritime Challenges. India an Indian Ocean Power has all the requisites to be identified as a Regional power of importance to global order and security. The growth of a balanced navy along with the necessary infrastructure has been moving at a decent phase though there have been hiccups now and then due to the long drawn processes which seem to decelerate the phase of naval growth. With a combined coast line of 7516 kilometers, nearly 1200 Islands, an Exclusive Economic Zone of two million square kilometers, Search and Rescue Region of four million square kilometers and the crisscrossing major Sea Lines of Communication, India is in an un-envious position when it comes to the challenges despite the natural geographical advantage in IOR.

The security challenges were accentuated with the Mumbai Terror attack on 26th November 2008 when ten terrorists from Pakistan used a hijacked Indian fishing vessel to land at Mumbai and carry out attacks on Iconic symbols and other assets in the commercial capital of India. The Maritime Security Architecture has never been the same and a lot of changes have been made to the traditional structures with overlapping responsibility.

The traditional maritime security challenges have not changed much and include:-

1. Actions by Violent Non State Actors

2. Asymmetric warfare (Unconventional attacks by improvised surface,

3. Sub surface or air units deployed by terrorists

4. **Cyber-attacks[7]**

5. SLOC safety

6. Jihadi terrorism-Al Queda, Al Shabaab,LeT and others

7. Illegal immigration/Trafficking in Drugs/Arms/contraband/

8. People smuggling

9. Fisheries and livelihood

10. Piracy in the West Arabian Sea

The Mumbai terror attack has brought about a paradigm shift in the way the concerned stake holders and the Government perceive the threats and shape required counters. There have been many structural and operational changes to the way the maritime security and intelligence agencies operated to achieve the common objective. While prior to the Mumbai terror attack, the agencies worked on their own, the post 26/11 environment has been fine tuned to engage all agencies in ensuring that there are no compromises on oceanic and coastal security. The specific concerns post Mumbai terror attacks are listed below:-

-   Porous Borders- Multiple Agencies Over lapping Centre and State responsibilities

-   Cross border terrorism ,Piracy and Environmental concerns

-   Developing economy with high stakes in the port and maritime sector

-   Large tracts of EEZ and SRR(2 mn and >4 mn Sqkms)

-   Long coast line-7516 kms, More than1200 Islands at extended ranges from mainland

-   Force levels- Gaps in capacity and capability

-   Technology , tools and techniques

-   Density of shipping, fisheries and oceanic activity

-   Expanding High Risk Areas in the Arabian Sea due to threat of piracy

The following actions have been initiated and it is expected that the slew of measures taken would make it extremely difficult for another repeat attack ala Mumbai terror attack. The measures implemented are as shown below:-

- Navy at the apex, JORs activated to work in tandem with other agencies.

- Creation of NW and NE Coast Guard Regions to focus on maritime borders with Pakistan and Bangladesh.

- Force level augmentation and new sanctions for CG and Marine Police Stations

- National Investigation Agency

- Multi Agency Coordination Centre

- National Technical Research Organisation

- Sagar Prahari Dal

- Enhanced levels of interaction between Int agencies, State and Central agencies

- National Security Guard Hubs in Metros

- Coastal Security Network- use of old light houses and Radar network

- Long Range Identification and Tracking

- S-AIS(Satellite Aided Automatic Identification System)

China Factor. Irrespective of what China does, the rest of the world keenly watches the developments in that part of the world as the Asian giant has taken strong strides in all spheres including the deep seas and the outer space. The initiatives in the maritime domain are equally disconcerting[8]. The scientific and technological advances have been rapid and the economic growth dramatic with a great degree of consistency. The huge investments in the military have unnerved[9] the neighbours who are involved in one manner or another as for as claims for territory is concerned. The South China Sea and the East China Sea witnessed some violent scenes in the last couple of years with increasing assertiveness and aggressiveness of China. The PLA- Navy has also embarked on a rapid modernization programme and the recent commissioning of an aircraft carrier Liaoning on 04 November 2012 has opened up new vistas for a navy aspiring to be a blue water navy. The Anti-Ship Ballitic Missile DF 21(ASBM)[10] which has been credited with the ability to strike a carrier at ranges of thousands of kilometers has been touted as a game changer. Likewise, the launch of stealth aircraft, deep ocean submersibles , Anti Satellite capability which was demonstrated way back in 2007 are all indicators that have been taken seriously by military analysts the world over. Dedicated studies[11] have been made on the implications particularly between US and China when they may engage in space wars. The most potent of all the capability is in the cyber domain where it is clear that clandestinely, China is fine tuning its capability to interfere with Command and Control systems, weapon systems, warning systems and Information support systems to degrade the potential of the adversary in a run up to a conflict scenario.

Anti Piracy Measures. Piracy assumed centre stage particularly from 2005 till 2011. The number of ships hijacked peaked in 2010 as illustrated in the graphs below. All the data is from the Piracy Reporting Centre report generated up to 2012. The increased successful attacks brought about greater concerns about the safety and security of ships, cargo and crew. While total elimination is indeed very difficult, there was a need for coordinated concerted action to bring this menace under control.

Various organisations such as the International Maritime Organisation (IMO), United Nations Security Council (UNSC), Piracy Reporting Centre(PRC)[12], Regional Cooperative Agreement against Armed Robbery and Piracy(ReCAAP)[13] and the navies of the world came together to work out strategies to combat piracy. The results at the end of 2012 clearly illustrate that the measures are succeeding.

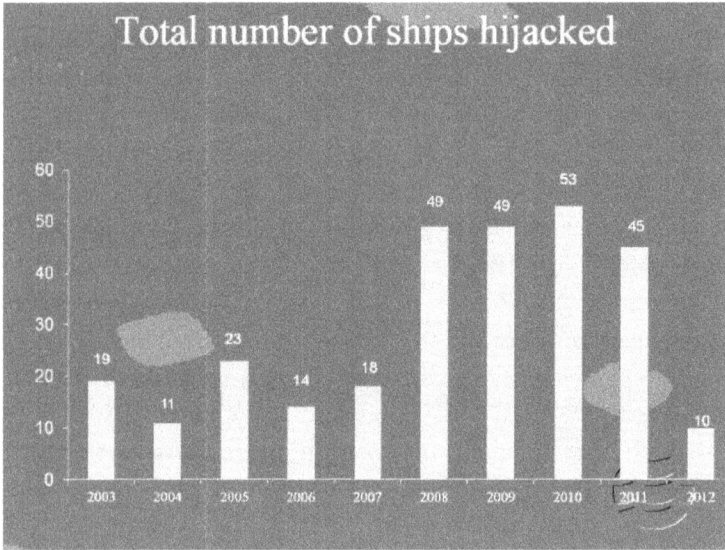

Total number of ships hijacked

	2012	2011	2010	2009	2008	2007	2006
Incidents	40	237	219	217	111	31	10
Hijacking	8	28	49	47	42	12	5
Success Ratio	20% (1:5)	11.8% (1:8.5)	22.4% (1:4.5)	21.6% (1:4.6)	37.8% (1:2.6)	38.7% (1:2.5)	50% (1:2)
Hostage	115	470	1016	867	815	177	87

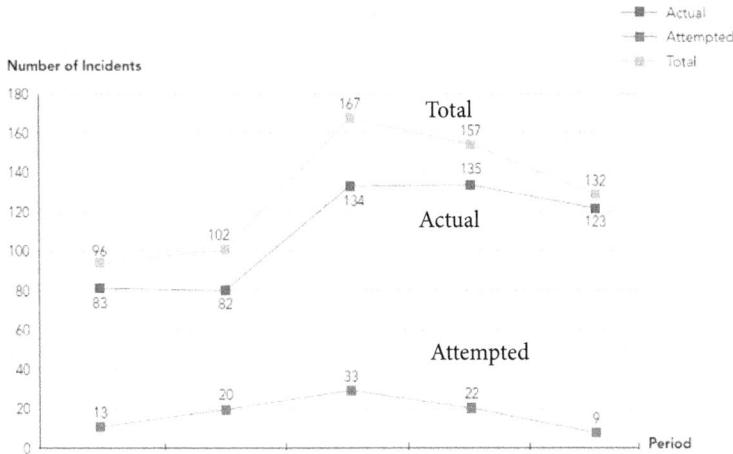

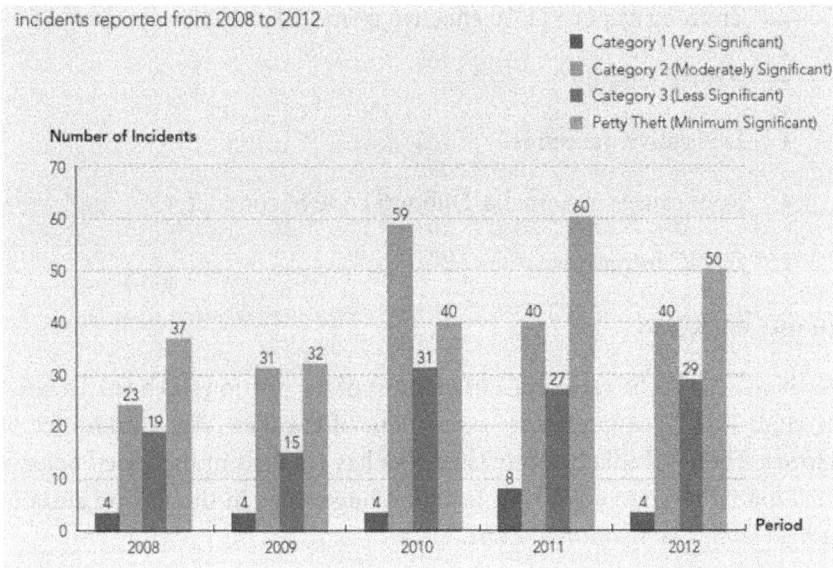

incidents reported from 2008 to 2012.

The statistics above clearly illustrate that the maritime industry and seafarers faced severe challenges due to acts of piracy and armed robbery in different parts of the world. The piracy incidents off Somali coast brought enormous hardship to crew who were held hostage for months due to the delays in negotiating the ransom sum. The meteoric rise of the number of attacks compelled the international community to initiate measures as given subsequently. It is clear that these measures have brought the scourge under control though one cannot be complacent. While the piracy attacks on the Somali coast are coming down, the incidents off Nigeria in the Gulf of Guinea have been alarming both in intensity and the violent nature of such attacks where crew members have been killed to take over cargo.

- Coordinated action by CMF, EUNAVFOR,NATO and navies of the world

- UKMTO in Dubai

- ReCAAP in Singapore +IFC +DFC

- PRC

- Best Management Practices for vessel hardening

- Training as per STCW effective from 01 Jan 2012.

- Armed Guards

- Legislative measures

- Root causes in Somalia-Djibouti code of conduct

- UNSC Initiatives.

In our backyard

Arabian Sea –As brought out earlier, most of the portion has been declared as High Risk Area due to the assessment of the Joint War Committee of Lloyds. Though India has protested this has resulted in increased density of shipping close to coast thus bringing huge ships in the fishing areas of India's Exclusive Economic Zone.

The case of MV EnricaLexie[14] in which the serving Italian marines shot dead two Indian fishermen on 15th February 2012 is a case in example of the ill effects of piracy and deployment of armed guards on board. The Italian marines are being tried in Indian courts and it has led to diplomatic row. It has also raised many questions about the legality and jurisdiction of states to prosecure related offences in such cases. In another similar case on 16th July 2012, USS Rappahonnak fired at a fishing boat presuming that it was a suicide boat intent on ramming the support ship of the US Navy. Unfortunately, here again the victim was an Indian fishermen who was on contract with a fishing company in Dubai who paid with his life.

New Ports and Infrastructure including private owners. With the economic liberalization and greater emphasis on ports and infrastructure, there are many private players now who are investing in the maritime sector. However India has a long way to catch up with China which has efficient ports and supporting infrastructure[15]. This brings in additional challenges for management of safety and security in a dynamic environment on both coasts. This also throws up challenges of environmental management .

Fisheries and Livelihood. With dwindling living resources, there has been acute competition in both Arabian Sea and the Bay of Bengal. The fishermen from neighbouring states are coming in to conflict over fisheries rights. Poaching in each other's territory is rampant. In the case of both Bangladesh and Pakistan it is due to non-demarcation of the maritime boundaries. In the case of Sri Lanka though the International Maritime Boundary Line has been demarcated, there is constant encroachment from the Indian side quoting their historical rights to fish in and around Kacchativu Island which was ceded in 1974 to Sri Lanka. This will be a major source of conflict in the coming decades.

Tri Lateral Initiatives. Despite the entry of the dragon in our backyard, it is refreshing that India, Sri Lanka and Maldives were able to come together to work in the areas of interest together.[16] Similar initiatives are needed with other maritime neighbours who could gain from the experience and expertise of India in handling maritime matters.

As a part of the Initaitives, the way ahead options also should include:-

1. Enhancing the scope of IOR-ARC to include security.

2. Initiatives in the East similar to Tri lateral initiative in the Arabian Sea.

3. Careful study of impact of US's "pivot to Asia" in terms of regional and military impact.

4. Making the Anti piracy bill work over time.

5. Resolving the maritime boundary issues.

6. Pro active engagement of maritime neighbours of India.

In conclusion it is clear that the maritime environment in the Indian Ocean Region is beset with many challenges. India has to take a lead role in managing the maritime domain by combination of cooperative arrangements, technology, procedures, legal support, force levels and above all innovative leadership. The list of such initiatives would include:-

1. Both long term and short term measures.

2. Drawing up of appropriate contingency plans.

3. Initiation of Collaborative Efforts and Cooperation.

4. Planned induction of newer platforms and shoring up of force levels.

5. Regular drills, exercises, audits and reviews to assess the efficacy of implemented measures.

6. Efforts to have a robust Maritime Security Architecture that caters for the present century challenges.

7. Greater emphasis on Information and system security due to sophisticated cyber threats.

8. Regional initiatives being the most eminent and equipped maritime nation in the region.

9. Working and promoting the concept of "Maritime Clusters" which brings in all the stake holders on the common page and gets them to work together to implement pro-active measures.

10. Bringing about greater awareness through campaigns, media and education at all levels.

Endnotes

1 Gunther Hauser, Franz Kernic-China: The Rising Power-Peter Lang GmbH-2009 p 32

2 Andrew T. H. Tan, 'East and South-East Asia: International Relations and Security Perspectives'Routledge Publishers 2013 pp 19-20

3 Galle Luft and Anne Korin*Energy Security Challenges for the 21ˢᵗ Century,* Greenwood publishers 2009- pp73

4 Robert J. Byer--A Rational Energy Policy, Library of Congress 2011 p 77

5 HeikoMeiertöns,-The Doctrines of US Security Policy: An Evaluation Under International Law,Cambridge 2010 p 154

6 Mingjiang Li --China and East Asian Strategic Dynamics: The Shaping of a New Regional Order,Lexington Maryland 2011p 263

7 *In a recent study undertaken on "The Critical Infrastructure Gap: US Port facilities and cyber vulnerabilities" by a USCG officer Commander Kraemik he brought out that the entire Maritime Enterprise would grind to a hald in a matter of days; shelves at grocery stores and gas tanks at service stations would run empty" and a halt in "energy supplies would likely send not just a ripple but a shock wave through the US and even global economy.*

8 China's Maritime Ambitions : Implications for Regional Security Article by Commodore RS VasanIN(Retd) carried by SAAG available at http://www.southasiaanalysis.org/papers43/paper4281.html

9 Steven Saxonberg-Transitions and Non-Transitions from Communism: Regime Survival in China,Cuba, Noth Korea and Vietnam- Cambridge University Press 2013 p 299

10 Andrew .S Erikson -Chinese Anti-Ship Ballistic Missile (ASBM) Development:Drivers, Trajectories, and Strategic ImplicationsJameston Foundation 2013 – fully dedicated to the study of the DF 21 related study.

11 David C. Gompert–The Paradox of Power: Sino-American Strategic Restraint in an Age of Vulnerability National Defense University Press Washington 2011, p92-99..

12 Marco Carine and Flora Macalan –Pirates, Paragon Publishing Limited India p 215

13 Shicun Wu, KeyuanZou, Maritime Security in the South China Sea: Regional Implications and International CooperationAshgatePublilshing Limited Surrey 2009 p 97

14 In an analysis by Commodore RS Vasan of Center for Asia Studies on the incident http://www.asiastudies.org/index.php?option=com_content&task=view&id=262&Itemid=79

15 SarafVishnu,,India And China : Comparing The Incomparable ,Macmillan India New Delhi p 112-113

16 As listed in the outcome document of the Ministry of External Affairs vide http://www.mea.gov.in/in-focus-article.htm?21922/Outcome+Document+of+the+Second+NSALevel+Meeting+on+Trilateral+Cooperation+on+Maritime+Security+between+India+the+Maldives+and+Sri+Lanka

Coast Guard and Indian Naval Diplomacy

P. V. Rao

Maritime security is the direct consequence of a coastal state's definition of its maritime sovereign zones and the perception of possible threats to such zones. Over the centuries coastal states had essentially depended on only the naval military forces of the country as the saviour of not only the security of the state concerned from external maritime threat/invasion, but also to safeguard the territorial sea and the national assets located within the defined waters adjacent to the coast. The need to increase vigil on the coasts changes as the state increases its dependence on maritime resources for development purposes and encourages establishment of more installations on the shores.

All modern states are found to be greatly using their marine resources–fishing, seabed and subsoil – and hence raising the technological inputs that could enable the maximum utilisation of available resources in their maritime domains. Hence one finds today not only just the shipping infrastructure and related properties that in any case have been the most ancient coastal possessions of any state concerned, but a large number of non-shipping assets or infrastructure being located onshore and offshore-oil drilling platforms, storage tanks, marine research stations and vessels, tourist and entertainment parks, water sport clubs, and several other. The demand for turning the seawater into more national economic and entertainment objectives has seen a phenomenal rise in the recent decades, thanks to the advent of globalisation and the attendant expansion of the public and private encroachment on the adjacent seas.

During the earlier eras coastal domains were under the total control of the states concerned. In other words, governments had controlled, managed, administered and developed the coastal onshore endowments such as salt lakes, sand, sand dunes, mangroves, beaches, creeks, backwaters of the seas, fishing zones and the rest. Similarly, coastal surface assets and infrastructure including ports, harbours, oil platforms and terminals, petrochemical and other related industrial establishments, transport and transit hubs, ship-building activities and many such movable and immovable properties on and offshore the maritime zones. Similarly, seabed resources such as oil and gas, hydrocarbon exploration activities, minerals, flora and fauna and other such natural properties were essentially state properties and states alone administered them.

However, maritime states have been increasingly reducing often losing their sovereign control over their coasts. Seas in general and adjacent maritime properties in recent decades are undergoing phenomenal transformation in terms of development, administration and even ownership of the maritime properties. Modern maritime states have been transferring and delegating their maritime properties and administration to the private agencies as part of the globalisation process. All states in the world – developed and developing- have broadly accepted the philosophy of global economic integration which in policy terms amounts to transferring sovereign controls over public properties, including maritime properties, to private individuals and corporate operators. A direct consequence of such major paradigmatic shift in transferring state control over public properties to private stakeholders is, from strictly maritime point of view, is leasing coastal properties to business interests and the corporate sector. Maritime states have handed over to the private groups their controls over coastal resources mentioned above. Broadly speaking the compulsions of globalisation have forced the state simply to become a facilitator of private management of its seashore assets.

Sovereign maritime zones have gained immense additional spaces under the UNCLOS (United Nations Law of Sea) regime. Littoral states like India are entitled to a territorial sea of twelve nautical miles, contiguous zone of twenty four and an expansive exclusive economic zone (EEZ) measuring 200 nautical miles from the coast. India would have exclusive rights of enjoying and exploiting ocean resources in these extended ocean spaces. In effect it meant the country's coastal security forces would have additional responsibility of protecting these zones.

The cumulative impact of above factors – globalisation, increased coastal assets and extended maritime sovereign spaces –on maritime security of a coastal state is the compelling need to expand or create additional maritime security forces. India hence took early steps to establish a coastal security forces, called the Indian coast guard – in 1978. Almost immediately following the Indian Maritime Zones Act was passed in August 1976 claiming the above ocean spaces sanctified by the UNCLOS under the national sovereign domain, another significant legislation aimed at creating a separate maritime security force, the Coast Guard Act was passed on august 19, 1978. Its mandate was to be the "principal national agency for enforcing all national legislation in the Maritime Zones of India, policing, surveillance, patrolling 7,683 kilometres of coastline and over two million square kilometres of sea within national jurisdiction...."[1]

Since its establishment the ICG has grown into a matured and efficient maritime armed force of the country undertaking a multitude of responsibilities to ensure a maritime stable order in the Indian sea zones. It is true in its over three decades of serving as the sentinel of national on and offshore coastal waters, it encountered formidable challenges –organisational and operational – to cope up with the kind of non-conventional security threats on the sea some of which, like maritime terrorism, were not foreseen when its functions were designed. The ICG, in the words of its former director general Admiral Prabhakaran Paleri gained considerable expertise in combating piracy and armed robbery at sea, law enforcement, endangered species protection, disaster relief operation, search and rescue, etc.

Apart from these peacetime operations ICG is involved in national defence in the protection of maritime borders, military or defence operations, higher conflict intensity situations and it modifies its role along with the Indian Navy's Identified Controlling Force (ICF).[2] The ICG was involved along with the IN, in *Operation Tasha,* a low-intensity conflict exercise, introduced following the IPKF withdrawal from the Sri Lankan civil war in 1990. To protect Tamil Nadu coasts.

Coast Guard and Indian Diplomacy

Maritime Security is the protection of a nation's territorial and maritime jurisdiction from foreign invasion by sea. It is necessary against military threats from sea. However, today maritime security denotes more than the armed protection provided by a country's navy. Maritime security has acquired a broader holistic meaning. Twentieth and twenty-first centuries, as noted above have added new and non-military dimensions to maritime security, viz; threats from non-state actors (pirates, drug-traffickers, terrorists), maritime pollution and safety of oil and cargo ships. Relief from natural disasters, exploring sea-bed resources, construction of ports and harbours are also covered by contemporary concept of maritime security. The ICG is therefore is entrusted with the responsibilities of guarding these expanding sea based activities.

Maritime security forces today are less of coercive instruments and more of goodwill agents. Non-combatant and peacetime (benign) utilities of naval power and capabilities are in greater evidence today than in the previous centuries. Analysing the naval uses of foreign policy, Ken Booth, who authored a systematic treatise, *'Navies and Foreign Policy'* states: "The diplomacy role of navies is concerned with the management of foreign policy short of the actual employment of forces." Indian Navy (IN) has today emerged as India's major instrument of foreign policy today. Its role mirrors India's aspiration to be recognized as a greater power in Asia-Pacific region. IN is thus called upon to address India's redefined geopolitical interests in the extended neighbourhood whose outer limits and reach are evident more on the sea than on land. In brief, sea constitutes the crucible of India's strategic outreach today and the navy is designed to serve as the means. What is interesting is that the Indian Coast Guard is also involved in serving some of India's foreign policy objectives in the Indian Ocean.

Naval diplomatic objectives are broadly divided into three categories by Ken Booth: negotiation from strength; manipulation; prestige. While the first two have greater relevance for specific and conflict borne scenarios, it is the third objective, building prestige that draws closely to the IN's current diplomatic postures. The Indian Naval forces today are largely engaged in this task of gaining the good will of countries, projecting at the same time the country's armed capabilities on the sea. The distinguished maritime scholar, Geoffrey Till has captured rightly the IN's current strategy of building synergies with other navies in the following language: "(This) maritime consensus building can be developed by ship visits, fleet reviews, joint procurement and combined exercise. India is well along this track in this age of engagement and its look east policy... has conducted a series of important exercises with locals and outsiders and has also participated in patrols in the waters off Southeast Asia."[3] The ICG is also playing some of these friendly strategies adopted by the Indian Navy in pursuit of its diplomatic objectives.

Port Visits and Exercises

Port visits and joint naval exercises are a common and traditional means of promoting friendly relations between the visiting and hosting maritime powers. Such naval interactions serve the broader foreign policy objectives of the countries concerned. Indian Navy had chosen the peacetime goodwill missions to the several littoral states in the Indian Ocean Region (IOR). More naval missions are sent in recent years to the Southeast Asian counties as part of India's look east policy and the drive to deepen strategic relations with them in several fields including defence sector. In so far as maritime cooperation between the ASEAN countries are concerned it is not the Indian Naval forces which are involved but interestingly the ICG forces are also engaged in goodwill, port visit, naval aid and training and joint exercises with the naval coast guard forces of their counterparts. Rather the ICG, supplementing the Indian naval diplomatic roles, is mandated to engage in similar exercises with countries beyond the Southeast Asian region, the East Asian powers, Japan in particular. In fact as Paleri notes, the IN-ICG cooperative interaction is a function of strategic assessment of maritime balance in the IOR, to promote peaceful ties with extra-regional powers and ensure the tranquillity of SLOCs (Sea   Lanes of Communication) and SLOT (Sea Lanes of Traffic) in the region.

To illustrate the ICG roles in the Asia-Pacific region, a few cases of its interaction with the regional maritime forces are discussed below. India's maritime security is closely intertwined with those of her seven maritime neighbours in the Bay of Bengal and the Arabian Sea. It is a recognition of the fact that ensuring maritime peace and order, or what is called 'maritime good order,' for smooth flow of seaborne vessels and other coastal activities in these two regions of intense activity by poachers, arms smugglers, narco-traffickers closely in nexus with insurgent/terrorist forces and similar criminal agents, is possible only with close cooperation and regular interaction between the security forces of the neighbouring coastal states. India has signed various bilateral, trilateral and multilateral agreements with the Malacca Strait and Bay of Bengal littorals to jointly check and combat the maritime threats posed by the criminal networks in the region.

ICG ships have been visiting Malaysian ports, and also offering training to the Royal Malaysian Navy (RMN) in coastal surveillance and defence of ports. Two ICG ships visited the Malaysian ports recently.[4] ICG is engaged in goodwill visits to Myanmar so also it interacts with Bangladesh coast guard and their respective coast guard ships exchange visits as a means of confidence-building measures (CBM). ICG and Bangladesh coast guard periodically engage in cross-border visits as a means of developing CBMs between these two neighbours which share very porous maritime and as well as land borders.

The ICG, as mentioned above, has gone beyond the Southeast Asian waters into the western Pacific Ocean in developing maritime synergies. Japan is in fact a Pacific country which deserves special mention in this case. As early as in 1990, when the cold war had collapsed and the geo-political contours of Indian strategic involvement in the Asia-Pacific region were yet to be shaped, pro-western Japan never a close friend of non-aligned India, mooted the idea of developing friendly relations with the Indian coastal forces. Two Japanese coast guard ships visited the Madras port on goodwill mission in 1987 and 1989 successively. Then followed the well-known*Alondra Rainbow*incidentin 1999 when the ICG had rescued the Japanese cargo vessel hijacked by pirates in the Bay of Bengal waters. The hijacked vessel was successfully apprehended by the ICG off western coast near Goa and handed over to the Japanese. This particular act of saving the merchant vessel by the Indian coastal maritime force had persuaded a grateful Tokyo to build long-tern maritime cooperative relationship with the ICG as also with the IN. Ever since Indo-Japanese maritime security forces are engaged in regular interaction in the Indian and Japanese maritime domains.

Bilateral exchanges between the coast guard forces of India and Japan became a regular feature. In 2001, Indian ICG patrol vessel *Sangram* visited Japan and participated in joint exercise with the Japanese counterpart. Next year in 2002 a Japan Coast Guard vessel reciprocated by participating in the joint SAR (search and rescue) exercise with the ICG at Chennai. Emphasising the crucial importance for Japan to seek close engagement with the Indian maritime security agencies, Prof. Hajime HIROSE of Japan Coast Guard Academy said:

> In all cases, SLOC between Japan and India means life or death. It is a matter of big concern for the safety of Japan's oil route, especially the route in South Asian waters. It is natural for Japan to consider the responsibility divided roughly for the two lanes, which are from the Indian Ocean to Malacca and from

the Malacca to Japan…And it is a matter of course to establish cooperation within coast guard agencies of the countries established between Japan and India.[5]

Periodic naval and coastguard operational exercises in anti-piracy, counter-terrorism, SAR, etc. between the respective forces of India and Japan have assumed prominent place in the overall Indo-Japanese strategic relations.

In the western maritime domain of India, in the Arabian Sea the ICG is engaged in maritime security exercises with some of the coastal states including Pakistan. Pakistan Maritime Security Agency and the ICG signed a MoU for regular contacts between their respective chiefs to diffuse any volatile situations, particularly with regard to the illegal encroachment of their fishermen into each other's sovereign domain. India has close strategic ties with Maldives, another western maritime neighbour of India bordering the Laccadive archipelago.Amidst reports of Chinese naval involvement in this strategically located central Indian Ocean republic, India has intensified her political and maritime interaction with Maldives. The archipelagic character of this Islamic republic provides easy penetrability to maritime criminal agents and of late *al-Quieda* elements are reportedly making inroads into it. India hence is closely interested in ensuring stability and security of the coastal and archipelagic surroundings of Maldives. Goodwill missions and joint exercises are exchanged since 1992 between the ICG and coast guard service of Maldives. A MoU on bilateral cooperation between these coastal security agencies is under active consideration.

Conclusion

From the above narration of the ICG cooperative ventures in varying ways with neighbouring and foreign maritime forces one can conclude that it has gone far beyond the originally mandated responsibilities safeguarding Indian coastal assets and ensuring the overall maritime security in India's EEZ. Its services to other coastal security agencies in a way amounts to offering the Indian maritime soft power endowments to the countries concerned. Rather in a broader sense, ICG is co-opting the Indian Navy's diplomatic roles in advancing the Indian strategic objectives and power projection in Indian Ocean and beyond.

References:

1. GM Hiranandani, *Transition to Eminence, the Indian Navy 1976-1990*, Lancer Publishers, New Delhi, 2004, 368.

2. Prabhakaran Paleri, *Role of the Coast Guard in the Maritime Security of India*, Knowledge World, New Delhi, 2007, p.325

3. "*International* maritime trends and Indian Ocean in 21st century," *Journal of Indian Ocean Studies*, August 2001

4. *Journal of Indian Ocean Studies*, December 2012, p.334

5. *Japan-India Dialogue in Ocean Security*, 2009, Ship & Ocean Foundation, Tokyo, p. 157

India's Maritime Security Policy: Issues and Challenges in the 21st Century

Anil Kumar P

Besides containing tremendous amounts of resources, the seas have also provided a sense of security to the littorals that enabled them to concentrate on threats emanating from the land frontiers. With advancements in technology and seafaring, however, the scope and extent of challenges emerging from the seas has also enhanced. While on the one hand, having a coastline and access to open seas provides extensive opportunities to prosper and promote national interests; the ever-increasing issues of maritime security continue to weigh on the minds of the rulers, on the other hand. Maritime security is both multi-dimensional and multifaceted and involves military and non-military issues. These include naval threats and challenges (military security issues), arms trafficking and narco terrorism as well as piracy (hard non military security issues) along with shipping, fishing, sea bed minerals and offshore oil and natural gas resources, vulnerability of Sea Lanes of Communication (SLOC), and illegal immigration. Moreover maritime security includes environmental protection, nuclear issues, ballistic missile defence as also maritime management as the seas are indivisible.

History shows that India was most prosperous and secure when she was most connected to the world, and that this connection was mainly by sea. Jawaharlal Nehru's conclusion from our history was that: "We cannot afford to be weak at sea. History has shown that whoever controls the Indian Ocean has, in the first instance, India's sea-borne trade at her mercy and, in the second, India's very independence itself." An array of land-driven concerns has, however, since Independence, had a way of dragging India back to shore, thwarting its sporadic thalassocratic ambitions. Blessed by its geography, India is cursed by its neighbourhood. The pan-oceanic vision nurtured under the British colonial rule and shared by great post-Independence figures such as Nehru and K.M. Pannikar has been buried under numerous territorial disputes and festering insurgencies that have convulsed the subcontinent and consumed much of its leadership's strategic attention for the past six decades. But today we realised the fact that our maritime policies will be one of the major determinants of success or failure in our attempt to transform India into a secure and prosperous country. Now India realised the significance of Indian Ocean and the need for a better maritime security strategy. This paper is an attempt to analyses the maritime strategic and security policy of India and its problems and challenges in the 21st century.

Navy played a mostly peripheral part in most of India's past conflicts, it has also been hard pressed to define and justify its role. In such a context, the latest edition of the Indian Maritime Doctrine issued by the Naval Headquarters, which builds upon both an earlier version released in 2004 and India's Maritime Strategy (2007) provides a vital insight into how the Navy draws its inspiration and conceives of its present and future mandate in a strategically dynamic era.

Indian Maritime Doctrine aims to provide a better understanding not only of the *Maritime Doctrine* but also of the larger context surrounding it. Doctrinal developments do not emerge from a vacuum, and are best understood from both a cultural and organizational perspective. It will be argued that in the Indian context, the nation's complex civil-military and inter-service relations are key to better gauging some of the motivations underlying the Maritime Doctrine. The Navy views itself as being a multidimensional service, capable of taking on many roles, of which war fighting is but one aspect. This is reflected in the most absorbing section of the maritime doctrine, which lays out four roles for the Indian Navy: military, diplomatic, constabulary and benign. These four roles echo to a certain degree those already identified more than 10 years prior in the Indian Navy's first *Strategic Defence Review*, which were then defined as the following: sea-based deterrence, economic and energy security, forward presence and naval diplomacy. (Rahul Roy-Chaudhury, *India's Maritime Security* (New Delhi: Knowledge World, 2000), pp. 125–6.)

Regarding the *Maritime Doctrine* two important elements are worth noting- First, what was defined as naval diplomacy in 1998 has been split into two different roles – benign and diplomatic – in 2009. The Indian Navy has long recognized the potential offered by vessels in terms of diplomacy and soft power projection. This has been reflected both in words, via the earlier version of the maritime doctrine, which defined the Navy as an 'effective instrument of India's foreign policy by generating goodwill through maritime diplomacy'; and in actions, as over the past decade the Indian Navy has frequently displayed with a certain panache its desire and capacity to be viewed as a provider of public goods as well as a reliable partner. Indian ships have thus taken part in a wide range of humanitarian and disaster relief operations over the years, whether it be in the wake of the devastating 2004 tsunami, or in 2008 after the Nargis cyclone. India has also engaged in NEOs or Non-Combatant Evacuation Operations, such as in 2006, when four Indian warships successfully evacuated more than 2,000 Indian, Sri Lankan and Nepalese citizens from a war-torn Lebanon. Second was the sheer width of the gamut of potential military roles laid out for the Indian Navy, which, crammed into a small box, appear to encompass every possible wartime function.

The 2009 version of the maritime doctrine goes so far as to wax in lyrical terms that the mere presence of an Indian warship with its multi-ethnic and multi-religious crew in a foreign harbour will contribute to India's image as a vibrant democracy abroad. (Note: 'The warship, with a relatively young crew, hailing from all parts of India, symbolizes a mini-India and succinctly epitomizes all that modern India stands for a vibrant, multi-ethnic, multi-religious, secular democracy, firmly on the track to economic and technological development'. Integrated Headquarters, Ministry of Defence (Navy), *Indian Maritime Doctrine*, 2009, p. 113.)

In India's case, civil-military relations, long marked by Nehruvian fears of creeping praetorianism, have led to a highly unwieldy and cumbersome system which has had an acutely deleterious effect on doctrinal and organizational development. Fearful of a drift towards a militaristic state in the vein of Pakistan, India's post-Independence leaders rigorously implemented a tight bureaucratic control of the young nation's armed forces. The Raj-era post of commander-in-chief of the Indian military was abolished, and the service headquarters were downgraded to become 'attached offices', organizationally external to the MOD and therefore removed from major decision-making. Indeed, after a series of brutal frontier conflicts in which navies played at best a secondary role, India's main priorities were to strengthen its land borders and build up its Army and Air Force, which were the primary actors in the event of a conflict with China or Pakistan. The Indian Navy, no longer considered as relevant, was relegated to the backseat, its share in the defence budget even plummeting at one stage to a dismal 3 per cent. Under the tenures of Indira and Rajiv Gandhi, the Navy spasmodically regained impetus, but it has only really been over the past 15 years that India's political leadership has actively endorsed an ambitious blue-water role.

Indeed, the 2009 maritime doctrine indicates that the Indian Navy is clearly demonstrating its desire for: *Greater Prestige* by having a greater say in the definition of the country's core security interests. This is accomplished through a sustained defence of how the sea can bolster overall national strategy, as well as by the advancement of the unwavering 'logic of geography'. India's centrality in the Indian Ocean and peninsular formation, it is argued, are sure indicators of the nation's maritime destiny, and therefore, as a corollary, of the Navy's great importance. Mention is also made of the pivotal role the sea plays in India's economic development, as close to 90 per cent of India's external trade is maritime. The Navy, therefore, is to some extent the ultimate guarantor of India's sustained economic development, by virtue of its role in upholding freedom of navigation and ensuring the safety of SLOCs.

Challenges in the 21st century

According to Admiral Arun Prakash (Retd.), the maritime potential of India can be realised only if there is a centralized organisation that looks into every aspect of the maritime domain. At present there are as many as sixteen ministries, agencies and departments within the Government of India that oversee policies related to the seas. For example, while fisheries is under the care of the Ministry of Agriculture, offshore hydrocarbons is under the purview of the Ministry of Petroleum. Moreover, these sixteen organisations do not include the Indian Navy and the Coast Guard which report directly to the Ministry of Defence. Consequently, India has failed to coherently exploit the potential wealth of its exclusive economic zone (EEZ) of 2.02 million square kilometres.

The MA-20 envisages an ambitious vision to create, build and sustain a maritime infrastructure for the nation by 2020. It has a financial outlay of Rs. 5 lakh crores for the development of ports, cargo handling, shipping, shipbuilding, etc. Some experts have expressed doubts whether the nation has the capability and capacity to absorb and implement such an overarching plan—sceptics view it as overambitious, being 'divorced from the basic realities' and ignoring the existing infrastructural, political and economic conditions in the country.

A strong shipbuilding (both warship and commercial ships) and shipping infrastructure is imperative for enhancing the maritime capacity of any country. In the Indian context, however, the monopoly of Public Sector Undertakings (PSUs) has stalled progress—largely because of inefficient management practices, resulting in cost and time overruns that eventually nullify national implementation plans. Unfortunately, the captive customer base of these PSUs, in form of ships for the Indian Navy and the Coast Guard, has prevented the modernisation and upgradation of the state-owned maritime facilities. The limited participation of private players in this field has been due to the cautious approach of the State. Thus, in the absence of patronage and experience, the Indian private sector shipbuilding industry has been discouraged from undertaking important maritime projects for the nation. Vice Admiral Bhasin highlighted the situation in Indian PSU yards: the turnover of the Mazagon Docks Limited (MDL) was $0.5 billion in 2011 and $0.55 billion in 2010. MDL currently has orders worth $19 billion. Under present circumstances, it would take MDL 35-40 years to deliver all its standing orders; foreign yards have the capacity to meet such orders within 2-3 years. According to the Vice Admiral, the trends for other yards, like Garden Reach Ship Builders, Hindustan Shipyard Limited and Goa Shipyard Limited, are similar to that of MDL. There is an urgent need to improve the overall efficiency of all state–owned shipyards.

The importance of infrastructure in the maritime domain is underscored by history. During the early twentieth century, Germany was an advanced industrial nation but not a great power since its maritime footprint was small because of low infrastructural capacity. Similarly, today considerable progress has been made by many nations in Asia but, unfortunately, this has not always been matched by a proportional investment in their maritime infrastructure. Hence, it is imperative for Asian littorals that are dependent on the seas for their economic existence to develop their maritime capability. In case of India, the government should begin by stipulating a change of status of various entities that are part of the maritime domain. To begin with, ports, shipbuilding, ship repair, deep sea shipping, coastal shipping and offshore economic activities need to be grouped together and given the status of an Infrastructure Sector or Strategic Sector, highlighting their importance and placing emphasis on their rapid development. Moreover, the government should revisit its existing policies in this sector and focus on domestic capacity building. Ninety per cent of India's international trade is being carried out by foreign vessels. In addition to this, the national merchant fleet does not possess sufficient vessels to undertake specialised operations like transport of LPG. Further, India also lacks the financial capability to underwrite/finance and insure freight from conflict zones. These issues need immediate consideration and political will; failure to address them would be detrimental not only to the health of the sector, but to the larger national interest as a whole.

Above all, there is a need for the creation of a nodal organisation that would formulate policy and regulatory roadmaps and monitor all developments in the maritime field. This organisation could be staffed with competent professionals representing all stakeholders in this domain. Hence, it could include naval and Coast Guard personnel, customs officials, representatives from financial institutions (representing insurance and other finance companies that are associated with the shipping and chartering), shipyards and ship operators, officials from fisheries and hydrocarbons, security agencies, etc. The organisation could look into all aspects of the maritime domain and would have the expertise to manage and intervene when needed. India's 2009 Maritime Doctrine is the latest effort by India's most politically minded – and resource-deprived – armed service to lay out a clear path for its desired future. Didactic in tone, advocatory in intent, the document is also highly aspirational, charting out roles and missions for the Navy it would like to be, rather than for the force it currently is. The naval thinking at the heart of its vision is a fascinating fusion of different concepts and traditions, which gives credence to the notion that India's true strength lies in its innate syncretism. Strategically minded and outward-looking, the Indian Navy could add a much-needed direction to India's slow drift towards great power status. But in order for it to do so, both India's elephantine bureaucracy and wary political leadership will need to cast off the outdated perceptions which needlessly tether India to the shore. The nation's largely khaki-clad military will also need to undergo a profound transformation, which helps give birth to a more harmonious civil-military relationship, while producing a rebalancing in favour of a more powerful navy. India's rise in wealth, power and influence is manifest. The path to greatness, however, does not lie in the dusty plains and frozen passes of its northern reaches. If it is to be found at all, it will be at sea – out in the great dark blue of the Indian Ocean.

My question is therefore: if energy and trade flows and security are the issues, why not begin discussing collective security arrangements among the major powers concerned? Is it not time that we began a discussion among concerned states of a maritime system minimising the risks of interstate conflict and neutralising threats from pirates, smugglers, terrorists, and proliferators? India's concerns in the north-west Indian Ocean and China's vulnerabilities in the north-east Indian Ocean cannot be solved by military means alone. The issue is not limited just to the Indian Ocean but indeed is one of security of these flows in areas and seas which affect the choke points. These arrangements should deal with transnational issues such as piracy, crime and natural disasters. Now that Asian states and powers have evolved the capabilities and demonstrated the will to deal with these questions, it is time that a structured discussion among them and the major littorals took place.

PART - IV

Coastal Security of India: A Coastal Community & Legal Perspective

Travails of Fishermen in the Palk Bay: A Possible Solution

V. Suryanarayan

We can choose our friends, but we cannot choose our neighbours. The compulsions of geography are unrelenting and the pangs of proximity lead to extremely difficult and complex situations. In the case of India there is an additional dimension of bilateral relations intersecting with domestic concerns in her neighbourhood policy.

Preliminary Observations

India borders on Pakistan, China, Nepal, Bhutan, Bangladesh, Myanmar, Thailand, Indonesia, Sri Lanka and Maldives. India's relations with each neighbouring country will have its immediate fall out on contiguous Indian states. Thus India-Pakistan relations will have its fall out on Gujarat, Rajasthan, Punjab and Jammu and Kashmir; India-China relations will affect Kashmir, Uttarakhand, Himachal Pradesh, Sikkim and Arunachal Pradesh; India-Nepal relations will spill over to Bihar, Uttarakhand, Uttar Pradesh, Sikkim and West Bengal; India-Bhutan relations will impinge upon West Bengal, Sikkim, Arunachal Pradesh and Assam; India-Myanmar relations will have its fallout on Arunachal Pradesh, Nagaland, Manipur and Mizoram; India-Sri Lanka relations is closely intertwined with the politics of Tamil Nadu and India-Maldives relations will have an impact on Minicoy islands. I have not mentioned Thailand and Indonesia because relations with these countries have yet to take off in a big way.

During the era of one-party dominance, New Delhi pursued a neighbourhood policy which it considered to be in India's national interest. On several occasions the interests and sensitivities of the contiguous Indian states were not taken into consideration. To illustrate, the Sirimavo-Shastri Pact of 1964, which divided the people of Indian origin in Sri Lanka between the two countries, was concluded by New Delhi against the wishes of all sections of public opinion in Tamil Nadu. C. Rajagopalachari,

Kamaraj Nadar, VK Krishna Menon, CN Annadurai and P Ramamurthy expressed their opposition and indignation. It was not only a betrayal of Gandhi-Nehru legacy on India's policy towards Indians Overseas, it was also a bad precedent. The second example was the conclusion of the India-Sri Lanka maritime boundary agreements of 1974 and 1976 which not only ceded the island of Kachchatheevu to Sri Lanka, they also sacrificed the traditional fishing rights of Indian fishermen who used to fish in and around Kachchatheevu.

With the formation of coalition governments in New Delhi and the regional parties becoming coalition partners a qualitative change has taken place in the centre-state equation with particular reference to India's neighbourhood policy. The Alliance partners began to make their inputs into the making of India's foreign policy. The inclusion of the Sethusamudram project in the policies and programmes of the Man Mohan Singh Government was due to the persistent efforts of M Karunanidhi and the DMK. Of equal relevance, the Centre exerted its benign influence and softened the hard line stance of the DMK on the ethnic issue during the Fourth Eelam War.

How to bring about harmony in the thinking of the central and state governments with reference to neighbourhood policy will be a litmus test for the policy makers in New Delhi in the days to come. As far as India's Sri Lanka policy is concerned, differences have come into sharp focus during recent months between Chennai and New Delhi. On the travails of the Indian fishermen in the Palk Bay, on human rights violations in Sri Lanka during the Fourth Eelam War, on the training of the Sri Lankan military personnel in Indian defence establishments located in Tamil Nadu, Chief Minister Jayalalitha had been very critical of the Central Government. Jayalalitha's postures can be understood only if we keep in mind the competitive nature of Tamil Nadu politics where the two Dravidian parties are vying with one another in championing the cause of the overseas Tamils. This slinging match will gather momentum in the days to come, as the political parties will be chalking out their strategies for parliamentary elections due to be held next year.

Even though the Constitution gives the Central Government full and exclusive authority to conclude international agreements and treaties, the experience of Tamil Nadu *vis-à-vis* the Sri Lankan policy points to the need for a healthy convention of involving the concerned state governments in finalising treaties which would affect their vital interests. Such involvement should spread from informing to consulting to getting concurrence, depending upon the extent to which the state's interests are involved.

Maritime Boundary Agreements and Issues relating to Fishing

Fishermen, throughout the world, are no respecters of maritime boundaries, wherever there is fish, they go. This reality is applicable to the fisheries scene, which has become today a thorny issue in India-Sri Lanka relations. Let me illustrate this fact by a telling incident which took place in February 2000 in the Kerala waters. On 12 February, five Sri Lankan fishing vessels, with 29 crew members, were found fishing in the Indian Exclusive Economic Zone. The Indian Coast Guard apprehended them and handed them over to the police station in Kochi. The police registered cases against them and the case was heard in the Magistrate Court. The Magistrate was eager to hear the version of the accused and instructed the Government lawyer to examine Sisira, one of the 29 accused. I am giving below the verbatim report of the exchanges that took place between the Government lawyer and the accused.

Lawyer: Which country are you from?

Sisira: I belong to the fisherman community

Lawyer: Yes, where do you belong? Sri Lanka or India?

Sisira: To the Tamil Land.

Lawyer: Oh, which country, which place?

Sisira: I live in Sri Lanka. My forefathers lived in India. Relatives are here and there. I go off and on to meet them. I work and live in the sea. India or Sri Lanka does not come to me.

Lawyer: What is your citizenship? What passport do you hold?

Sisira: What is citizenship? Passport? I have none.

Lawyer: But you come from the Sri Lankan side. Your vessel is licensed there, Thus you are a Sri Lankan trespassing into India.

The Magistrate got tired of the exchange of words. He said, "There are many kinds of citizens and non-citizens under the State laws. You come from the Sri Lankan shores; you are not offering any mitigating proof to disprove that". Thereafter he gave the judgement, "Sri Lankan trespassing into India – a fit case to invoke the benevolent provisions of the MZI Act".

Here lies the dilemma, arising out of the symbiotic relationship between the fishermen and the sea. The Magistrate's legalistic statement reveals the determination of India and Sri Lanka to dominate their side of the seas, to safeguard the sanctity of their borders and to uphold the rights and responsibilities of citizenship. To fishermen like Sisira, maritime boundaries are man-made creations. Throughout centuries, they have been fishing in all areas, where there are plenty of fish. It is a universal phenomenon, the Sri Lankans enter the Indian and Maldivian waters, Indian fishermen enter Pakistani waters, and Bangladesh fishermen enter Myanmar and the Japanese and Taiwanese trawlers roam around the whole of Asian waters. The restriction imposed by the State on cross border movements of the fisher folk have led to strains in bilateral relations, loss of human lives and destruction of fishing crafts.

How can we reconcile the two conflicting views? Can India and Sri Lanka work out an arrangement which safeguard the livelihood of the fisher folk of the two countries, preserve and enrich the marine ecology and pave the way for harmonious bilateral relations? If this goal is to be accomplished, it is essential that we recognize the fisher folk as the primary stake holders in the issue and make them the focus of our policies.

There is a silver lining in the horizon. In a visionary step in the right direction, during the SAARC summit in Colombo few years ago, Prime Minister Man Mohan Singh offered to India's economically weaker neighbours "asymmetric reciprocity" in trade relations. The Prime Minister has also been harping on the point that if regional co-operation is to succeed the existing physical connectivity among countries and peoples must be strengthened. In the 15th SAARC Summit in Colombo in early August 2008, the Prime Minister called for a "change in our mind sets, and a new paradigm of thinking". He emphasized the importance of "physical connectivity" and the necessity to fully exploit the linkages. Man Mohan Singh went further and in his speech launching a new railway line in Jammu and Kashmir, said, "I cannot do much about the India-Pakistan border, but we must strive to make the border irrelevant".

Conflict of Interests

The root cause of the present tension in the Palk Bay is the conflict of interests. On the one side are the Governments of India and Sri Lanka, who in furtherance of good neighbourly relations concluded the maritime boundary agreements of 1974 and 1976. These placed the island of Kachchatheevu on the Sri Lankan side and also gave up the traditional fishing rights enjoyed by the Indian fishermen in and around Kachchatheevu. On the other hand are the Indian and Sri Lankan fishermen who will not easily give up a means of livelihood which they have enjoyed for several centuries. It would be imprudent to attempt to create a Berlin Wall in the Palk Strait, for the simple reason that the links between the population of two countries cannot be easily severed. We are like Siamese twins, what afflicts one will affect the other.

The intimate ties between the fishermen and the sea have affected the history, economy and culture of the coastal communities of both Tamil Nadu and the northern and eastern parts of Sri Lanka. The Palk Strait both unites and separates the Tamils of Sri Lanka and India, and, in so doing, it creates peculiar administrative, logistical and security problems for both countries. The shallow waters of the Palk Strait and the geographical proximity of the two countries facilitated the movement of ideas, goods and men. The rich cultural heritage of Sri Lanka is the cumulative result of cross cultural interaction spread over several centuries. In the 19th and 20th centuries thousands of Indian Tamil labourers were ferried across the Palk Bay to provide the much needed labour for the development of tea plantations. When immigration rules were tightened by Sri Lanka after independence, illegal migrants found their way to the island through *Kallathonis* (illegal boats). In a strange twist of history, after the communal holocaust of July 1983, Sri Lankan Tamils fled to Tamil Nadu through *Kallathonis* or what was popularly known as Eelam Shipping Service. After 1983 Tamil Nadu became the sanctuary and the support base for the Tamil Eelam struggle. However, the conflict over fisheries led to another development. When the cease fire agreement was signed in 2002 and the Sri Lankan fishermen started fishing again, they found poaching by Indian fishermen to be a major hindrance to their livelihood. After the decimation of the Tigers and the end of the Fourth Eelam War the problem of livelihood of the Sri Lankan fishermen assumed greater significance. There was another unfortunate development. Fanned by chauvinist elements, the fishermen started viewing each other with suspicion and hatred. Fishermen from

India and Sri Lanka began to be viewed as aggressors by some disgruntled elements on both sides.

The present policy of the two governments is to consider the issue of poaching as a humanitarian issue. As and when the fishermen get detained, the representatives of the two governments get in touch with each other, discuss the matter and finally release the fishermen and their boats. This policy can be termed as "fire fighting exercise", which involves taking immediate steps to extinguish the fire. But the need of the hour is to remove the causes of fire once and for all. As a result of sustained pressure exerted by the Government of Tamil Nadu, few years ago, the Government of India took up the matter with the Government of Sri Lanka. The end result was a joint statement issued on October 28, 2008 under which Colombo gave a solemn assurance that there "will be no firing on Indian vessels". The earlier Colombo stance had been that Indian fishing vessels should not cross the international maritime boundary. But in recent months Colombo's policy has undergone a big change. As and when they detain fishermen in Sri Lankan waters, they produce them before a court of law and after trial the fishermen get released but the trawlers are kept in Sri Lankan custody. Without trawlers the fishermen are not able to venture to the sea.

Perceptions of Tamil Nadu

How does the Government of Tamil Nadu view the problem? The prognosis of the Government of Tamil Nadu is that the root cause of the travails of the fishermen is the ceding of the island of Kachchatheevu to Sri Lanka in 1974 and the bartering away of the traditional fishing rights in 1976 Agreement. When the 1974 agreement was signed Karunanidhi was the Chief Minister. There are strong historical claims to prove that Kachchatheevu was part of the Zamindari of Raja of Ramand and when Zamindari was abolished it became a part of the Madras Presidency. The Government of India adopted a different stance. It considered the island to be a disputed territory and in the process of delimitation ceded the island to Sri Lanka. However, Articles 4 and 5 of the Agreement provided for the continuation of the traditional fishing rights, but these rights were also given away by the Agreement in 1976. When Jayalalitha came to power, she demanded that the island should be taken back from Sri Lanka. Since unilateral abrogation of international boundary agreements will cause irreparable damage to Indian image, the author suggested getting the back the island and surrounding seas in "lease in perpetuity". Sovereignty will be vested with Sri Lanka, but the Indian fishermen could fish in and around kachchatheevu as a result of lease in perpetuity. Both the DMK and the AIADMK Governments have accepted this suggestion and have suggested this course of action to the Central Government at regular intervals. But New Delhi considers the ceding of Kachchatheevu to be a closed chapter and does not want to reopen the issue. Complicating the situation the AIADMK took the initiative and has challenged the ceding of Kachchatheevu in the Supreme Court as unconstitutional. The DMK did not want to lag behind; it has also filed a similar case in the Supreme Court.

In order to protect the interests of Tamil Nadu fishermen, author had also suggested another course of action, which also has been accepted by both the DMK and the AIADMK Governments. Licensed Indian fishermen should be permitted to fish in Sri Lankan waters up to five nautical miles and as a quid pro quo Sri Lankan fishermen could be permitted to fish in the Indian Exclusive Economic Zone to catch Tuna. There is already a precedent. Under the 1976 maritime boundary agreement Sri Lankan fishermen were permitted to fish in the Wadge Bank near Kanyakumari for a period of three years. This suggestion made some headway and at the end of Foreign Secretary level meeting in July 2003 Colombo invited detailed proposals for its considered examination. According to informed sources the Ministry of Agriculture in the Central Government under which fisheries falls did not want to permit Si Lankan fishermen to fish in the Indian Exclusive Economic Zone. As a result the proposal could not make any headway.

Dialogue among Fishermen

If a lasting solution has to be found to the travails of fishermen it is necessary to bring the livelihood of fishermen into primary focus. A dialogue among fishermen of two countries is the need of the hour. A solution from below has greater chance of success than one imposed from above, by the Governments of Sri Lanka and India. The initiative for such a dialogue was taken by Thiruvanathanuram based Alliance for the Release of Innocent Fishermen (ARIF). Meetings were arranged between representatives of fishermen in Jaffna a well as in Chennai, but they could not make much headway for two reasons. Tamil Nadu fishermen were reluctant to give up the use of trawlers which is playing havoc with marine ecology on the Sri Lankan side of the maritime boundary. Equally important, Chennai, Colombo and New Delhi were indifferent to track two diplomacy. In fact sections in Sri Lankan Government were anxious to fuel the conflict among fishermen, so that Palk Bay could be spilled with Tamil blood. Fortunately wiser counsels began to prevail. New Delhi was the first to support the initiative wholeheartedly; after lot of dilly dallying the Government of Tamil Nadu has also extended its support. The Government of Sri Lanka is speaking in different voices. But with a popularly elected government in the Northern Provincial Council, it can be expected that the voice of sanity will prevail and Jaffna will exercise its influence on Colombo to support the proposal for dialogue among fishermen.

Palk Bay – Our Common Heritage

India must project a vision that the Palk Bay constitutes the common heritage of both India and Sri Lanka. Instead of viewing it as a contested territory, joint efforts should be made to enrich the sea. A Palk Bay Authority should be constituted, consisting of the representatives of both countries, fishermen's representatives, marine ecologists and fisheries specialists. The Palk Bay Authority could determine the ideal sustainable catch per year, the type of fishing equipments to be used, the number of days Indian and Sri Lankan fishermen could fish etc. Trawlers must be immediately decommissioned. Joint efforts should be made to enrich the marine resources. What is more, fishermen of both countries should be encouraged to embark upon joint ventures for deep sea fishing. Such endeavour could lead to a win win situation. And, what is more, it would give a fillip to bilateral and regional co-operation.

Coastal Security Of Tamil Nadu: An Empirical Study To Elicit A Community Perspective

S.Utham Kumar Jamadhagni

An oft-repeated term in the security lexicon after the 26/11 Mumbai terrorist attacks **is** Coastal Security. Though India is an ocean-based economy and is geographical peninsula or area surrounded on three sides by seas, there has been a neglect of this vital field in safeguarding our nation's security. The Mumbai attacks highlighted the vulnerability of our coasts to terrorist designs and urged for a revamp of existing coastal security infrastructure. A number of measures were taken for the strengthening of Coastal security in India, and one of the states that have gained in leaps and bounds in this regard is Tamil Nadu. It would be pertinent here to begin with a general understanding of what Coastal Security means.

Coastal Security refers to the security of or relating to a coast; located on or near or bordering on a coast.[1] Security is referred to in terms of more than merely a traditional state-centric military security; it refers to security on a wider more comprehensive level. Coastal Security it is felt is a primary requirement for the safety of the country. This is because, the coasts provide for an open, unhindered access route to any person wishing to do harm to the Union. There are no gates, no fences, and no security check posts all along the coast that would prevent any person from entering the country through the coast. Also, there are no measures or hindrances to the presence of foreign vessels in territorial waters. Though monitoring of all foreign vessels may seem irreducibly the easiest way to deal with the problem, however, it is neither practical, nor is it conducive to India's plans of growth and trade. The waters of India have to be open and safe to ensure that trade is not hindered in any manner. As a growing economy India would feel the need for such facilitation even more. With this urgency in mind, several steps were taken to ensure that some semblance of security could be attained in relation to the Coast. For this several Marine Police Stations were set up[2], a toll free number was established so that fishermen could report any suspicious activity seen by them or to report any other matter of importance or seek any assistance in distress[3].

With such steps being rapidly taken up across the entire coastal region of India, we decided to take up the case of Tamil Nadu. A state with a unique feature in terms of coastal security, Tamil Nadu has for long known the intricacies and complexities of the coast as a threat to national security.

Sharing Indian waters with Sri Lanka and the troubles that plagued that country, Tamil Nadu often had to grapple with the presence of asylum seekers and refugees spilling over from Sri Lanka due to the rise in tensions there. This meant that the Tamil Nadu police were all in favour of ways to curb this influx of people if it continued without any checks or balances, as it could present a security nightmare.

The Tamil Nadu Marine Police has been in the process of trying to complement the task of the Coast Guard to patrol the vast distances to ensure the security of the Coast. This was done by the setting up of Marine Police Stations[4] at strategic locations and then to arm these stations with the infrastructure (boats, firearms, and personnel) to deal with patrolling and other monitoring activities along the coast. In this light, the Marine Police has taken steps to deal with the fishing communities along the coast and to use them as the eyes and ears of the police. This method seemed and still provides for the best mechanism to monitor all activity along the coast as the fishermen are more equipped through their knowledge of the local terrain and population to identify people of different origins and report them.

Their knowledge is so sharp that they are able to identify if a person is from an adjacent village. This knowledge is assisted by the sheer numbers of persons who go out to sea. The number often ranging in the thousands in a particular area, it was considered then to increase the faith and trust the peoples had in their local marine police.

This was done through Village Vigilance Committees (VVCs), where the police would meet the people and educate them on several issues related to security and the presence of the toll free number 1093, as well as the various ways in which they could deal with the several scenarios that they might counter. This program was paired with several other activities to engage the youth of the villages and to ensure that they were inclined to help the police than side with anti-state activities.

It was in this general atmosphere, that the process of coastal security is examined to understand how this was being ensured. With reported skirmishes between the fishing community and the Sri Lankan navy, it was argued how much knowledge of national security was present with the fishing community, and in case such discourse existed in the community, what their idea of coastal security was. This would then allow us to understand what were felt to be missing in terms of coastal security or how they felt this security could be improved or in other words, how the gaps in the security apparatus present could be filled. Finally, it was important to know how the various steps taken by the Marine Police in gaining the hearts and minds of the people would be reflected in what the fishermen thought was the purpose of the presence of the Marine Police or Coastal Security Group.

Thus there was an imminent need to study:

1. the perception of "coastal security" for the people who live across the coast of Tamil Nadu and who primarily depend on the sea.

2. the vulnerabilities in coastal security as viewed by these people, the counter measures available and to suggest mechanisms in case these measures are absent.

3. measures of improvement in coastal security.

Basically it is learnt that:

1. Coastal security as understood by the fishing community was not the same as understood by the planners of such security.

2. Their idea of security was primarily regarding their own safety and the security of their livelihood.

3. Vulnerabilities (in relation to traditional security) as expressed by these communities would be in relation to patrols, and specific points of neglect along the coast.

4. Vulnerabilities (in relation to comprehensive security) as expressed by these communities would reflect in their sense of safety at sea and security of livelihood.

It was upon these assumptions that a study was planned and undertaken with sufficient leverage to expand the knowledge that was to be gained from the exercise of meeting people on the ground. It would be cumbersome on the audience to get a detailed a report of every village we visited and the deliberations we had at each of the villages and the conversations we had with each of the Police officials who were kind enough to guide us and talk to us throughout the journey. Hence what is presented below is a summary of the all such discussions divided according to the various aims of study.

The first aim was *"to study the perception of coastal security according to the people who live across the coast of Tamil Nadu and who primarily depend on the sea."*

In regards to this, the study, during the interactions confirmed the perception that what is security was greatly affected by the geography of the area. This may seem to be quite an obvious statement, but here it means that the proximity of the fishing community to what could be termed as troubled waters, or areas of tension. By this the proximity to Sri Lankan waters, and also, the past experiences with LTTE cadres and/or supporters is referred.

Travelling south, the hardships of fishing and how dangerous the lives of fishermen were brought to notice. The hardships of fishing including loss of numerous lives and limbs were complicated by the dwindling supplies of fish stock and the intrusion of the trawlers and other larger mechanized boats which reduced fish stocks in the region.

The districts that were closest to Sri Lanka indicated that people were more concerned with their safety, their well-being on the water from attacks of the Sri Lankan Navy and for things to be done to ensure their safety on the water. This apprehension was then converted to general fears of safety as was seen before about their lives on the water and not so much about being attack by Sri Lanka's Navy or how they never knew if they were going to be attacked by the Sea Tigers.

Nonetheless, their perception on Coastal Security was largely based on their own personal security. The understanding stemming from the fact that they required personal safety on the water and if that meant security then that should suffice. However, this is not to say that they have no clue about the larger role that is required of them to inform suspicious activity and persons in their area of dominance.

The difference in this activity being that they consider this part of their normal functioning; there is nothing unusual about it. This largely stems from the sense of territorial right over certain areas of the sea, that they are the legitimate people to fish over a certain area, and anyone else encroaching on this area should be known to them or friendly to them. This would be elaborated upon in the appropriate section below.

Thus, what is the perception of Coastal Security as regards the people who live across the coast and depend on them? Coastal security would refer to the security to their life and limb, and the sustenance of their livelihood. In terms of security, we figure this may be best summarily clubbed under the banner of human security as a theoretical backdrop to understand how this means security.

This brings us to our second aim, *"to understand the vulnerabilities in coastal security as understood by these people, the counter measures available and to suggest mechanisms in case these measures are absent."*

The vulnerabilities in a security situation depend upon your understanding of what security is, and how it has to be secured. And hence, in relation to the people along the coast, this vulnerability in their own security was seen from the forces of human intervention in their coastal region. In other words, the vulnerabilities to their livelihoods from extensive fishing, from dangers to their lives on the sea and other such problems faced from being on sea including encounters in foreign waters.

One of the ways in which vulnerabilities were seen was geographical points along the coast that were more accessible than others or out of the purview of the security apparatus that would allow for easy infiltration on to the Indian mainland. When we started our trip and as we reached the end of it, we could see that, there were vast open spaces that fell under this category. In fact, to use the words of Mr Rajesh Das, IPS, in a preliminary meeting we had with him, "every inch of coastline can be used to enter the mainland, and in those terms, every inch is vulnerable."

It was heartening to know of the measures that were in place to deal with this; however, we will get to that point a little later on in the text.

The last aim was *"to suggest measures of improvement in coastal security."* But to go into this, we would have to understand the measures already in place to address the issues that we raised above, and to understand some of the other vulnerabilities in terms of security that were raised (by both the police and the fishermen communities).

In the light of having summarized what vulnerabilities and the idea of security of the people along the coast, it is felt that we should turn our attention to some of the methods used in the daily routine of the police to watch over the coast, and some of the issues raised by them as far as they saw hindering their task in securing this coast.

The coastal security of Tamil Nadu is ensured through a series of steps taken by the police, among other things, to win the hearts and minds of the people along the coast. These steps are taken to fulfil the primary role of the Coastal Security Group, which is the protection of the Union of India from anti-state elements including terrorists and those planning to undertake terrorist acts. This primary role is augmented through several means which together help to attain this larger aim.

Patrolling is considered to be one of the important ways to monitor activities on the sea; this plays the dual role of not only monitoring illicit activities, but also ensuring the people that there is an active presence of the law on the water.

The presence of the police is dual in nature because of the area of jurisdiction under the CSG. This is both on water and on land. On land their presence is felt in the villages and in the communities through routine patrols and check posts set up at regular intervals close to these communities on the main roads.

VVCs

These patrols on land are also supported by an innovative method called the Village Vigilance Committees[5]. The VVCs facilitate periodic interaction between the police and the public, so that police personnel go in to the villages and interact with the locals and educate them on the various services of the CSG and how they can get in touch with the police at any time, whether on land or sea, by using the toll free number of 1093.

The VVCs also help to encourage local cooperation by engaging the population in friendly sporting activities. This keeps the youths busy and engaged in activities so that they do not fall prey to idleness which may lead them to join hands with anti-state activities that may provide better incentives.

Nonetheless, we feel that the VVCs play a crucial role in getting the larger message out of the responsibilities of the fisherman to the larger role of national security. This is because of the sheer complexity of trying to monitor all the activities of the sea by the police alone. The sheer magnitude of the problem can be seen from just taking a moment to look at how fishermen go for fishing and how they come back. They go in the thousands to the sea, and return the same way.

The VVCs, we feel play the role of educating a few, and allowing this education to spread to the larger populace over time. This allows for the knowledge to spread through the word of mouth, through peers, and a greater reception of this knowledge from those that they otherwise trust.

This brings us to the argument of whether these steps are adequate enough in the larger picture. Patrolling along the coast is a good exercise; this is something that allows us to ensure the speedy interception of suspected boats and also to monitor the activities of the fishing communities on the sea. However, due to the size of the boats and the technology available on the boats, they are limited in the time they can function, and the functions they can perform.

For instance, the 5-ton boats are designed for speedy interception, their use for patrolling at 10 knots is harmful for their engines, while the larger 12-ton boats although are more equipped for patrolling, do not have the ability to stay on the water for too long, hence their schedules can almost be predicted and evaders plan accordingly. This same problem exists for the 5-ton boat, as the only means of navigation on this boat is a compass.

Apart from this, patrolling of the villages on land is an exercise that is taken up over irregular and large intervals. For instance, a village would usually be visited once in a month to conduct the VVC and to gather some information from the locals. This was conducted by the policemen travelling to the villages on cycles or bikes, and sometimes using public transport. Nonetheless, it was ensured that the villages knew that the police did exist.

In some villages, and the numbers grew as we headed further south, villagers were unaware of the VVCs or even the toll free number. Boats that had to carry the number mandatorily did not have the number on them and the locals hardly ever heard of anything in relation to coastal security or any such group existing to deal with this. To add to this, women in most villages told us that they did not know the number to contact the CSG, now were they aware of the CSG. Some of them did know other numbers though, or would contact kin if something was required.

The police version of this was that meetings with the locals were held usually in plain clothes, so as to get closer to them, and to gain their trust. While on the converse, the locals said that if they had any issue, they used to call on the Coast Guard, or the fisheries, or Q-branch. This, however, did not mean that the CSG were not playing a role in these villages. The CSG knew of the activities in these villages, and were usually the ones acting on the calls of the people. The calls that the people did make, even though to other departments, found their way to the CSG showing great inter-department cooperation.

Also, with their dependence of kin on the sea in the Southern most districts, we found that knowledge of the presence of the CSG was almost zero. Yet, they felt it their duty to inform the Coast Guard or Navy or fisheries of unknown boats, suspicious characters on the sea and so on. If they came in to contact of outsiders in their villages, the persons had to prove they were innocent of being there. Else, these persons would be removed immediately from the village, and one of the several departments mentioned above would be informed of these persons presence. It seemed almost impossible for someone to infiltrate on to the mainland and use a village to "blend" into the local populace. This was found to be almost, if not completely, impossible. This notion of ours being reinforced through various exercises that the CSG and other departments have held, where the simulation of such an infiltration was conducted. The persons have always been apprehended.

There are some issues relating to police infrastructure too. Each station has an allotted strength of police personnel. Most of the police were not in the stations as they had to travel to the villages that were some distance from the stations to conduct VVCs. While the police complained that they were over stretched it was also seen that the frequency of such visits was varied.

In light of all these, we can now safely head to the section where we can talk about some of the suggestions of the fishermen, our understanding of such suggestions, and what we felt are recommendations that should be or could be considered seriously.

Among the many suggestions that we got, one of the main ones that kept glaring at us was training. Training was insisted to be something that would be essential to carry out better patrolling, and to carry out functions more effectively.

While we were present only for a limited amount of procedures by the Marine Police, and we can't claim to know all the functions of the marine police or to see the complexities of their entire work, we could still understand that it doesn't need any specialised training. Apart from the possibility of getting sea sick, a clear head, wearing life jackets and following the instructions of the captain on board should help any person during the entire sea-borne experience. And hence, even though basic concepts should be taught to the police assigned to a marine police station, it is suggested that a small handbook would suffice to fulfil this function.

The establishment of a separate part to the police for the purposes of recruitment and appointments so that professionalism remained high was another suggestion. We do feel that this is a very valid possibility. Although at the same time we also see the need for police officers to be interchangeable between the branches of the police. It is absolutely necessary for the police to be open to the idea of transfers from "Law and Order" to "Marine Police" to other sections, as this allows for the cohesiveness of the policing body than independent bodies. Nonetheless, if police officers were to be transferred from a marine police station to another police station, it would take less time for them to perform and could carry forward their experience from the previous post.

As mentioned earlier, the frequency of visits to a certain village was few and far between. This gap between visits and interaction seemed to increase the distance or not close the gap between the people and the police. This is a problem because the effectiveness of the VVC program comes with winning the hearts and minds of the people. In the worst scenarios of police interaction, the police were seen as the enemies as the police were against some of the fishing practices of the locals. The police were doing their job of preventing the illegal use of certain nets or the capture of fishermen with endangered species of marine wildlife.

A method to tackle this was to improve relations with the fishing communities through increased patrols and activities. However, with the current infrastructure, this frequency cannot be achieved. On the positive side, we have come to learn that these strains on the infrastructure are now being dealt with in the subsequent plans of the implementation of Marine Police Stations (MPS). The new phases allows for the area under each MPS to be reduced considerably, allowing more frequent patrols, more regularity in VVCs, and most of all, more efficiency from the police in carrying out their routine jobs in relation to the communities that come under their jurisdiction.

More modern arms were another suggestion that we often heard. It was something that was discussed, and it was understood also that, the police had all the firearms that was required considering the threats they faced, and even the possible escalation of threats (to a certain limit of course). Either way, the present 303 rifles provided for the most range and accuracy, and the semi automatics present where always available when the need arose. Some officers were hoping that arms could be extended to further ranks. It was justified by the thought that fishing communities would garner more respect and cooperation from those personnel carrying a weapon than otherwise, and it would always help to defend the personnel from a possible attack. Either way, this would be counterproductive. Police personnel dealing with the threat at hand are armed accordingly, and get the right response from the people, winning their hearts and minds being the goal, we feel that being armed to the teeth wouldn't help this cause.

One of the problems that also seemed to arise was from fishermen not being able to identify the International Maritime Boundary Line (IMBL) physically. This is a contested notion, as we also met numerous fishermen who told us that they were absolutely aware of their crossing the IMBL, and knew where to fish. It was only for the sole purpose of getting a decent catch that they crossed the IMBL, without doing so, fishing would not be profitable, and they'd have to starve.

The people who told us that they'd not cross the boundary if they knew where it lay suggested that some sort of demarcation be made. However, their wants of some form of demarcation are physically not feasible. It was in relation to this that we were wondering about the use GPS systems on the water. Fishermen are told to always carry their GPS systems to sea, and use life jackets while at sea. While almost all of them have no regard for the use of life jackets at sea, they suggest that the GPS is something that not all of them have because of the cost of the module. Others, with the GPS, say that it is not possible to know where the IMBL is on the machine. This notion was proved false by our observation of the most basic device that they used. It is possible to program the GPS to show when they cross the IMBL. In this regard, it may be considered a suggestion to program the GPS modules available with the fishermen to show them the IMBL so that that is not a reason under which they may put their lives in danger.

Another fact that struck us was that the people wanted to know how or if the government could help them during the rough seasons when they couldn't fish. And methods the government could adopt to help them 'feed their families'. While women wanted to know if proper education could be imparted to their wards.

While this might be out of the scope of this report, a comprehensive sense of security would allow for the inclusion of these concerns in to the larger security framework of these people.

In relation to this, it was also understood that the women folk were open to idea of other occupations, provided, they receive adequate training and help to be successful in other occupations. Feasibility of fish farming could be taken so that families may be able to sustain themselves on that during the tough months, while it also provides for another source of income. Also, during the 90 days that they are not allowed to go on the sea, some sort of the opening up of their lives to tourism could also be thought about, creating opportunities for them to expand their sources of income, as well as allowing people to understand better the lives of these wonderful people. This would also allow for planned sustained development through limited controlled tourism.

In conclusion, it may be said that this study to understand the perception of coastal security according to the people who live across the coast of Tamil Nadu and who primarily depend on the sea, to understand the vulnerabilities in coastal security as understood by these people, the counter measures available and to suggest mechanisms where they are absent and to suggest measures of improvement in coastal security have been completed in the above paragraphs.

We hope that these may be taken into consideration during the processes of planning and implementation, as the voices from below are as important to effective policy planning as those voices of planning and guidance from above.

Endnotes

1 http://www.kgbanswers.co.uk/whats-the-definition-of-coastal/1319078#ixzz1FdttzHQZ

2 http://mha.nic.in/pdfs/BM_Costal(E).pdf

3 http://www.marinebuzz.com/2009/11/27/india-tamil-nadu-police-is-first-to-launch-toll-free-coastal-security-help-line/

4 30 more marine police stations sanctioned for Tamilnadu , the Hindu, February 3, 2010 http://www.hindu.com/2010/02/03/stories/2010020354520600.htm

5 Vigilance committee to be formedineveryvillage in TN, The Hindustan Times, July 4, 2009 http://www.hindustantimes.com/India-news/TamilNadu/Vigilance-committee-to-be-formed-in-every-village-in-TN/Article1-428679.aspx

Coastal Security of India: The Role of Coastal Community

Suresh R & Rakhee Viswambharan

Introduction

The concept of security has various dimensions. In the cold war period threat to security to nation was mainly from the other nation states. However, in the post-cold war period the threat to national security emanates from non-state actors also. There are some non-traditional threats to national security including international terrorism. This new threat can be addressed only with the active support of other nation states as well as people. Similarly in the post-cold war period the human security issues assume great significance. Thus it is the responsibility of nation to address both national security and human security simultaneously. Interestingly the coastal security is an area where the national security interests and human security interests converge.

Coastal security is one of the subset of maritime security. The coastal security has become an urgent necessity especially in the context of Mumbai terrorist attack and the threat it poses to the national security. In the post cold war period the threat to the security of nation states emanates mainly from non state actors. Unlike the attack from state actors the non state actors mode of attack is different. It demands a constant vigil throughout the land and maritime borders. The recent Italian marine issue adds a new dimension to the security of the coastal people engaged in fishing.

When we look into the coastal security a convergence of the national security concerns and human security concerns is visible. The overall development of the coastal area would lead to better human security and better human security would result in enlisting the support of the coastal community to ensure national security programme, especially the coastal security. However the task of guarding the vast coastline, unlike our land borders, is a complex issue involving multiple stake holders such as shipping, fisheries, offshore exploration and production, tourism, and scientific community. In short, coastal security is not only about protecting our coastal terrain and territorial waters from direct attacks by state actors or non state actors, but also safeguarding the interests of all stake holders.

India's Maritime Security Interests

India has a coast line of 7516 kms and a territorial limit extends to 12 nautical miles from the coast and Exclusive Economic Zone (EEZ) of 200 nautical miles, which covers 2 million sq kms. There are nine States and four Union Territories that have coastal area. Though it is the duty of the Indian navy and the Indian Coast Guard to provide the security of the maritime borders they cannot keep a constant vigil on the movement of men and materials along the entire coastal region. The Indian navy is mainly stationed to the area beyond 200 nautical miles in international waters and Indian Coast Guard to look after the area from 12 nautical miles up to 200 nautical miles and the coastal police is responsible for the area up to 12 nautical miles from the shore. Therefore the coastal policing are necessary to supplement and not supplant the security responsibility of the Indian defence forces. It is also important to note that the coastal policing through coastal police stations alone cannot ensure a foolproof security arrangement in the coastal area or through the construction of fencing along the coastal area. Therefore the cooperation and support of the coastal community is sine quo non for the coastal security.

India has to step up surveillance and protection of India's vast coastline of 7,516 kms. India's maritime zones, over which it has certain rights and obligations, include a territorial sea up to 12 nm (22 kms) from the baseline, a contiguous zone from 12 to 24 nm (22-44 kms), an Exclusive Economic Zone (EEZ) from 12 to 200 nm (22-370 kms) and a continental shelf up to 200 nm. These zones currently comprise 2.013 million sq km area of sea which is the 12th largest in the world and equivalent to two-thirds of the total land area. India's has thousand-plus island territories and offshore installations. Again nearly 70 per cent of India's energy requirements of crude oil are currently shipped from abroad, increased focus would be required on the ability to maintain the safety and security of energy shipments and the prevention of any disruption of supply through multilateral cooperation. Another important maritime security interest of India is the prevention of maritime terrorism not only through multilateral efforts but also through comprehensive coastal security programme with the involvement of coastal community.

The task of providing security to the vast coastline, unlike the land borders, is a complex phenomenon involving multiple stake holders such as shipping, fisheries, offshore exploration and production, tourism, and scientific community. It is not only important to protect and promotes the multifarious interests of different stake holders but also involve them in the coastal security programme.

Coastal Security and Maritime Security Agencies

There are nine states and four union territories that have coastal area. Though it is the duty of the Indian navy and the Indian coast guard to provide the security of the maritime borders they cannot keep a constant vigil on the movement of men and material along the entire coastal region. There is currently a fragmentation of organizations, policies and legal and enforcement measures relating to maritime security issues. This results in overlapping of jurisdiction and inability to provide quick decisions or respond effectively to fast evolving situations. Currently, as many as 12 ministries and eight departments of the central government are involved in maritime-related policy formulation and implementation, as are nine coastal states and four union territories, with defence left to the Indian Navy and the Indian Coast Guard.

To deal with such a situation, a formal mechanism for coordination among the multiple users of the sea is urgently required. This would enable effective and time-urgent coordination among varied maritime related ministries/departments of the Government, as also the concerned states and union territories. In this respect, the Group of Ministers' report has recommended the formation of "an apex body for management of maritime affairs". Such an apex body would coordinate the activities of various agencies operating form different regions and having different mandates. The coastal security scheme is one such comprehensive initiative to address the problem of coastal security with the involvement of the coastal community.

Coastal Security Scheme and the role of Coastal Community

The Coastal Security Scheme has been formulated for strengthening infrastructure for patrolling and surveillance of country's coastal areas, particularly the shallow areas close to coast to check and counter illegal cross border activities and criminal activities using coast or sea. The Ministry of Home Affairs has been implementing Coastal Security Scheme in two phases (Phase-I -2005 to 2011 and Phase-II – 2011 – 2015). The scheme also aims at establishing institutional arrangements at state and district level for coordination among various agencies including the Indian Coast Guard and the Indian Navy.

The Coastal Security Scheme is under implementation in the nine coastal States and four coastal Union Territories since 2005. Under the scheme, in the first phase (2005-2011) assistance has been given to all the coastal states of Gujarat, Maharashtra, Goa, Karnataka, Kerala, Tamil Nadu, Andhra Pradesh, Orissa and West Bengal and the Union Territories of Daman & Diu, Lakshadweep, Puducherry and Andaman & Nicobar Islands to set up 73 coastal police stations 97 check posts 58 outposts. Under the Phase-II (2011 - 2015) of the Scheme it has been proposed to provide 131 Marine Police Stations, 60 jetties, 10 Marine Operation Centres,

The proposal of the Phase-II Coastal Security Scheme has been formulated on the basis of vulnerability/gap analysis carried out by the coastal States and Union Territories in consultation with the Indian Coast Guard. The proposal was approved by the Government of India on 24 September 2010 for implementation from 1 April 2011 for a period of five years. The Scheme has provided support to coastal States/Union Territories to upgrade their coastal security apparatus. Nevertheless the task of securing India's vast coastline is immense. There are 12 major ports and around 200 minor ports in the country. The 12 major ports are International Ship and Port Facility Security (ISPS) compliant and are subject to security audit once in two years. However, there is no such mechanism of security audit for the non-major ports. Apart from 12 major ports, 53 minor/non-major ports and 5 shipyards in the country are ISPS compliant.

As per the report of the home ministry of India a three tier coastal security ring all along India's coast is provided by Marine Police, Indian Coast Guard and Indian Navy. Extensive surveillance and patrolling has been put into place across the Eastern and Western coastlines by the security forces in a co-ordinated manner. The Indian Coast Guard is undertaking extensive patrolling and surveillance along the eastern and western coast in coordination with other Central and State agencies viz Indian Navy, Marine Police, Customs, CISF, Port Authority etc. Further, for effective surveillance, the deployment of assets by Indian Coast Guard in the Exclusive Economic Zone has been enhanced. On an average, every day about 18-20 ICG Ships are on patrol whereas about 8-10 aircrafts are on aerial surveillance sortie. At least one ship is being maintained on maritime borders with Pakistan and Sri Lanka. In addition, waters off Lakshadweep and Minicoy islands are maintained under constant surveillance during non-monsoon period by deployment of assets alternatively by Indian Coast Guard and Indian Navy.

Costal Security Scheme

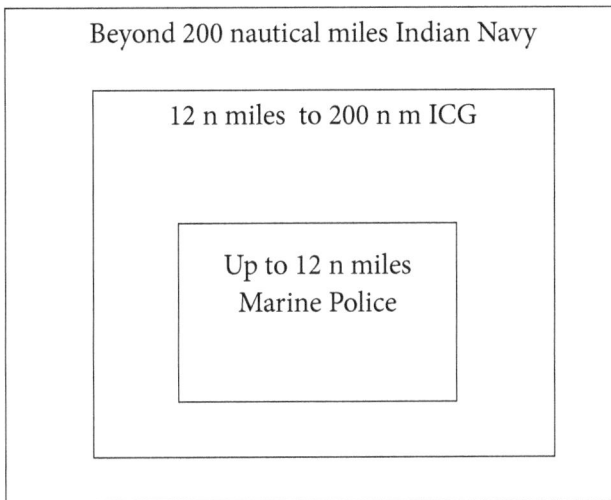

```
┌─────────────────────────────────────────────────┐
│  Beyond 200 nautical miles Indian Navy           │
│   ┌─────────────────────────────────────────┐    │
│   │   12 n miles  to 200 n m ICG            │    │
│   │    ┌─────────────────────────────┐       │    │
│   │    │                             │       │    │
│   │    │   Up to 12 n miles          │       │    │
│   │    │   Marine Police             │       │    │
│   │    │                             │       │    │
│   │    └─────────────────────────────┘       │    │
│   └─────────────────────────────────────────┘    │
└─────────────────────────────────────────────────┘
```

Further Indian Coast Guard is regularly conducting community interaction programmes in the fishing villages along the coast. The community interaction programmes are aimed at sensitizing the fishing community on the prevailing security situation and develop them to be the 'eyes and ears' for intelligence gathering. It was started in 2009, and a total of 1919 community interaction programmes have been conducted by Indian Coast Guard. Thus the security agencies have well accepted the role of the coastal community in the coastal security scheme.

Again on 15 May 2013 Defence Minister of India called upon various agencies to work together to ensure a seamless and robust coastal security architecture and stated that fishermen should be made an integral part of the security planning. He also said that an integrated approach was essential for a strong coastal security and noted that fishermen were the "eyes and ears" for overall coastal security. However, so far the involvement of coastal community in coastal security scheme is limited to sensitising them through periodic awareness programme undertaken by Indian Coast Guard and Marine police.

In this connection the proposal put forth by Professor K R Singh is an innovative step to gain the support of the coastal community in coastal security programme on a permanent basis. He had suggested the setting up of a Marine Guards on the lines of Home Guards by recruiting coastal people from each coastal locality. These trained Marine Guards would help the coastal security agencies in intelligence gathering which is a very vital input to the coastal security agencies to monitor the movement of men and materials along the vast coastal area. The gathering of intelligence through human being would also support the surveillance through electronic gadgets. This proposal if implemented will not only help to solve unemployed among coastal people but also help to enlist the support and cooperation of the coastal community in security related activities on a permanent basis. It is important to note that the Karnataka state has already selected 200 fishermen to be employed in coastal security police. The people from coastal villages can be recruited to the marine police force as marine guards and their seafaring experience is likely to be an asset to the security agencies.

In addition the coastal people can be trained to gather information which would support and supplement the necessary intelligence inputs to the marine police. India has a long coastal stretch and at several places the stretch lacks security forces. Hence, the fishermen if trained can be used to alert and inform in case they find anything unusual such as a person photographing or sketching, contacting ships with torch signals, transferring goods from a ship to a boat, transferring people, fisher folk fishing in areas not meant for fishing and are acting suspiciously or people urging fisher folk in buying their boats or renting them by paying a huge amount of money. One of the major problems with the new recruits in marine police is that they do not know the local language. Therefore it is necessary to concentrate on area-wise recruitment to marine police. And through periodic awareness programme the coastal community can be trained to gather vital intelligence inputs to the security agencies. Thus when it came to protecting the coastal borders of the country, the fishing community could play a big role. In fact, every sea-faring fisherman can be trained to be a front man of coastal security.

The Triton mock-drill, a coastal security exercises conducted by the Indian Navy had shown that terrorists could still find passages into the country through the sea. It has been pointed out that at one instance during the Triton exercise, "enemies" sent through the sea by the security agencies could bribe and gain entry into the country at one or two points. Therefore, there should be more awareness on coastal security. During this exercise it was also found that certain coastal area remained vigilant and the "terrorists" were captured with the cooperation of the fishing community. It shows that sea-faring fishermen were the eyes and ears of coastal security and no amount of modernised coastal security measures would equal them. As part of the coastal security programme, it had been decided to equip all categories of fishing vessels with radio-frequency identification gadgets. It would enable the security agencies to identify each and every fishing vessel out at sea. This, in turn, would enable checking of vessels without the gadget. Even then the fishing community would continue to be the vital aspect of coastal security.

The task of providing security to the vast coastline, unlike the land borders, is a complex phenomenon involving multiple stake holders. Among these stake holders the role of coastal community assumes significance in the coastal security programme. They are considered as the eye and ears of the coastal security. Now the question arise how to enlist the cooperation and support of the coastal community for effective coastal policing. Such support and cooperation are necessary on a permanent basis and round the clock. The cooperation and support of the coastal people are needed day in and day out to ensure coastal security. The livelihood for the fishing community comes from the sea. In this connection they also require protection from the security agencies involved in anti-piracy and related security operations of the defence forces.

In order to ensure the support of the coastal community it is important to build a better coastal community - police relations. Unlike other areas the coastal area is mainly occupied by the fishing community. Their problems are different from the problems of the people living in other area. Generally the coastal areas lag behind in basic amenities. This includes lack of safe drinking water, sanitation, proper housing, education, and other infrastructural facilities such as roads, hospitals, markets etc.

Since the livelihoods of the coastal community come from fishing it is difficult to replace the coastal area settlers. The whole hearted cooperation and support of the coastal community can be ensured only thorough improving the living conditions of the coastal people. The coastal community faces natural calamities such as sea erosion, tsunami etc. They are also the victims of climate change pollution, and poverty. In short the human security issues are numerous and imminent as far as the coastal community is concerned.

Thus when we look into the coastal security a convergence of the national security concerns and human security concerns is visible. The overall development of the coastal area would lead to better human security and better human security would result in enlisting the support of the coastal community in national security programme. Thus the development of infrastructural facilities in the coastal area not only improves the human security but also to enhance the coastal security and maritime security.

The security agencies in India had already maintained that the coastal community is the eyes and ears of coastal security. It is this understanding on the part of the security agencies which led to formal interaction between the coastal community and security agencies. The mass awareness drive has been initiated by the Indian coast guard in association with the department of fisheries at various location for the fishing community. The main objective of the drive was to re-emphasize the responsibility of fishing community towards the coastal security setup and their role as "Eyes and Ears" of the security agencies. This programme was also utilized to educate fishermen on safety and security aspects while operating at sea. Such interactions are beneficial to both the security agencies and the fishing community. It also enhances better police community relationship.

Again the coastal security projects have also envisaged the construction of coastal roads along the coastal areas and the development of infrastructural facilities. Such development along the coastal area would also promote coastal (beach) tourism. The development of tourism along the coastal area would also enhance the employment opportunities to the coastal people. One of the major problems before the coastal community is unemployment. This problem can be well addressed by development of tourism along the coastal area.

Thus particular attention needs to be paid to the maritime dimensions of national security as it is closely linked to India's political stability and economic prosperity. Concomitantly in the maritime security the coastal security aspect need to be focused. Along with enhancing the operational capabilities of the security agencies the problems of the coastal community also need to be addressed. A comprehensive programme needs to be initiated to address all aspects of coastal security with the active support of the coastal community. And the investments in the coastal security with the involvement of coastal people will not only enhance the national security but it also augments the human security.

References

Professor K R Singh Coastal Security- Maritime Dimensions of India's Homeland Security, Vij Books India Pvt Ltd, New Delhi, 2013.

Annual Reports of the Ministry of Home Affairs, Government of India 2005 – 2011

Annual Reports of the Ministry of External Affairs, Government of India 2005 – 2011

Annual Reports of the Ministry of Defence, Government of India 2005 – 2011

Suresh R Peace in the Indian Ocean: A South Asian Perspective, Serials Publishers, New Delhi, 2012 ISBN : 9788183875059

Suresh R India's Security Policy in the Post Cold War Period in Prof. Mohanan B Pillai (Ed.) India's National Security Concerns and Strategies, New Century Publications, New Delhi 2013 ISBN 9788177083569

India's Maritime Military Strategy, Ministry of Defense, Government of India, New Delhi. Also see The Indian Navy's Vision Document, May 2006. www.indiannavy.nic.in

Suresh R, Human Security A Canadian Perspective, Holistic Thought, Vol. V No 1 & 2, Jan Dec 2006.pp 103-113.

The details of assistance provided to coastal States and Union Territories under the Coastal Security Scheme Phase I 2005 -2011

S. No.	Name of State/ UT	Coastal Police Stations	Ves-sels	Jeeps	Motor Cycles	Check Post	Out Post	Bar-racks	Rub-ber In-flated Boats
1	Gujarat	10	30	20	101	25	46	-	-
2	Maharashtra	12	28	25	57	32	-	24	-
3	Goa	3	9	6	9	-	-	-	10
4	Karnataka	5	15	9	4	-	-	-	-
5	Kerala	8	24	16	24	-	-	-	-
6	Tamil Nadu	12	24	12	36	40	12	-	-
7	Andhra Pradesh	6	18	12	18	-	-	-	-
8	Orissa	5	15	10	15	-	-	-	-
9	West Bengal	6	18	12	12	-	-	6	-
10	Pondicherry	1	3	2	3	-	-	-	-
11	Lakshadweep	4	6	8	8	-	-	-	-
12	Daman & Diu	1	4	3	5	-	-	-	-
13	Andaman & Nicobar Islands	-	10	18	20	-	-	-	-
	Total	73	204	153	312	97	58	30	10

Piracy, Use of Force And Criminal Jurisdiction: An Analysis of Enrica Lexie Case In The Light of International Conventions, Guidelines And National Legislations

Sandeep Menon N.

Abstract

The debate that ensued as a result of the incident where two Italian marines shot and killed the Indian fishermen on the ground of alleged piracy attack was primarily focused on the jurisdiction that could be exercised by the Indian courts. This paper examines the relevant Kerala High Court Judgment as well as the Supreme Court judgment and analyses the criminal jurisdiction that could be exercised by Indian Courts beyond the territorial waters. This paper also considers whether it is empowered to do so under the national legislations in accordance with International principles. The International Conventions such as UNCLOS of 1982, Territorial Waters, Continental Shelf, Exclusive Economic Zone and other Maritime Zones Act of 1976 (in short Territorial Waters Act, 1976) as well as SUA Convention are carefully analysed and discussed together with the provisions of IPC, CrPC and SUA Act to understand and appreciate the definitions of territorial waters, contiguous zones and Exclusive Economic Zones, to understand as to what constitutes piracy and to examine which state can exercise jurisdiction over this matter. This paper proceeds to prove that Indian Courts do have the jurisdiction and examines whether it is the State or the Union that can exercise jurisdiction over this matter. Most importantly, various guidelines by the IMO, submissions made by different countries before the Maritime Safety Committee and Best Management Practices in case of piracy attack are examined in detail to check whether the use of force by the Italian mariners was proportionate or whether it exceeded than what was necessary. This paper also focuses on various factors that should be taken into consideration during deployment of armed guards on board a ship as per IMO Guidelines. The Italian Regulation on the same will also be discussed in detail in this paper.

Introduction

The unpleasant incident where two Indian fishermen were shot and killed by the Italian marines on the ground of alleged piracy attack sparked a lot of uncertainty in the Indian Courts. This incident, where the Italian Marines on board the vessel 'MT Enrica Lexie' that is registered in Italy shot down two Indian fishermen, onboard a fishing boat 'St. Antony', the issue that arose into consideration were the following. 1) Whether the Italian marines are liable to be prosecuted under the Indian laws for the alleged killing of Indian fishermen? 2) If yes, is it the state of Kerala or the Union of India which has the jurisdiction in the matter? This paper examines these two main issues along with many other in the light of the High Court and Supreme Court judgments in the matter of Enrica Lexie and on the basis of various national laws and international principles.

The place of incident – Legal Implications

In the matter of *Massimilano Latorre & Salvatore Girone (Italian marines)* v. *Union of India*[1], there was confusion with regard to the exact place at which the firing took place. Though the FIR stated that it is 33 nautical miles (NM) from the coastal police station, the remand report mentioned the same as 22.5 NM from the baseline. Though the petitioners claimed that it is only 20.5 NM from the baseline, the Kerala High Court observed that the incident took place in Contiguous Zone and not in the territorial waters. The same observation is true and it is very pertinent in the instant case. Had it been in the territorial waters, much of the controversies could have been avoided. This issue will attain clarity only by analysing the provisions of UNCLOS, 1982 and Territorial Waters, Continental Shelf, Exclusive Economic Zone and other Maritime Zones Act, 1976 (in short Territorial Waters Act, 1976). The definitions of Territorial Waters, Contiguous Zone, EEZ and Continental Shelf can be seen in Articles 3, 33, 55 & 57 and 76 of UNCLOS and sections 3, 5, 7 and 6 of the Territorial Waters Act, 1976 respectively.

It is clear from the provisions of UNCLOS and Territorial Waters Act, 1976 that the territorial waters extend up to 12 nautical miles from the baseline and the contiguous zone extend up twenty-four nautical miles from the nearest point of the baseline. Unlike in territorial waters where the coastal state can exercise full sovereignty, in the contiguous zone the coastal State may exercise control that is necessary to prevent infringement of its customs, fiscal, immigration or sanitary laws and regulations within its territory or territorial sea and punish infringement of the same.[2]

The alleged case of piracy and the permitted legal use of force to combat piracy

In order to analyse whether the firing and the resultant killing of two Indian fisherman by the Italian Marines amount to an offence, it is important to analyse whether the act of the fishermen comes within the definition of piracy and the measures taken by the Marines had exceeded than what was required during a threat of piracy. Article 101 of UNCLOS defines the term 'piracy' which basically include any illegal acts of violence or detention, or any act of depredation, committed for private ends by the crew or the passengers of a private ship.[3] Article 3 of the Convention for the Suppression of Unlawful Acts against the Safety of Maritime Navigation as amended by 2005 Protocol also specifies the instances where one could be said to have committed an offence.[4] It can never be inferred from either of these conventions that the acts of the fishermen would constitute piracy or could even cause an imminent threat of piracy. It should also be noted that the Kerala High Court has made a specific observation in this regard. The Honourable High Court has observed that "in this context, it is pertinent to peruse the statement in Exhibit P2 (copy of the FIR) that there were 11 persons in the fishing boat including the first informant. Except two, all others were sleeping when the Italian Marines opened fire at the fishing boat. They fired continually for about two minutes. One of the deceased, late Valentine was sitting in the driving seat and the other deceased Pink was at the stern of the fishing boat when they were shot down to death. It was also stated that the fishing boat was 200 meters away from the vessel. The respondents have also submitted that all the fishermen in the boat were unarmed. There is nothing in the writ petition to suggest the contrary. For that reason itself, the story of attempted piracy attack is not a credible one."[5]

It has been specifically mentioned in the Supreme Court judgment[6] that St. Antony, the Indian fishing vessel was allegedly 'mistook' to be a pirate vessel and after the incident, the Italian vessel continued on its scheduled course to Djibouti. So there is a clear cut idea at present to the effect that Indian vessel was not engaged in piracy and was an ordinary fishing vessel which suggests the fact that there were no acts from its side which could have reasonably thought to be an act of piracy.

Steps to be taken in case of a pirate attack

Though the measures to combat piracy cannot be held to be illegal, it is to be analysed whether there was at least a reasonable apprehension of a pirate attack, if not an actual attack of piracy. It is submitted that the Italian marines have not followed the measures that they ought to have followed and in addition to that, they did exceed the use of force than that was necessary.

The Guidance to Ship Owners and Ship Operators, Shipmasters and Crews on Preventing and Suppressing Acts of Piracy and Armed Robbery against Ships issued by International Maritime Organization via Circular MSC.1/Circ.1334 dated 23 June 2009[7] aims at bringing to the attention of ship owners, companies, ship operators, masters and crews the steps that should be taken to reduce the risk of pirate attacks, possible responses to them and the vital need to report attacks, both successful and unsuccessful, to the authorities of the relevant coastal State and to the ships' own maritime administration. As regards the use of defensive measures, the guidance states that robust actions from the ship which is approached by pirates may discourage the attackers and outrunning attacks may be an appropriate preventive manoeuvre against pirate attacks. Use of water hoses, increase of speed and heavy wheel movements to ride off attackers thereby causing the effect of the bow wave and wash to deter the attackers by making it difficult for them to attach poles or grappling irons to the ship are also suggested defensive measures.[8]

There is a specific mentioning in the 2009 guidelines that early detection of suspected attacks must be the first line of defence and a pirate attack or a similar attack can be detected if the vigilance and surveillance are successful. The guidelines mandate the shipowners, company, ship operator and master to be aware of any UN Security Council, IMO or any other UN resolutions on piracy and armed robbery against ships and any recommendations therein relevant to the shipowner, operator, master and crew when operating in areas where piracy or armed robbery against ships occur. It is true that the options available to the master and crew will depend on the extent to which the attackers have secured control of the ship but if the master is certain that all the crew are within secure areas and that the attackers cannot gain access or make the ship at imminent danger then he/ she may consider undertaking evasive manoeuvres of the type referred to above to encourage the attackers to return to their craft. The only thing which is clear so far the factual circumstances of this case is concerned is the fact that none of these above mentioned measures were resorted to by the Italian marines apart from firing shots at the fishermen and murdering them. It is submitted that Italian marines being trained military personnel ought to have fired warning shots rather than fatal ones.[9]

The 2009 guidelines[10] allow the use of unarmed security personnel so as to provide security advice and use of privately contracted armed security personnel. Though the use of privately contracted armed security personnel on board merchant ships and fishing vessels has been left as a matter for the flag State to determine in consultation with shipowners, operators and companies, it specifically states that if armed security personnel are allowed on board, the master, shipowner, operator and company should take into account the possible escalation of violence and other risks. The guidelines allow the use of Military teams or law enforcement officers duly authorized by Government but it is specifically mentioned that the carriage of military personnel may be recommended when the ship is transiting in areas of high risk. The guideline also requires the masters, shipowners, operators and companies to contact the flag State and seek clarity of the national policy with respect to the carriage of armed security personnel and to meet all the legal requirements of flag, port and coastal States. It is true that the privately contracted armed personnel may be empowered under the laws of the flag state to use firearms so as to prevent piracy or other maritime crimes but whenever a ship is in transit it is not just the flag state jurisdiction that comes into action. Due regard should be given to the port/coastal state's jurisdiction as well.

The Italian regulation on the use of armed security personnel

The Supreme Court judgment on *Republic of Italy and ors* v. *Union of India and ors*[11] starts by stating that the marines were deployed as per an agreement entered into between the Ministry of Defence – Naval Staff and Italian Shipowners' Confederation pursuant to the Law Decree No.107/2011 which was converted into Italian law No.130 of 2nd August 2011. Article 5 of the same legislation authorises deployment of military navy contingents on Italian vessels to counter piracy. It allows deploying of armed guards, governmental or private contractors, in case of unavailability of governmental ones on board Italian flagged vessels. The National Official Guidance states that the shipowners will bear the entire cost with regard to embarking armed guards on board from the Naval Forces that may also appeal to personnel of others military forces, and use of arms to ensure the protection of the ship and crew. It specifically states that private contractors can be deployed in case of non availability of governmental guards.[12]

In this context, the Regulation on the Employment of contractors on board the Italian flagged ships sailing in International Waters under piracy risk was issued on 29th March 2013[13]. It came into force on 13th April 2013 and it integrates the piracy measures adopted by Law Decree No.107/2011. Article 5(2) (d) of the said Regulation limits the use of weapons to the case of the exercise of right to self-defence under Article 52 of the Code of criminal procedure. There is absolutely no mentioning on the use of minimal/proportional force in the said regulations and there is no reference made to the The Guidance on Rules for the Use of Force (RUF) by Privately Contracted Armed Security Personnel (PCASP) in Defence of a Merchant Vessel (MV) issued by BIMCO[14]. The GUARDCON which is a model contract for the employment of security guards on vessels provides under Section 4(c) that the security personnel shall always have the sole responsibility for any decision taken by him for the use of any force, including targeting and weapon discharge, always in accordance with the Rules for the use of Force and applicable national law.[15] It seems that the latter part of the said section which talks about following the Rules for the use of Force has not been taken into consideration in the said Regulation. It is said that "the effects of the ISM Code[16], the Risk Management Procedures and the Best Management Practices for Protection, which any shipowner has to comply with, do not seem to be considered by the Regulation."[17]

What the regulation gives importance to can be clearly understood from clause 2 to Article 4 which talks about the characteristics of the vessels for the performance of services protection wherein it is stated that, merchant ships must be prepared for the storage of weapons for the performance of protection services and be equipped with special cabinets for custody of the weapons with the characteristics specified in Article 6 paragraph 3 of this Decree[18]. The object behind his regulation is clear from sub section (2) to Article 6 as well which provides that the security guards, in the performance of security services and only within the limits of international waters in the areas at risk of piracy, may use the common firearms, as well as those ship equipment. In case of use of the weapons held regularly by the same security guards, applies the current legislation on detention, port, import and export of common firearms.

The Best Management Practices

The Best Management Practices for Protection against Somalia Based Piracy (Version 4 – August 2011) which provides for Suggested Planning and Operational Practices for Ship Operators and Masters of Ships Transiting the High Risk Area states that the measures to protect ship described in BMP are the most basic effective solutions but it does not prevent the owners from considering measures beyond the scope of BMP even if it is related to providing additional equipments or manpower so as to counter a piracy attack[19]. Having said that, BMP under section 8 that talks about Ship Protection Measures provides for use of razor wires, water sprays, fire hoses, water cannons, anti-piracy manoeuvres whilst maintaining the best possible speed, unarmed as well as armed private maritime security contractors. There is a specific mentioning that armed Private Maritime Security Contractors are to be used as an additional layer of protection and not as an alternative to BMP.[20] This suggests the fact that measures such as increasing the speed, evasive manoeuvring and like techniques as stipulated under BMP has to be resorted to before using firearms even in case of apprehension of piracy. It is true that BMP suggests only the best management practices and it does not detract the master of the ship from his overriding authority to protect the ship and its crew. But whether other such overriding authority was warranted in this specific case of Enrica Lexie is the question that has to be answered and it should be answered in the negative after having perused through facts of the case. A clear reading of BMP suggests that it is only self defensive measures that need to be employed during approach stage and other measures short of murdering that needs to be employed during the attack stage.[21]

Other Guidelines

Moreover it should also be noted that the IMO's Revised Interim Guidance to Shipowners, Ship Operators, and Shipmasters on the use of Privately Contracted Armed Security Personnel on Board Ships in the High Risk Area (MSC.1/Circ.1405/Rev.1 dated 16 September 2011) prohibits the use of unnecessary force than is required in a case of an attack on the ship[22].

According to Rule 3.5 which lays down the rules for the use of force "it is essential that all Privately Contracted Armed Security Personnel (PCASP) have a complete understanding of the rules for the use of force as agreed between shipowner, PMSC and Master and fully comply with them and they should be fully aware that their primary function is the prevention of boarding using the minimal force necessary to do so." The rule specifically states that PMSC should require their personnel to take all reasonable steps to avoid the use of force and it should not exceed what is necessary and should be proportionate to the threat and appropriate to the situation. The interesting fact is that the rule is clear about the fact that PMSC should require that their personnel should not use firearms against persons and it can be allowed only in cases of self defence or defence of others against the imminent threat of death or serious injury. It is submitted that there is no proof to show that there existed imminent threat of piracy for the Italian marines to open fire shoot down the Indian fishermen.

The IMO's Interim Guidance To Private Maritime Security Companies Providing Privately Contracted Armed Security Personnel On Board Ships in The High Risk Area issued vide circular MSC.1/Circ.1443 dated 25 May 2012 clearly provides that PMSC should ensure that PCASP operating for them have a complete understanding of, and fully comply with, the applicable laws governing the use of force and they should take all reasonable to avoid the use of force and, if force is used, that force should be used as part of a graduated response plan in particular including the strict implementation of the latest version of Best Management Practices.[23] All these guidelines prove the fact that the immediate measure that could be taken in the case of an actual pirate attack is not to open fire and the force which could be used in such circumstances should not exceed the reasonable force that is required.

It has been specifically stated in the submission by Italy before the Maritime Safety Committee on Safety issues related to the use of armed personnel on board ships in the high risk area during the 90th session[24] that the Italian Administration has allowed the use of Military Teams of Protection of the Italian Navy (NMP) on board Italian merchant ships and fishing vessels, sailing in high risk areas following the approval of the revised interim recommendations for flag States regarding the use of privately contracted armed security personnel on board ships in the high risk areas.[25] It is submitted that if the decision to employ armed personnel was in pursuance of the revised interim recommendations, they ought to have fulfilled the other conditions stipulated under the same revised recommendations.

In relation to deployment of Armed Guards, certain submissions have been submitted by India before the Maritime Safety Committee in its 90th session vide MSC 90/20/16 dated 27 March 2012[26]. They are the follows:

1. when privately contracted armed security personnel (PCASP) or members of armed forces are deployed on board merchant ships, the command of the vessel, for both security and safety purposes, should only be with the master of the vessel;

2. there should be verifiable linkages between the flag State, the private maritime security company and the PCASP when PCASP are deployed;

3. ships carrying armed security guards should have the permission/ clearance from the flag State for carriage of specific personnel and the firearms and ammunition on board; and

4. ships carrying armed security guards should report the details of on board armed security guards to the coastal State while they are within the limits of the exclusive economic zone of the concerned coastal State.

It should be noted that the discussion on these by India are specifically because of the Enrica Lexie incident. This has been stated by India along with the above mentioned submissions.[27]

It is pertinent to note an interesting observation made in an article[28] and it is as follows: "Currently the right of a master and crew to defend against piracy includes lethal force and there is no obligation to file public reports. Private security companies are also not required to file public incident reports. Internally both the shipping industry and maritime security keeps records but neither are eager to be pushed into the public spotlight over their choice of self defence methods in international waters." This clearly shows that the many of the measures resorted to by the master and crew of vessels to defend against piracy, in general, are not brought into the limelight and hence it cannot be said that they follow a proper procedure and stick on to the guidelines wherever necessary.

Reasonable use of force

The Guidance on Rules For the Use of Force (RUF) by Privately Contracted Armed Security Personnel (PCASP) in Defence of a Merchant Vessel (MV) issued by BIMCO specifically states that RUF should be in accordance not just with the laws of flag state but should also be in accordance with the coastal state laws[29]. The RUF should be consistent with the use of force only being used when essential and not otherwise. It specifically states that even when force has to be used, minimum levels of the same should be used. The guidance also mentions that RUF should contain guidance to the effect that use of force should be proportionate and appropriate to the situation, should not exceed what is strictly necessary and should take all reasonable steps to avoid the use of lethal force.

The basic principle as suggested by this guideline is an attempt towards non-violent means primarily in case of an attack and it also gives some examples of the same. The matter of Enrica Lexie does not highlight the use of any non-violent means first and that they resorted to lethal means only as a measure of last resort. Rule 7(g) of the guideline specifically states that lethal force should be used only as a last resort and opening of fire may be resorted to only when the attackers have failed to heed warning shots.

In this context, it is submitted that regulations relating to deployment of armed forces and carrying of firearms can be stipulated by the flag state but once the vessel is within the jurisdiction of the coastal state, it is bound to observe the national laws of the coastal state.[30]

Jurisdiction: Flag state jurisdiction

It is true that though Article 97 of UNCLOS provides for penal jurisdiction to be exercised based on flag state jurisdiction (Italy in this matter) or the principle of nationality, the matters in which such jurisdiction may be resorted to are restricted to collisions and any other incidents of navigation[31]. Under no stretch of imagination one could say that the act of the Italian marines would fall under 'any other incident of navigation'. It is submitted that the Supreme Court has correctly appreciated this issue by observing that an incident of navigation as intended in Article 97 of UNCLOS do not involve a criminal act and hence the matter cannot be left to the flag state.[32] Moreover Chelameswar, J in *Republic of Italy and ors* v. *Union of India and ors*[33] rightly points out the fact that Article 97 has been placed under Part VII of UNCLOS which is dealing with High Seas and

Article 86 restricts the provisions of Part VII to all parts of the sea that are not included in the exclusive economic zone, in the territorial sea or in the internal waters of a State, or in the archipelagic waters of an archipelagic State.[34]

Jurisdiction: State of Kerala or Union of India

An analysis of the international principles relating to jurisdiction supports the fact that Indian courts can exercise jurisdiction in the Enrica Lexie incident. Territorial principle in relation to criminal jurisdiction which states that the courts of the place where the crime is committed may exercise jurisdiction can be used with the help of section 188A of the CrPC[35], which has been brought out by the Notification No. SO 67/E dated 27th August, 1981, to support the fact that Indian courts can exercise jurisdiction in this matter. The objective territorial principle that states that jurisdiction could be exercised by a state if any essential constituent element of a crime is consummated on that state territory can be squarely made applicable in this case as the victims which is a part of the whole criminal activity are Indian fishermen. The passive nationality principle by which aliens may be punished for acts committed abroad that are harmful to the nationals of the forum[36] could also be made applicable here so as to charge the marines of murdering the Indian fishermen. There is nothing wrong in Indian courts assuming jurisdiction over the marines even according to protective or security principle that states that all states assume jurisdiction over aliens for acts done abroad which affect the security of the state. It seems quite weird to analyse the factual situation of Enrica Lexie on the basis of every single principle of international law regarding jurisdiction. It could be said that there is no point in segregating each international principles as they all are inter related and mutually operative. This can be verified from the following observation. "It may be that each individual principle is only evidence of the reasonableness of the exercise of jurisdiction. The various principles often interweave in practice. Thus, the objective applications of the territorial principle and also the passive personality principle have strong similarities to the protective or security purpose."

It may be true that the Italian marines are empowered under the flag state jurisdiction to carry firearms but once they have crossed over to the Indian jurisdiction, they are bound by the national laws of India. One may argue that they were not in the territorial waters, but section 188A of CrPC extends the criminal jurisdiction of India beyond its territorial waters up to its EEZ. The submission by Mr. Harish Salve, the learned counsel appeared for the Republic of Italy in the matter of *Republic of Italy* v. *Union of India*[37] has specifically stated that once a convention is ratified (UNCLOS in this case), the municipal law on similar issues should be construed in harmony with the Convention, unless there were express provisions to the contrary. He has also relied on *Maganbhai Ishwarbhai Patel* v. *UOI & anr.*[38] to show that unless there is a law in conflict with the treaty, the treaty must stand. It is submitted that the learned counsel assumes that there are no provisions to the contrary in the national law. The Notification No. SO 67/E dated 27th August, 1981 that brought out section 188A of the CrPC has been done as per section 7(7) of the Territorial Waters Act, 1976[39] and it has to be noted that the Notification is a law according to Article 13(3) (a) of the Constitution of India.[40] UNCLOS 1982 has been ratified by India on 29th June 1995 and it should be noted that there has been no reservations or declarations made by India at the time of ratification pertaining to extension of criminal jurisdiction beyond territorial waters. On one hand, it may be argued that by ratifying UNCLOS India ought to restrict the exercise of criminal jurisdiction especially when no reservations or declarations pertaining to the same has not been made thereby signifying the intention to be bound by the principles of UNCLOS. But it is also true that as per Article 309 of UNCLOS reservations and other exceptions are not allowed and by virtue of Article 310 declarations and statements should be in such a way that it do not purport to exclude or modify the legal effects of this Convention in the particular state and these may be the reasons why India restricted itself from making appropriate reservations or declarations. One may even go to the extent of saying that in case of conflict between international law and municipal law, municipal law should prevail and thus section 188A can still be applied in the instant case contrary to the provisions of UNCLOS.

In this context, it is pertinent to note down the observations of Justice Strong in the case of *The Scotia*[41] which has been quoted with approval in the case of *The Paquete Habana*[42] which is as follows, "Undoubtedly no single nation can change the law of the sea. The law is of universal obligation and no statute of one or two nations can create legal obligations for the world. Like all the laws of nations, it rests upon the common consent of civilised communities. It is of force, not because it was prescribed by any superior power, but because it has been generally accepted as a rule of conduct. Whatever may have been its origin, whether in the usages of navigation, or in the ordinances of maritime states, or in both, it has become the law of the sea only by the concurrent sanction of those nations who may be said to constitute the commercial world. Of these facts we may take judicial notice. Foreign municipal laws must indeed be proved as facts, but it is not so with the law of nations". This would fundamentally go against those who may argue that section 188A CrPC may be made squarely applicable in this matter, but it is submitted that The Suppression of Unlawful Acts Against Safety Of Maritime Navigation and Fixed Platforms on Continental Shelf Act, 2002 (in short, SUA Act) alone is sufficient to bring the Italian Marines before the jurisdiction of the Indian courts.

The Supreme Court in *Republic of Italy and ors.* v. *Union of India and ors.*[43] makes the following observation that "the submission made on behalf of the Union of India and the State of Kerala to the effect that with the extension of Section 188A of the Criminal procedure Code to the Exclusive Economic Zone, the provisions of the said Code, as also the Indian Penal Code, stood extended to the Contiguous Zone also, thereby vesting the Kerala Police with the jurisdiction to investigate into the incident under the provisions thereof, is not tenable. The State of Kerala had no jurisdiction over the Contiguous Zone and even if the provisions of the Indian Penal Code and the Code of Criminal Procedure Code were extended to the Contiguous Zone, it did not vest the State of Kerala with the powers to investigate and, thereafter, to try the offence. What, in effect, is the result of such extension is that the Union of India extended the application of the Indian Penal Code and the Code of Criminal Procedure to the Contiguous Zone, which entitled the Union of India to take cognizance of, investigate and prosecute persons who commit any infraction of the domestic laws within the Contiguous Zone. However, such a power is not vested with the State of Kerala."[44]

Though the word used in UNCLOS 1982 in relation to exercising of jurisdiction is 'coastal state' the corresponding provisions in the Territorial Waters Act, 1976 uses the words 'India' and 'Central Government'. It is of no doubt that the term 'state' implies 'nation' in the international context. Moreover it is true that SUA Act under section 12 and Territorial Waters Act, 1976 under section 14 require the sanction of the Central government. But no where it is suggested that the requirement of sanction from the Central Government to prosecute certain offences means that only the centre has the jurisdiction to try the matter and not the state government. Moreover it becomes extremely difficult and in addition to that the admiralty jurisdiction conferred on our High Courts becomes obsolete if the centre decides to take all the matters coming within the SUA Act and Territorial Waters Act, 1976 within the jurisdiction of the Supreme Court.

Sections 179 and 183 of the CrPC coming under Chapter XIII that deals with the Jurisdiction of the Criminal Courts in Inquiries and Trials specifically permits the court of local jurisdiction to try this matter. According to section 179, "when an act is an offence by reason of anything which has been done and of a consequence which has ensued, the offence may be inquired into or tried by a Court within whose local jurisdiction such thing has been done or such consequence has ensued." Further according to section 183, "when an offence is committed whilst the person by or against whom, or the thing in respect of which, the offence is committed is in the course of performing a journey or voyage, the offence may be inquired into or tried by a Court through or into whose local jurisdiction that person or thing passed in the course of that journey or voyage." It is of no doubt that by virtue of sections 179 and 183 CrPC, the state of Kerala has the jurisdiction over this matter as the words specifically used in both the sections are "the court within/through local jurisdiction".

It is also pertinent to note that Article 1(3) of the Constitution of India states that the territory of India shall comprise of the territories of the States, the Union territories specified in the First Schedule and such other territories as may be acquired. It has been specifically held in the case of *Masthan Sahib* v. *Chief Commissioner, Pondicherry*[45] that the expression 'territory of India', wherever used, means the territory which, for the time being, falls within Article 1(3). This clearly shows that the territory of India will definitely mean the territory of the state. It should also be noted that the definition of India as a Union of States emphasises the fact that states play an important role in the Constitution of India, as apart from the States, India does not exist.[46]

Criminal Jurisdiction

According to Article 27 of UNCLOS, the criminal jurisdiction can be exercised on board a foreign ship only in cases where the consequences of the crime extend to the coastal State or if the crime is of a kind to disturb the peace of the country or the good order of the territorial sea or if the assistance of the local authorities has been requested by the master of the ship or by a diplomatic agent or consular officer of the flag State or if such measures are necessary for the suppression of illicit traffic in narcotic drugs or psychotropic substances.[47] It is true that the firing by Italian marines definitely had consequences which extended to the coastal state but the same happened not in the territorial waters but in the contiguous zone. Section 27 of UNCLOS applies to cases concerning exercise of criminal jurisdiction on board a foreign ship passing through the territorial sea and not otherwise.

Section 3 of the Indian Penal Code which deals with punishment of offences committed beyond, but which by law may be tried within, India is wide enough in as much as it makes not only Indian citizens liable for offences committed abroad, but also those covered by any special law bringing them under Indian jurisdiction.[48] Section 3 states that any person liable, by any Indian law, to be tried for an offence committed beyond India shall be dealt with according to the provisions of this Code for any act committed beyond India in the same manner as if such act had been committed within India. Hence this section, when it is wide enough to cover not only Indian citizens but also any person covered by special law bringing them under Indian jurisdiction, should be taken as capable of including Italian Marines as well. The only requirement for that purpose here is to have a law bringing them under Indian jurisdiction. A combined reading of section 3 of the IPC and the two statutes namely the Admiralty Offences (Colonial) Act, 1849 and SUA Act 2002 highlights the fact that Indian courts have the jurisdiction to try the Italian Marines.[49]

Section 1(2) of the SUA Act states that it extends to the whole of India including the limit of territorial waters, continental shelf, the exclusive economic zone or any other maritime zone within the meaning of section 2 of the Territorial Waters Act, 1976. Hence it is of no doubt that the SUA Act squarely applies to the Enrica Lexie incident that had happened outside the territorial waters of India. The issue can be more clarified by looking into section 1(3) of the act which states that it applies to any offence under section 3 committed outside India by any person. Section 1(3) is sufficient enough to bring even a non-citizen under its ambit. Section 1(4) provides that the act applies only to offences committed by an offender when such offender is found in the territory of a convention state. India is a party to the convention state and is thus a convention state. Section 3(1) of the Act which provides for offences against ship, fixed platform, cargo of a ship, maritime navigational facilities makes it an offence to unlawfully and intentionally cause death to any person in the course of commission of or in attempt to commit, any of the offences specified in clauses (a) to (d) of section 3(1) and also offers punishment in the form of death to such offenders under its sub-clause (g) (i).

Section 3(7) of the Act which is subject to sub-section 8 provides that where an offence is committed outside India, the person committing such offence may be dealt with in respect thereof as if such offence had been committed at any place within India at which he may be found. A combined reading of section 3(7) with section 3(8) (c) makes it clear that the Indian courts can exercise jurisdiction over this matter as the sub-section 8 specifically states that the court shall take cognizance of an offence punishable under this section which is committed outside India if the alleged offender is on a fixed platform or on board a ship in relation to which such offence is committed when it enters the territorial waters of India or is found in India. It has been rightly pointed out that "in the case of Enrica Lexie the Italian marines were on Enrica Lexie when she entered Indian Territorial waters and moreover the Marines and the Captain are still in India and hence the Act squarely applies to the facts of the case."[50]

It is true that the previous sanction of Central Government is necessary for prosecution under SUA Act[51] but once the same is given, the Sessions Court which can be designated by the State Government with the concurrence of the Chief Justice of the High Court may try the offences under this Act.

The appropriateness of punishment

As regards the punishment that could be provided to the Italian Marines, it is submitted that the punishment that exists according to section 575 of the Italian Penal Code, 1931 for murder is 21 years and the maximum punishment that could be awarded in case of aggravating circumstances is life imprisonment according to sections 576 and 577. It is submitted that the same is considerably different in the Indian punitive sanctions where the maximum punishment that can be awarded is death for an act of murder under section 302 IPC. It is not intended to argue that the marines should be awarded death sentence for their acts but to show the considerable amount of difference that exists in the realm of criminal law sanctions in the two jurisdictions. Moreover capital punishment is out of question in the Italian criminal justice administration as it is generally out of use. According to Article 27 (as amended by the Constitutional Amendment Law of 2007) of the Constitution of Italy, "Criminal responsibility is personal. A defendant shall be considered not guilty until a final sentence has been passed. Punishment may not be inhuman and shall aim at re-educating the convicted. Death penalty is prohibited." This clearly aims at reforming and rehabilitating the offender. But in India, we still give importance to deterrent and retributive forms of punishment as it is evident from the fact that we still retain death penalty. This is further clear from the fact that Italy has signed and ratified the Second Optional Protocol to ICCPR aiming at the abolition of Death Penalty, 1989 whereas Indian has not done that yet.[52] Furthermore, India being a common law country does have the advantage of precedents like *Nilabathi Behera* v. *State of Orissa*[53] and *The Chairman, Railway Board & Ors* v. *Mrs. Chandrima Das & Ors*[54] where the Supreme Court have clearly ruled that compensation could be granted when the violation of fundamental rights are so patent and incontrovertible. It cannot be guaranteed that Italian laws which are based on civil law could adapt to the particular facts and circumstances like it is being done by the Indian courts.

Conclusion

Once we take all the factors that were discussed into consideration, it could be said that the Italian marines could be prosecuted in India for the offences they have committed. Without a doubt, it could be established that the marines had exceeded in the use of force especially when there is no concrete evidence to show that at least a reasonable apprehension of a pirate attack by the deceased Indian fishermen existed. It is true that the incident happened in the contiguous zone but by virtue of section 188A CrPC, which has been brought out by way of a notification in the Official Gazette it is not possible to completely agree to the claim made by Italy that they have the sole jurisdiction in this matter. The fact that the Italian marines have blatantly violated international norms which have been laid down in the form of BMP and Rules for the Use of Force should have been noted down by the court while disposing of the matter. The judgment of the Supreme Court which observed that it is only the Union of India and not the State of Kerala which has jurisdiction over this matter may be true considering the fact that the issue itself has become international and has attracted international attention. But an analysis of the provisions of the sections 179 and 183 of the Criminal procedure code compels us to think that there is some error in the judgment and it should have left the jurisdiction to the state itself.

Endnotes

1. (2012) 252 KLR 794

2. The same is clear from Article 33 of UNCLOS which defines Contiguous zone. Article 33 is as follows: 1. In a zone contiguous to its territorial sea, described as the contiguous zone, the coastal State may exercise the control necessary to: (a) prevent infringement of its customs, fiscal, immigration or sanitary laws and regulations within its territory or territorial sea; (b) punish infringement of the above laws and regulations committed within its territory or territorial sea. 2. The contiguous zone may not extend beyond 24 nautical miles from the baselines from which the breadth of the territorial sea is measured.

    Section 5 of the Territorial Waters Act, 1976 (1) The contiguous zone of India (hereinafter referred to as the contiguous zone) is an area beyond and adjacent to the territorial waters and the limit of the contiguous zone is the line every point of which is at a distance of twenty-four nautical miles from the nearest point of the baseline referred to in sub-section (2) of section 3.

3. Article101of UNCLOS: Definition of piracy: Piracy consists of any of the following acts:(a) any illegal acts of violence or detention, or any act of depredation, committed for private ends by the crew or the passengers of a private ship or a private aircraft, and directed:(i) on the high seas, against another ship or aircraft, or against persons or property on board such ship or aircraft;(ii) against a ship, aircraft, persons or property in a place outside the jurisdiction of any State;(b) any act of voluntary participation in the operation of a ship or of an aircraft with knowledge of facts making it a pirate ship or aircraft;(c) any act of inciting or of intentionally facilitating an act described in subparagraph (a) or (b).

4. Article 3(1) of SUA Convention: Any person commits an offence within the meaning of this Convention if that person unlawfully and intentionally: 1. seizes or exercises control over a ship by force or threat thereof or any other form of intimidation; or 2. performs an act of violence against a person on board a ship if that act is likely to endanger the safe navigation of that ship; or3. destroys a ship or causes damage to a ship or to its cargo which is likely to endanger the safe navigation of that ship; or4. places or causes to be placed on a ship, by any means whatsoever, a device or substance which is likely to destroy that ship, or cause damage to that ship or its cargo which endangers or is likely to endanger the safe navigation of that ship; or 5 destroys or seriously damages maritime navigational facilities or seriously interferes with their operation, if any such act is likely to endanger the safe navigation of a ship; or 6 communicates information which that person knows to be false, thereby endangering the safe navigation of a ship. (2) Any person also commits an offence if that person threatens, with or without a condition, as is provided for under national law, aimed at compelling a physical or juridical person to do or refrain from doing any act, to commit any of the offences set forth in paragraphs 1 (b), (c), and (e), if that threat is likely to endanger the safe navigation of the ship in question.

5. *Massimilano Latorre & Salvatore Girone (Italian marines)* v. *Union of India*, (2012) 252 KLR 794

6.   *Republic of Italy and ors* v. *Union of India and ors*, (2013) 4 SCC 721

7.   Available at <http://www.imo.org/OurWork/Security/PiracyArmedRobberyGuidance/ Documents/MSC.1-Circ.1334.pdf> last accessed on July 2, 2013

8.   The Flag State Framework for Implementation of Avoidance, Evasion, and Defensive Best Practices to Prevent and Suppress Acts of Piracy against Ships submitted by the United States before the Maritime Safety Committee at its 90th session via MSC 90/20/14 dated 13 March 2012 also talks about these self defensive measures.

9.   Andrew Palmer, "The Use of Armed Guards, Legal and Practical Issues", September 5 2012, available at <http://www.idaratmaritime.com/wordpress/?p=386> last accessed on July 3, 2013

10.   The Guidance to Ship Owners and Ship Operators, Shipmasters and Crews on Preventing and Suppressing Acts of Piracy and Armed Robbery against Ships issued by International Maritime Organization via Circular MSC.1/Circ.1334 dated 23 June 2009

11.   *Republic of Italy and ors* v. *Union of India and ors*, (2013) 4 SCC 721

12.   Available at <http://www.ukpandi.com/fileadmin/uploads/uk-pi/Documents/Piracy/ privatearmedguardsflagstateregs.pdf> last accessed on July 11, 2013

13.   See<http://www.gazzettaufficiale.it/atto/serie_generale/caricaDettaglioAtto/ originario?atto.dataPubblicazioneGazzetta=2013-03-29&atto.codiceRedazionale=13 G00072&elenco30giorni=true> last accessed on July 6, 2013

14.   The Guidance on Rules for the Use of Force (RUF) by Privately Contracted Armed Security Personnel (PCASP) in Defence of a Merchant Vessel (MV) issued by BIMCO is detailed out in the latter part of this article under the heading "Reasonable use of force".

15.   For a better understanding on GUARDCON, See <https://www.bimco.org/ Chartering/Documents/Security/~/media/Chartering/Document_Samples/Sundry_ Other_Forms/Sample_Copy_GUARDCON__04_01_2013.ashx> last accessed on July 16, 2013

16.   International Safety Management Code, 2010; For a detailed understanding, see <http:// www.imo.org/OurWork/HumanElement/SafetyManagement/Pages/ISMCode.aspx>

17.   See<http://www.skuld.com/Documents/Topics/Voyage_and_Port_Risks/Piracy/ on%20the%20wave%202013%20-%201%20English%20version.pdf> last accessed on July 10, 2013

18.   See<http://www.gazzettaufficiale.it/atto/serie_generale/caricaDettaglioAtto/ originario?atto.dataPubblicazioneGazzetta=2013-03-29&atto.codiceRedazionale=13 G00072&elenco30giorni=true> last accessed on July 6, 2013

19.   The full text is available at <http://www.liscr.com/liscr/Portals/0/BMP4.pdf> last accessed on June 29, 2013

20.   R. 8.15 Armed Private Maritime Security Contractors: The use, or not, of armed Private Maritime Security Contractors onboard merchant vessels is a matter for

individual ship operators to decide following their own voyage risk assessment and approval of respective Flag States. This advice does not constitute a recommendation or an endorsement of the general use of armed Private Maritime Security Contractors. Subject to risk analysis, careful planning and agreements the provision of Military Vessel Protection Detachments (VPDs) deployed to protect vulnerable shipping is the recommended option when considering armed guards.

21. R. 9.3 Attack stage: Reconfirm that all ship's personnel are in a position of safety. As the pirates close in on the vessel, Masters should commence small alterations of helm whilst maintaining speed to deter skiffs from lying alongside the vessel in preparation for a boarding attempt. These manoeuvres will create additional wash to impede the operation of the skiffs. Substantial amounts of helm are not recommended, as these are likely to significantly reduce a vessel's speed.

22. See < http://www.imo.org/MediaCentre/HotTopics/piracy/Documents/1405-rev-1. pdf> last accessed on July 15, 2013

23. It is true that para 1.5 of the interim guidelines states that this interim guidance is not legally binding and is not in itself a set of certifiable standards. But in the absence of any valid legally binding instruments, this in itself should be considered as at least a persuasive legal instrument.

24. Agenda item 20; MSC 90/20/3, 22 February 2012

25. Draft Msc Circular Guidance To Port State Control Officers On Life-Saving Appliance Arrangements On Board Italian Ships Due To The Additional Security Personnel Engaged For A Single Voyage Through The Areas At High Risk Of Piracy Attacks; MSC 90/20/3 Idem. Safety issues related to the use of armed personnel on board ships in the high risk area. Submitted by Italy

26. Piracy And Armed Robbery Against Ships - Armed security personnel on board ships Comments on MSC 90/20/5 (Secretariat), Submitted by India

27. According to India, in a recent incident on the Indian coast, armed security guards mistook a fishing boat in the vicinity of their ship to be a pirate boat and fired upon the boat, killing two fishermen.

28. David Isenberg, "The Rise of Private Maritime Security Companies", July 12, 2012, available at <http://www.seasecurity.org/mediacentre/the-rise-of-private-maritime-security-companies/> last accessed July 5, 2013

29. <http://www.ukpandi.com/fileadmin/uploads/ukpi/Latest_Publications/Circulars/2012/BIMCO%20Guidance%20on%20the%20Rules%20for%20the%20Use%20of%20Force.pdf> last accessed July 18, 2013

30. Andrew Palmer, "The Use of Armed Guards, Legal and Practical Issues", September 5 2012, available at <http://www.idaratmaritime.com/wordpress/?p=386> last accessed on July 3, 2013. The author has stated that another incident similar to the Indian fisherman issue happened in 2010 in Oman where a crew from a passing cargo ship fired upon a group of fishermen, thinking they were pirates, killing one of them and injuring another and according to him there have been many similar incidents, and most have gone unreported because the victims were killed far out at sea.

31. Article 97 of UNCLOS: Penal jurisdiction in matters of collision or any other incident of navigation: In the event of a collision or any other incident of navigation concerning a ship on the high seas, involving the penal or disciplinary responsibility of the master or of any other person in the service of the ship, no penal or disciplinary proceedings may be instituted against such person except before the judicial or administrative authorities either of the flag State or of the State of which such person is a national.

32. Paragraph 94 of the judgment in *Republic of Italy and ors* v. *Union of India and ors*, (2013) 4 SCC 721

33. (2013) 4 SCC 721

34. Article 86: Application of the provisions of this Part: The provisions of this Part apply to all parts of the sea that are not included in the exclusive economic zone, in the territorial sea or in the internal waters of a State, or in the archipelagic waters of an archipelagic State. This article does not entail any abridgement of the freedoms enjoyed by all States in the exclusive economic zone in accordance with article 58

35. Section 188A, CrPC: Offence committed in exclusive economic zone: When an offence is committed by any person in the exclusive economic zone described in sub-section(1) of Section 7 of the Territorial Waters, Continental Shelf, Exclusive Economic Zone and Other Maritime Zones Act, 1976 (80 of 1976) or as altered by notification, if any, issued under sub-section (2) thereof, such person may be dealt with in respect of such offence as if it had been committed in any place in which he may be found or in such other place as the Central Government may direct under Section 13 of the Said Act.

36. Ian Brownie, *Principles of Public International Law*, OUP, New Delhi (6th edn., 2004), p. 302

37. (2013) 4 SCC 721

38. (1970) 3 SCC 400

39. Section 7(7): The Central Government may , by notification in the official Gazette,- (a) extend, with such restrictions and modifications as it thinks fit, any enactment for the time being in force in India or any part thereof to the exclusive economic zone or any part thereof; and (b) make such provisions as it may consider necessary for facilitation the enforcement of such enactment, and any enactment so extended shall have effect as if the exclusive economic zone or the part thereof to which it has been extended is a part of the territory of India.

40. It has been stated by Dilip Rao in his article on Italian Marines V. Union of India that "s.188A, CrPC has not been notified under the CrPC and a new provision cannot be introduced through a gazette notification under the Maritime Act, 1976 but must be incorporated only through an amendment enacted by parliament – in simple words, this is an expansion of the scope of a criminal law which cannot be accomplished in this manner." <http://centreright.in/2013/03/italian-marines-v-union-of-india/> last accessed on July 3, 2013

41. *The Scotia*, 81 U.S. 170 (1871)

42. *The Paquete Habana*, 175 U.S. 677 (1900)

43. (2013) 4 SCC 721

44. Paragraph 84 of *Republic of Italy and ors* v. *Union of India and ors*, (2013) 4 SCC 721

45. AIR 1962 SC 797

46. H.M. Seervai, *Constitutional Law of India: A Critical Commentary*, Vol 1, N.M. Tripathi Pvt. Ltd., Bombay (2nd edn., 1975), p. 119

47. Article 27, UNCLOS: Criminal jurisdiction on board a foreign ship: 1. The criminal jurisdiction of the coastal State should not be exercised on board a foreign ship passing through the territorial sea to arrest any person or to conduct any investigation in connection with any crime committed on board the ship during its passage, save only in the following cases: (a) if the consequences of the crime extend to the coastal State; (b) if the crime is of a kind to disturb the peace of the country or the good order of the territorial sea; (c) if the assistance of the local authorities has been requested by the master of the ship or by a diplomatic agent or consular officer of the flag State; or (d) if such measures are necessary for the suppression of illicit traffic in narcotic drugs or psychotropic substances.

48. K.D. Gaur, *Commentary on the Indian Penal Code*, Universal Law Publishing Co., New Delhi (2nd edn., 2013), p.46

49. Shyam Kumar, "The Long Arm of Indian Law – Enrica Lexie Incident and Jurisdiction of Indian Courts to Try the Italian Marines", available at <http://admiraltylawkochi. blogspot.in/2012/04/long-arm-of-indian-maritime-law-enrica.html> last accessed on July 6, 2013 specifically argues that a According to the author, section 3 of the Admiralty Offences (Colonial) Act, 1849, which provides that "where any person shall die in any colony of any stroke, poisoning, or hurt, such person having been feloniously stricken, poisoned, or hurt upon the sea, or in any haven, river, creek, or place where the admiral or admirals have power, authority, or jurisdiction, or at any place out of such colony, every offence committed in respect of any such case, whether the same shall amount to the offence of murder or of manslaughter, or of being accessory before the fact to murder, or after the fact to murder or manslaughter, may be dealt with, inquired of, tried, determined, and punished, in such colony, in the same manner and in all respects its if such offence had been wholly committed in that colony; and if any person in any colony shall be charged with any such offence as aforesaid in respect of the death of any person who, having been feloniously stricken, poisoned, or otherwise hurt, shall have died of such stroke, poisoning, or hurt upon the sea, or in any haven, river, creek, or place where the admiral or admirals have power, authority, or jurisdiction, such offence shall be held for the purpose of this Act to have been wholly committed upon the sea" clearly empowers the authorities in India to deal with offences committed outside India.

50. Shyam Kumar, "The Long Arm of Indian Law – Enrica Lexie Incident and Jurisdiction of Indian Courts to Try the Italian Marines", available at <http://admiraltylawkochi. blogspot.in/2012/04/long-arm-of-indian-maritime-law-enrica.html> last accessed on July 6, 2013

51. According to Section 12, no prosecution for an offence under this Act shall be instituted except with the previous sanction of the Central Government.

52. Available   at   <http://treaties.un.org/pages/ViewDetails.aspx?src=TREATY&mtdsg_
     no=IV-12&chapter=4&lang=en> last accessed on July 17, 2013

53. (1993) 2 SCC 746

54. AIR 2000 SC 988

www.ingramcontent.com/pod-product-compliance
Lightning Source LLC
Chambersburg PA
CBHW060838100426
42814CB00016B/421/J